Some pencil marks

£2.99

C000150161

Margaret Cavendish

The Convent of Pleasure

Recent Books by Sharon L. Jansen

Mary Astell: Some Reflections upon Marriage. Saltar's Point Press, 2014.

Mary Astell: A Serious Proposal to the Ladies. Saltar's Point Press, 2014.

Anne of France: "Lessons for My Daughter." The Library of Medieval Women. Boydell & Brewer, 2012.

Reading Women's Worlds from Christine de Pizan to Doris Lessing: A Guide to Six Centuries of Women Writers Imagining Rooms of Their Own. Palgrave Macmillan, 2011.

The Monstrous Regiment of Women: Female Rule in Early Modern Europe. Queenship and Power, ed. Carole Levin and Charles Beem. Palgrave Macmillan, 2010.

Debating Women, Politics, and Power in Early Modern Europe. Palgrave Macmillan, 2008.

Margaret Cavendish

The Convent of Pleasure

Edited by

Sharon L. Jansen

Saltar's
Point
Press

First published 2016 by
Saltar's Point Press,
dedicated to producing
quality teaching texts for classroom use.

ISBN-13: 978-0692654620
ISBN-10: 0692654623

Grateful acknowledgment is made to the National Portrait Gallery (London) for permission to reproduce the frontispiece from Margaret Cavendish's *Playes* (London, 1662).

Grateful acknowledgment is made to the Folger Library for making the image of the title page of Margaret Cavendish's *Plays, Never before Printed* (London, 1668) available for use under a Creative Commons Attribution-ShareAlike 4.0 International (CC BY-SA 4.0) license.

Grateful acknowledgement is made to Tagul (https://tagul.com) for its commercial license permitting use of the word cloud generated through its web service as cover art for this book.

That my ambition of extraordinary fame is restless and not ordinary I cannot deny, and since all heroic actions, public employments, as well civil as military, and eloquent pleadings are denied my sex in this age, I may be excused for writing so much, for that is the reason I have run, more busily than industriously, upon every subject I can think of.

Margaret Cavendish, *Nature's Pictures Drawn by Fancy's Pencil* . . . (1656)

Contents

List of Figures

Acknowledgments

In preparing this edition of *The Convent of Pleasure*, I am deeply grateful to the many students with whom I've read Cavendish's play over the course of my teaching career. This edition actually began in the classroom, with photocopies of my own transcription of the text from the 1668 *Plays, Never before Printed*. My students' responses to their experience of reading Cavendish have contributed to my work here; their engagement with the play first inspired me to begin the process of editing *The Convent of Pleasure* for them, their puzzlement with some of Cavendish's language indicated where they needed clarifications, definitions, and explanations, and their overwhelming enthusiasm and delight led to the present volume. I owe them my deepest thanks.

Any new edition of *The Convent of Pleasure* must also begin with an acknowledgment of a debt of gratitude to previous editions. The first of these is Jennifer Rowsell's *The Convent of Pleasure. A Comedy* (The Seventeenth Century Press, 1995), produced as "almost a facsimile, retaining the original grammar and punctuation" but with modernized spelling. This was followed in 1999 by Anne Shaver's excellent *The Convent of Pleasure and Other Plays* (Johns Hopkins University Press), a volume that made six of Cavendish's plays available to contemporary readers for the first time. About her editorial method, Shaver explains, "With a few noted exceptions, I have retained Cavendish's eccentric spelling, grammar, and punctuation because they are aspects of her works that have occasioned comment from the moment they appeared." The play is also included in Sylvia Bowerbank and Sara Mendelson's anthology, *Paper Bodies: A Margaret Cavendish Reader* (Broadview Press, 2000), an edition that also "reproduced verbatim spelling and punctuation of primary sources."

Two editions place Cavendish's play in different literary contexts: Stephanie Hodgson-Wright's *Women's Writing of the Early Modern Period, 1588-1688, An Anthology* (Columbia University Press, 2002) and Hero

Chalmers, Julie Sanders, and Sophie Tomlinson's *Three Seventeenth-Century Plays on Women and Performance* (Manchester University Press, 2006). Hodgson-Wright notes that her aim as editor is "to make the texts user-friendly to the first-time reader." In her edition of *The Convent of Pleasure*, Hero Chalmers provides not only helpful notes but a useful collation of the press variants found in nineteen copies of the play. Finally, *The Convent of Pleasure* is also included in the *Broadview Anthology of British Literature* (2nd ed., 2012), the text based on Shaver's edition of the play and edited in conformity to the anthology's practices.

My effort here is a complementary one—this teaching edition of *The Convent of Pleasure* offers the text of the play in a single affordable volume. The introduction surveys Cavendish's life and work in the context of women's performance and playwriting in early-modern England. The text has been carefully edited and modernized, supplying the reader ample notes and aids. The volume is completed by a bibliography with suggestions for further reading and a chronology of Margaret Cavendish's published work.

And one final note. A great deal of contemporary critical debate has focused on the issue of *The Convent of Pleasure*'s "performability." The question of the play's stage potential seems to originate from the assumption that, since the play was not performed during Cavendish's lifetime, it was not—and is not—performable. Several essays found in the bibliography here challenge this assumption and argue the case for the play's "stage readiness." Another way of answering the question may be to read the plays of William Cavendish, Margaret's husband, all of which *were* performed and none of which seems to be any more "performable" than *The Convent of Pleasure*. But I would suggest that the best way of deciding the question is to focus on Cavendish's play itself and to enjoy all of the theatrical possibilities it offers. The many students with whom I have read the play over the years have never doubted the play's "performability." In fact, when I've raised the question with them, they've looked at me as if I were crazy. I hope this edition will enable the play's readers to answer for themselves the question of the play's stage potential for a theater audience.

Introduction

of

Many readers first encounter Margaret Cavendish in the pages of Virginia Woolf's *A Room of One's One*. There, after her discussion of the fictional Shakespeare's sister, Woolf turns her attention to several early-modern women writers, Cavendish among them. Woolf's assessment is memorable. "What a vision of loneliness and riot the thought of Margaret Cavendish brings to mind!" Woolf exclaims, "as if some giant cucumber had spread itself over all the roses and carnations in the garden and choked them to death." Woolf acknowledges Cavendish's "passion for poetry" but concludes that her writing is "disfigured and deformed." Disfigured and deformed by her "rage," disfigured and deformed because "no one taught her."[1]

Cavendish was keenly aware of the deficiencies of her education. She would later write that she "never went to school" but "only learned to read and write at home," where she was "taught by an ancient decayed gentlewoman" who was "kept for that purpose."[2] Beyond those basic skills, the young Margaret was provided with lessons in singing, dancing, music, and needlework but, as she concedes, these were arranged "rather for formality than for benefit."[3] Even so, she

---

[1] Virginia Woolf, *A Room of One's Own* (1929; rpt. New York: Harcourt / Harvest Edition, 1989), 61-62.

[2] Margaret Cavendish, Letter 175, *CCXI Sociable Letters* (London, 1664), 367. I have silently modernized the spelling and punctuation.

[3] Margaret Cavendish (1623-1673) published an account of her life, *A True Relation of my Birth, Breeding and Life*, as the eleventh and final book in her *Natures Pictures Drawn by Fancies Pencil to the Life* . . . (London, 1656). In the second edition of *Natures Pictures* (London, 1671), *A True Relation* was omitted. Cavendish's auto-biography is included in Charles H. Firth, ed., *The Life of William Cavendish, Duke of Newcastle, to which is added "The True Relation of My Birth Breeding and Life" by Margaret,*

claims to have been something of reader when she was a child; though her "study of books" may have been "little," she still "chose rather to read" than to spend her time "in any other work or practice."[4] She also loved to write, and she later describes the way she filled sixteen "little baby-books" with her scribbles and blots. The contents were "as confused as the chaos, wherein is neither method nor order, but all mixed together without separation."[5] Still, however much she may have enjoyed reading and filling up pages with her "sense and no sense," the time she spent with "serious study" was limited, she confesses, "by reason that I took great delight in attiring, fine dressing, and fashions, especially such fashions as I did devise myself."[6]

Cavendish claims to have read and reread the plays of Shakespeare when she was a girl and reports that "going to plays" in London was among the "harmless recreations" enjoyed by female members of her family.[7] But while she might have enjoyed going *to* the theater with her mother and sisters, there was no role for women *in* the theater. The "golden age" of English drama glittered and shone for men only. Thousands of men and women attended performances at the London playhouses each week during the early seventeenth century, but they never heard a single word of dialogue *spoken* by a woman much less *written* by a woman.[8] Women did not perform on stage in the public theaters, nor did they write any of the plays that were acted there. A very few aristocratic women translated dramatic texts, even fewer

---

Duchess of Newcastle, 2nd rev. ed., (New York: E. P. Dutton, 1907). The quotation is from pp. 157-58. I have silently modernized the spelling and punctuation.

[4] Cavendish, *True Relation*, in Firth, ed., *Life of William Cavendish*, 175. I have silently modernized the spelling and punctuation.

[5] Margaret Cavendish, Letter 131, *Sociable Letters*, 267. I have silently modernized the spelling and punctuation.

[6] Cavendish, *True Relation*, Firth, ed., *Life of William Cavendish*, 175. I have silently modernized the spelling and punctuation.

[7] On her love for Shakespeare when she was a "very young maid," see Cavendish, Letter 123, *Sociable Letters*, 244-48, and Letter 162, 338-39, for example; on the Lucas family's attending the theater in London, see Cavendish, *A True Relation*, in Firth, ed., *Life of William Cavendish*, 159-60. I have silently modernized the spelling and punctuation.

[8] According to theater historian Tanya Pollard, "up to twenty-five thousand people attended theatrical performances in London each week between 1580 and 1640." Pollard, ed., *Shakespeare's Theater: A Sourcebook* (Malden, MA: Blackwell, 2004), xii.

attempted to write an original comedy or tragedy—but no early-modern woman writer could ever hope to see her play acted on the English stage.[9] And if writing a play was difficult and performance impossible, publication was just as problematic for women writers. Publication—public speech—violated gender ideologies that expected women to be chaste, silent, and obedient. Finally, as if all these obstacles were not enough for her when she eventually made the decision to write and publish plays, Margaret Cavendish faced another difficulty after the outbreak of the English Civil Wars: in 1642, the great London playhouses were closed by order of parliament.[10]

Limited by her education and sex, stung by criticisms of her intellectual ambitions, and knowing that professional theaters had been closed in England, Margaret Cavendish nevertheless began writing plays, both comedies and tragedies, at some point in the 1650s. By the time she published her first collection of dramatic work in 1662, the world had changed, once again, for English playwrights, performers, and audiences—in August of 1660, just weeks after Charles II landed in England, the new Stuart king, now restored to the throne, reopened the theaters under a royal charter, offering patents to two dramatic companies, the King's Company, under the management of the dramatist Thomas Killigrew, and the Duke's Company, managed by the poet and playwright William Davenant. Among the many theatrical innovations Killigrew and Davenant introduced, one was remarkable: for the first time, Englishwomen began to act on the public stage.[11] But the possibilities for Margaret Cavendish as a woman writing drama were still limited. Despite the obstacles, she dared to offer a second volume, *Plays, Never before Printed*, in 1668.

While Margaret Cavendish was not the first Englishwoman to write a play or to publish one, she was first woman to present her dramatic

---

[9] On the difficulties for women writing drama in the generation before Cavendish, see Marion Wynne-Davies, "The Theater," in *The History of British Women's Writing*, vol. 2, *1500-1610*, ed. Caroline Bicks and Jennifer Summit, The History of British Women's Writing (New York: Palgrave Macmillan, 2010), 175-95. On the very few early-modern women writers of dramatic texts in England, see below, 38-49.

[10] An Ordinance concerning Stage Plays, 2 September 1642. In *Acts and Ordinances of the Interregnum, 1642-1660*, ed. C. H. Firth and R. S. Rait (London: His Majesty's Stationery Office, 1911), 26-27.

[11] For a discussion of women, performance, and the stage before 1660, see below, 30-38.

work in a folio collection. As critic Shannon Miller observes, the production of such folio volumes was crucial to the "emerging seventeenth-century canonical hierarchy of playwrights" and "central in establishing reputations."[12] The playwright Ben Jonson was the first to publish a folio edition of his dramatic work in his 1616 *The Works of Benjamin Johnson.*[13] This was followed in 1623 by *Mr. William Shakespeare's Comedies, Histories, and Tragedies, Published According to the True Original Copies*, an edition now commonly referred to as the "First Folio"; in 1632 by the Second Folio of Shakespeare; in 1640 by a second edition of Jonson's *Works*; and in 1647 by the publication of the *Comedies and Tragedies Written by Francis Beaumont and John Fletcher, Gentlemen, Never Printed before, and Now Published by the Authors' Original Copies*. Into the midst of this dramatic print contest, Cavendish wedged herself and her two folio volumes, the 1662 *Plays* and the 1668 *Plays, Never before Printed*. But, as Jeffrey Masten notes, such large-format publications constituted a "theatrical discourse perceived as conversation between men." A "woman's entrance" into this territory was both "treacherous and heavily policed," and neither one of Cavendish's folios appeared in a second edition.[14] Meanwhile, the works of male playwrights continued to appear with mind-numbing regularity: a Third

---

[12] Miller, "'Thou art a Moniment, without a tombe': Affiliation and Memorialization in Margaret Cavendish's *Playes* and *Plays, Never before Printed*," in *Cavendish and Shakespeare, Interconnections*, ed. Katherine Romack and James Fitzmaurice (Burlington, VT: Ashgate Publishing, 2006), 9. The term "folio" refers to the size of the book, in this case a large volume in which the sheet of paper has been folded only once (producing two leaves and four pages), as opposed to the quarto volume, with the sheet folded twice (producing four leaves and eight pages), and the octavo, with the sheet folded three times (producing eight leaves and sixteen pages).

[13] Before Jonson's use of the folio for his *Works*, play texts were printed in quarto and octavo formats. As Lynne S. Meskill notes, "Folios were large, unwieldy, expensive and luxurious. They were destined for aristocrats, the rich, the learned; smaller formats were akin to pamphlets: cheap, easily available and widely disseminated." By contrast, the folio format "was reserved for serious literature: namely epic and poetry and serious readers, possessors of libraries and reading lecterns." Jonson's decision to use print his plays in this format was thus a "revolutionary" act, "with its implicit assertion" that dramatic work was also "serious literature." Meskill, "Ben Jonson's 1616 Folio: A Revolution in Print?" *Études Épistémè* 14 (2008): 179.

[14] Masten, *Textual Intercourse: Collaboration, Authorship, and Sexualities in Renaissance Drama* (New York: Cambridge University Press, 1997), 120, 156. For more on Cavendish's use of the folio format for her plays, see below, 55-70.

Folio of Shakespeare's work in 1663, a second folio of Beaumont and Fletcher, titled *Fifty Comedies and Tragedies*, in 1679, a Shakespeare Fourth Folio in 1685, a third edition of the Jonson's *Works* in 1692. Even today, well into the second decade of the twenty-first century and some 350 years after Cavendish dared to publish two collections of her plays, her folios have never been republished. For Margaret Cavendish there were no second acts.

But that should not surprise us.

Today, in many parts of the world, but most particularly in North America and western Europe, significant numbers of women have made undeniable progress in their effort to achieve equality. And yet, despite the enormous progress that has been made, women's participation in many areas of society remains limited—women are under-represented in politics and government, in business and technology, and in far too many professions, and they still suffer economic disparity simply because they are female. Nowhere do we see this gender gap more clearly than in the field where Margaret Cavendish sought a place among her male contemporaries. Whether their professional careers are in theater, film, or television, women are still not equal participants.

In commenting on the opportunities for women in theatrical productions, playwright Marsha Norman recently noted, "Women have lived half of the experience of the world, but only 20 percent of it is recorded in our theatres."[15] In a comprehensive study of 153 U.S. theaters, published in 2015, the Dramatists Guild of America reported that only 22 percent of the plays produced in a three-year period were by women writers. In other words, "if life worked like the theatre, four out of five things you had ever heard would have been said by men."[16] Onstage and back stage, there is also a colossal gender gap: significantly fewer roles for female actors than male, and noticeably fewer female

---

[15] Quoted in Suzy Evans, "The Gender Parity Count Ticks Up—Slightly," *American Theater*, 20 July 2015, http://www.americantheatre.org/2015/07/20/the-gender-parity-count-ticks-up-slightly/.

[16] Marsha Norman, "Why 'The Count' Matters," *The Dramatist* 18, no. 2 (2015): 18. The study covered three consecutive seasons, 2011-12, 2012-13, and 2013-14. For the methodology used in the study, see pp. 20-21. A complete list of "all the theaters counted" is found on p. 29.

directors, set designers, lighting designers, sound designers, and choreographers, among other crucial roles.[17]

At the same time, on screens both large and small, women face similar inequities.[18] Recent studies of the top 100 films released in 2015 reveal women accounted for only 11 percent of the writers, 7 percent of the directors, 22 percent of the producers, 20 percent of the editors, and 3 percent of the cinematographers.[19] On screen, women played leading roles in only 21 percent of the top 100 films of 2014—but not a single woman over the age of forty-five "performed a lead or co lead role."[20] And none of these numbers address issues of pay equity.[21]

---

[17] See Suzy Evans, "Women Push for Equality On and Off Stage," *American Theatre*, October 2014, http://www.americantheatre.org/2014/09/17/women-push-for-equality-on-and-off-stage/; Martha Wade Steketee and Judith Binus, *Women Count: Women Hired Off-Broadway 2010-2015* (New York: League of Professional Theatre Women, 2015), http://theatrewomen.org/women-count/; and Gordon Cox, "When Will Broadway's Onstage Diversity Carry Over Behind the Curtain?" *Variety*, 10 November 2015, http://variety.com/2015/biz/features/broadway-diversity-behind-the-scenes-1201636823/. For a similar analysis of theaters on the West Coast, see, for example, Valerie Weak, *Not Even: A Gender Analysis of 500 San Francisco/Bay Area Theatrical Productions from the Counting Actors Project, 2011-2014* (San Francisco: WomenArts, 2015), http://www.womenarts.org/not-even/.

For a brief overview of the issues in Canada, see Yvette HeyLiger's report on the Equity Theatre Symposium in Canada, *The Dramatist* 18, no. 2 (2015): 48-50. For the UK, see, for example, Tonic Theatre, "What We Learned," *Advance: Gender Equality in England's Theatres* (September 2014), http://www.tonictheatre-advance.co.uk/learning/ #stats.

[18] For a comprehensive study of women in both film and television, see Stacy L. Smith, et al., *Inclusion or Invisibility? Comprehensive Annenberg Report on Diversity in Entertainment* (Los Angeles: USC Annenberg School for Communication and Journalism's Media, Diversity, & Social Change Initiative, 2016).

[19] For these figures, see Martha M. Lauzen, *The Celluloid Ceiling: Behind-the-Scenes Employment of Women on the Top 100, 250, and 500 Films of 2015* (San Diego: Center for the Study of Women in Television and Film, 2016), 3. For a study focused on the numbers of women directors of films released in 2015, see Directors Guild of America, "Feature Film Diversity Report," *Directors Guild of America* (December 2015), http://www.dga.org/News/PressReleases/2015/151209-DGA-Publishes-Inaugural-Feature-Film-Diversity-Report.aspx.

[20] Stacy L. Smith et al., "Key Findings," *Inequality in 700 Popular Films: Examining Portrayals of Gender, Race, & LGBT Status from 2007 to 2014* (Los Angeles: USC Annenberg School for Communication and Journalism's Media, Diversity, & Social Change Initiative, 2015), 1. In addition to this longitudinal study, see Martha M. Lauzen, *It's a Man's (Celluloid) World: On-Screen Representations of Female Characters in the Top 100 Films of 2014* (San Diego: Center for the Study of Women in Television and Film, 2015).

While women are more fully represented on television screens than they are in film—in the 2014-15 prime-time season, 40 percent of the "major characters" on broadcast, cable, and Netflix programs were female—they still comprised only 25 percent of the writers, 12 percent of the directors, 38 percent of the producers, 20 percent of editors, and 1 percent of directors of photography, among other roles.[22]

As Stacy Smith concludes in her study of inequality in the portrayals of women in film, "The landscape of popular cinema . . . remains skewed and stereotypical." Films "continue to distort the demographic reality of their audiences," and even after years of "activism, attention, and statements about addressing the issue, Hollywood's default setting for characters and content creators remains fixed on 'status quo.'"[23] Or, as Martha Lauzen, director of the Center for the Study of Women in Television and Film, says, more succinctly, when it comes to the big screen, women still encounter a "celluloid ceiling." And on the small screen, it's much the same: women are, even now, "boxed in."

Virginia Woolf's description of Margaret Cavendish in *A Room of One's Own* is both memorable and memorably horrifying. But those comments were a kind of second draft for Woolf—she had first written at some length about Cavendish a few years earlier. In *The Common Reader*, a collection of essays and reviews published in 1925, Woolf reveals that she is familiar not only with Cavendish's biography of her husband, William Cavendish, but also with her *Poems and Fancies*, her "female orations" and "philosophical letters," and her plays. "[H]er poems, her plays, her philosophies, her orations, her discourses," Woolf writes, "all those folios and quartos in which, she protested, her

[21] On pay equity for film actors, see Ramin Setoodeh, "Equal Pay Revolution: How Top Actresses Are Finally Fighting Back," *Variety*, 10 November 2015, http://variety.com/2015/film/news/hollywood-gender-pay-gap-inequality-1201636553/.

[22] Martha M. Lauzen, *Boxed In: Portrayals of Female Characters and Employment of Behind-the-Scenes Women in 2014-15 Prime-Time Television* (San Diego: Center for the Study of Women in Television and Film, 2015), 5. See also Maureen Ryan, "ACLU's Melissa Goodman on Gender Discrimination: It's a Legal and Civil Rights Problem," *Variety*, 10 November 2015, http://variety.com/2015/tv/news/aclu-melissa-goodman-diversity-tv-directors-gender-discrimination-1201635880/.

[23] Smith, *Inequality in 700 Popular Films*, 21.

real life was shrined—moulder in the gloom of public libraries, or are decanted into tiny thimbles which hold six drops of their profusion."[24]

In this essay Woolf is more nuanced about Cavendish. Not that Woolf is unabashedly glowing in her praises of Cavendish, but neither does she condemn her with that terrible image, the ugly cucumber vine smothering the roses and carnations. Woolf seems to appreciate the "wild streak" in Cavendish that was "forever upsetting the orderly arrangements of nature," and she is quite clear about the reasons why Cavendish drew upon herself such heaps of public "ridicule." "People were censorious," Woolf observes, "men were jealous of brains in a woman; women suspected intellect in their own sex."[25] Though "her philosophies are futile, and her plays intolerable, and her verses mainly dull," Woolf can't quite resist or dismiss Margaret Cavendish: "One cannot help following the lure of her erratic and lovable personality as it meanders and twinkles through page after page. There is something noble and Quixotic and high-spirited, as well as crack-brained and bird-witted, about her." Despite everything, "the vast bulk of the duchess is leavened by a vein of authentic fire."[26]

Despite the spark of this "authentic fire," as Woolf observes, Cavendish's "terrible" critics "sneered and jeered," and her "torment-tors," who could little appreciate her ambition, much less her accomplishments, "mocked her." For her part, Cavendish claimed to disregard all the criticism and ridicule. When she dared to publish her second collection of plays in 1668, for example, she brushed her critics aside, declaring, "I write . . . only for my own pleasure and not to please others." Well aware of her "envious detractors," she was defiant: "malice cannot hinder me from writing, wherein consists my chiefest delight and greatest pastime." She insisted that she would continue to publish her books regardless of whether "anybody reads them or not" and that, in any case, she wasn't writing for her contemporaries: "I regard not so much the present as future ages, for which I intend all my

---

[24] Woolf, *The Common Reader, First Series* (1925; rpt. New York: Houghton Mifflin /Mariner Books, 2002), 69.

[25] Woolf, *The Common Reader,* 71.

[26] Woolf, *The Common Reader,* 77.

books," adding that, if future readers liked her work, that was all that mattered.[27]

The future readers that Cavendish once imagined—or hoped for—have indeed emerged, and the "terrible" critics who loved to sneer and jeer at her work are no longer mocking her. Today there is an International Margaret Cavendish Society, with members in the UK, the US, Canada, Australia, New Zealand, France, Italy, Germany, Greece, the Netherlands, Norway, Portugal, India, Israel, and Japan. There are regular panels at scholarly conferences exploring Cavendish's contributions to literature, philosophy, political theory, economics, medicine, science, gender and sexuality studies, and ecofeminism. Cavendish's work is debated and analyzed in the pages of academic articles as well as in college classrooms, but she's equally present online—you'll find Margaret Cavendish at the Poetry Foundation website, for example, but she's also to be found at the Kids Philosophy Slam site, where she was recently named "Philosopher of the Week." While there is still no article on Margaret Cavendish in the *Encyclopedia Britannica*, her work has found its way into the *Norton Anthology of Literature* and the *Stanford Encyclopedia of Philosophy*. There is also a lively Cavendish presence in popular culture: a graphic novel, *Mad Madge*, in the Dawn of the Unread series; a place in *Shape and Situate: Posters of Inspirational Women in Europe*, a zine dedicated to "remembering who we are"; an episode in the Stuff Mom Never Told You podcast; and dozens of YouTube videos and Prezi presentations, most of them created and posted by students from all over the world. Critic Jonathon Sturgeon recently named Danielle Dutton's "anti-historical historical novel," *Margaret the First*, as one of the "50 most anticipated books of 2016."[28]

---

[27] Margaret Cavendish, "To the Reader," *Plays, Never before Printed*, A1r. I have silently modernized the spelling and punctuation.

[28] The *Mad Madge* graphic novel, written by Mhairi Stewart and illustrated by Gary Erskine, is issue 15 (2015) of the Dawn of the Dead series ("When the dead go unread there's gonna be trouble"), produced by Nottingham Trent University, available online at http://www.dawnoftheunread.com/issue-15-01.html. Anne-Marie Atkinson's Cavendish poster is in *Shape and Situate*, issue 5 (2013), http://remember-who-u-are.blogspot.co.uk/p/shape-situate-posters-of-inspirational.html. Cavendish is included in the "Empresses of Science Fiction" episode, Stuff Mom Never Told You (6 July 2015), http://www.stuffmomnevertoldyou.com/podcasts/empresses-of-science-fiction/. For Sturgeon's comments, see "The 50 Most Anticipated Books of

In ways Virginia Woolf could never have predicted (and that may well have surprised Cavendish herself), Margaret Cavendish has not only gained the appreciative readers she once anticipated but something she did not: worldwide status as an early-modern feminist icon.

Margaret Cavendish's Life and Work

B orn in 1623, Margaret Cavendish began life as Margaret Lucas, youngest of the eight children of Sir Thomas Lucas and his wife, Elizabeth Leighton. Although her father was not a "peer of the realm," Cavendish was proud of her family's status: "My father was a gentleman, which title is grounded and given by merit, not by princes."[29] The Lucas family lived comfortably and happily at St. John's Abbey, their estate near Colchester, and managed to maintain their affluent style of life even after Thomas Lucas's death in 1625 when Margaret was, in her own words, still "an infant."[30] The Lucas estate

---

2016," *Flavorwire* (5 January 2016), http://flavorwire.com/554364/the-50-most-anticipated-books-of-2016/25.

[29] Cavendish, *True Relation*, in Firth, ed., *Life of William Cavendish*, 155. I have silently modernized the spelling and punctuation. In addition to her autobiography, there are four principal biographical accounts of Margaret Lucas Cavendish's life: Douglas Grant, *Margaret the First: A Biography of Margaret Cavendish, Duchess of Newcastle, 1623-1675* (London: Rupert Hart-Davis, 1957); Kathleen Jones, *A Glorious Fame: The Life of Margaret Cavendish, Duchess of Newcastle, 1623-1673* (London: Bloomsbury Publishing, 1988); Katie Whitaker, *Mad Madge: The Extraordinary Life of Margaret Cavendish, Duchess of Newcastle, the First Woman to Live by Her Pen* (New York: Basic Books, 2002); and James Fitzmaurice, "Cavendish, Margaret, duchess of Newcastle upon Tyne (1623?-1673)," *Oxford Dictionary of National Biography* [online] (Oxford: Oxford University Press, 2004-), http://oxforddnb.com.

[30] Cavendish, *True Relation*, in Firth, ed., *Life of William Cavendish*, 156. I have silently modernized the spelling and punctuation.

Elizabeth Leighton was pregnant with her first child in the summer of 1597, although she and Sir Thomas were not married, a fact Cavendish omits in *A True Relation*. Cavendish does, however, reveal that her father killed Sir William Brooke—adding, in his defense, that her father was compelled, "in honor" to challenge Brooke and "in justice" killed him (155). Declared an outlaw, Sir Thomas fled to the continent, where he remained until after Queen Elizabeth's death in 1603. He was ultimately pardoned by James I, and on 18 March 1604, the new king issued a warrant restoring Lucas to his status and property. Only then could Sir Thomas Lucas return home—his eldest son, named for his father, was by that time six years old. Sir Thomas married Elizabeth Leighton in 1604, but because of the circumstances of the younger Thomas's birth, the eldest Lucas son could not be his father's heir. A second

was necessarily divided between Thomas Lucas's sons and his wife, as Cavendish notes in her autobiography, but Elizabeth Lucas did not suffer the kind of economic loss so many women in her situation faced; since the widow and her children "agreed with a mutual consent," Margaret writes, "all their affairs were managed so well as she lived not in a much lower condition than when my father lived."[31]

The idyllic life of the Lucas family was disrupted after the outbreak of the English Civil Wars in 1642—Cavendish laments that her family was "ruined" by the "unhappy wars" descending on them "like a whirlwind," separating members of the family from one another, depriving them of their income, destroying their property, and taking the lives of far too many of them. At the very outset of the war, on 21 August 1642, while John Lucas, Margaret's older brother, was mustering troops for the royalist cause, St. John's Abbey was attacked by a huge crowd of men, women, and children from nearby Colchester; in addition to taking horses and armor, they seized "plate, money, books, boxes, writings and household stuff."[32] John Lucas was captured and transferred to a prison in London (he was released on bail in September and promptly joined the king's army); John's wife, Anne Neville, and his mother, Elizabeth, were threatened and held in the town jail. The crowd was still not satisfied. Throughout the next day, angry members of the town attacked the house itself, breaking windows and doors, destroying the gardens, pulling down fences, even killing livestock and deer.

It's not clear from surviving records whether Margaret Cavendish, then about nineteen years old, was at St. John's Abbey when it was attacked, or whether she was in London at the home of her married sister, Catherine Lucas Pye. After being forced out of their home, members of the Lucas family eventually assembled in London and then relocated to Oxford, where Charles I had set up his court. The years of war that followed continued to be as devastating for the Lucas family as the first few weeks of that war had been. Margaret's youngest

---

son and heir, John, was born in 1606, followed by Mary (born c. 1608), Elizabeth (born c. 1612), Charles (b. 1613), Anne (b. c. 1614-16?), and Catherine (born 1617). Margaret's birth followed six years later, in 1623.

[31] Cavendish, *True Relation*, in Firth, ed., *Life of William Cavendish*, 156. I have silently modernized the spelling and punctuation.

[32] Contemporary accounts quoted in Grant, *Margaret the First*, 52.

brother, Charles Lucas, was captured in 1648 at the siege of Colchester, condemned for treason by a parliamentary court, and executed on 28 August 1648. Her eldest brother, Thomas Lucas, died of wounds he received in 1649. John Lucas was again captured and imprisoned in 1655. Nor were the Lucas women spared. Margaret lost her eldest sister, Mary Lucas Killigrew, in 1646, "her death being . . . hastened through grief of her only daughter," a little girl who had died of consumption six months earlier. Margaret's own mother, Elizabeth, died soon after Mary: "my mother lived to see the ruin of her children, in which was her ruin, and then died," Cavendish writes.[33] As if all that were not enough, St. John's Abbey, which had been looted in 1642, was destroyed in the 1648 siege that ended with Charles Lucas's execution—heavily damaged by artillery bombardment during the siege, the abbey's destruction was complete when royalist munitions, stored inside, exploded. Finding nothing left to loot, the besieging troops broke open the Lucas family tomb in St. Giles's Church, on the abbey grounds, scattering the bones "with profane jests." The bodies of the recently buried Elizabeth Lucas and her daughter, Mary Killigrew, were still intact; the soldiers cut off the women's hair and wore it in their hats, a grim talisman of their victory.[34]

Meanwhile, in 1643, while she was with her family in Oxford, Margaret secured a place as lady-in-waiting to Queen Henrietta Maria, the French-born wife of King Charles I; when the queen fled the strife-torn country in 1644, Margaret Lucas left England with her. While the grieving and extremely shy young woman was in Paris with the English court-in-exile, she met and married William Cavendish, a widower some thirty-four years her senior.[35] Having suffered a humiliating military defeat at the battle of Marston Moor—and despite the king's wishes—William Cavendish had fled England with his two sons and brother, living in Hamburg before joining English exiles in Paris. The young Margaret was noted for her bashfulness and her beauty, William

---

[33] Cavendish, *True Relation*, in Firth, ed., *Life of William Cavendish*, 165. I have silently modernized the spelling and punctuation.

[34] Contemporary accounts quoted in Grant, *Margaret the First*, 101.

[35] William Cavendish (1592-1676) was the grandson of the formidable "Bess of Hardwick," Elizabeth Talbot, countess of Hardwick (the second of her four marriages was to Sir William Cavendish). William Cavendish became the Viscount Mansfield in 1620, earl of Newcastle-upon-Tyne in 1628, marquess of Newcastle-upon-Tyne in 1643, and first duke of Newcastle-upon-Tyne in 1665.

for his wealth and his devotion to the royalist cause. After her marriage, Margaret began the education she had not had when she was a child. Her husband read to and with his young wife, engaged with her, challenged her, and fostered her interests in a broad range of topics, including politics, philosophy, literature, and science. She characterized herself as his "apprentice," adding that no one ever had "a more abler master to learn from than I have."[36]

Under her husband's tutelage, she began to write once more—even more daring, she would publish her work. Ambitious, inventive, and prolific, Cavendish knew the risks she was taking. In an introductory letter included in her first published book, she acknowledged the difficulties she faced as a writer: "I shall be censured by my own sex, and men will cast a smile of scorn upon my book because they think thereby women encroach too much upon their prerogatives, for they hold books as their crown and the sword as their scepter, by which they rule and govern." She was well aware of the virulent personal attacks that Mary Sidney Wroth had endured three decades earlier when she published her romance, *Urania*; Cavendish imagined that the reaction to her own efforts might be similar. Scornful male readers were likely to respond to her "as to the lady that wrote the *Romancy*, 'Work, lady, work, let writing books alone, / For surely wiser women ne'er wrote one.'"[37]

---

[36] Margaret Cavendish, *The Worlds Olio* (London, 1655), n. p. The passage is from the epistle between Book 1, part 1 and Book 1, part 2 (the last page in Book 1, part 1 is numbered 26; Book 1, part 2 begins on a page numbered 27). I have silently modernized the spelling and punctuation.

[37] Margaret Cavendish, *Poems, and Fancies* (London, 1653), "To All Noble, and Worthy Ladies," n. p. I have silently modernized the spelling and punctuation. Cavendish is quoting Lord Edward Denny's scurrilous attack on Lady Mary Wroth after the 1621 publication of *Urania*; Denny condemned Wroth as a "hermaphrodite in show, in deed a monster / As by thy words and works all men may conster." His twenty-six line poem ends, "leave idle books alone / For wise and worthier women have writte none." Quoted in *The Poems of Lady Mary Wroth*, ed. Josephine A. Roberts (Baton Rouge: Louisiana State University Press, 1983), 33. Denny's letter to Wroth was not published, but the verse must have circulated widely, since Roberts reports that "it appears in two seventeenth-century manuscripts." And, as Cavendish's reference makes clear, this bitter comment must still have concerned women writers more than thirty years later. Cavendish alludes to this warning several years later in the prefatory address to her husband, "To His Excellency the Lord Marquis of Newcastle," in *Sociable Letters* (1664): "It may be said to me, as one said to

During the years of exile the couple endured, Margaret Cavendish's intellectual development was not only fostered by her husband, but she was also privileged to meet some of the greatest philosophers of her day, including Thomas Hobbes and René Descartes. Yet Cavendish was keenly aware of how disadvantaged she was in making their acquaintance and how ill equipped she was to profit from any intellectual exchange with them.

Thomas Hobbes had a long association with the Cavendish family—he had been the tutor of an earlier William Cavendish (our William's cousin). When he was still a young man, Margaret's husband had met Hobbes at the Cavendish family home, Welbeck Abbey, and William eventually became a great patron of the philosopher (Hobbes dedicated his 1640 *Elements of Law, Natural and Politic*, among other works, to William). In Paris, Hobbes frequently dined with William Cavendish, and so, Margaret writes, "I have had the like good fortune to see him."[38] But her interaction with the philosopher was limited: she never heard him discuss philosophy (though she does describe a conversation between Hobbes and her husband about witches), and, she claims, "I never spoke to Master Hobbes twenty words in my life."[39] Those twenty words must have included an invitation she extended to him to come to dinner: "I cannot say I did not ask him a question, for when I was in London, I . . . asked him if he would please to do me that honor to stay at dinner, but he with great civility refused me, as having some business, which I suppose required his absence."

---

a Lady, *Work Lady, Work, let writing Books alone, For surely Wiser Women ne'r writ one*" (n. p.)

Although Lady Mary Wroth's *Urania* had been published three decades before Cavendish published her *Poems, and Fancies*, James Fitzmaurice reminds us that, while "a great many respected women wrote and shared what they had written within coteries," Wroth was the "last woman of good birth to write for the press" before Cavendish began to publish her work, and that Wroth's "fate was not to be envied." Fitzmaurice, "Fancy and the Family: Self-Characterizations of Margaret Cavendish," *Huntington Library Quarterly* 53, no. 3 (1990): 202.

[38] Cavendish, "An Epilogue to My Philosophical Opinions, *The Philosophical and Physical Opinions*, 2nd ed. (London, 1663), n. p. I have silently modernized the spelling and punctuation.

[39] Margaret Cavendish, *The Life of . . . William Cavendishe . . .* (London, 1667), 143-46; in Firth, ed., *Life of William Cavendish*, 106-108. I have silently modernized the spelling and punctuation. She makes no mention of Descartes in her biography of her husband.

She read Hobbes's *Leviathan* when it was published in 1651, the same year she could finally read his 1642 *De cive*, published for the first time in an English translation.[40]

As for Descartes, who corresponded with the young William Cavendish and later debated with him while William was in exile in Paris, Margaret writes, "upon my conscience I never spoke to Monsieur Descartes in my life, nor ever understood what he said, for he spoke no English, and I understand no other language, and those times I saw him, which was twice at dinner with my lord at Paris, he did appear to me a man of the fewest words I ever heard."[41] To read any part of Descartes's major works, including his *Principia philosophia* and his *Discours de la méthode*, she had to have sections translated for her into English.[42]

Thus, despite her avid interest in philosophy, politics, and government, Margaret Cavendish could not debate with men like Hobbes and Descartes even when she met them. She could only engage with their ideas textually—as she did in her 1664 *Philosophical Letters*.[43] There in a series of 157 letters "sent" by a fictional and unnamed female correspondent, Cavendish is able to explore the philosophies of "several famous and learned authors," including Hobbes and Descartes. In each letter, her imagined letter-writer outlines her critique of the philosophers' arguments, offers her own opinions and theories, and solicits a response. Thus Cavendish can "debate" their ideas in her epistles, but she can never engage the great men directly, either in person or in print.

In 1648, pressed by debts, the couple left Paris and moved to Antwerp, which William Cavendish judged to be "the most pleasantest and quietest place to retire himself and ruined fortunes in"; there Cavendish busied herself by writing about poetry, history, and drama, gathering her essays, reflections, poems, and opinions into a collection. But her work was interrupted in 1651 when, Cavendish writes,

---

[40] On Cavendish's reading of translations of Hobbes, see Whitaker, *Mad Madge*, 116.

[41] Cavendish, "An Epilogue to My Philosophical Opinions," *Philosophical and Physical Opinions*, n. p. I have silently modernized the spelling and punctuation.

[42] Whitaker, *Mad Madge*, 259.

[43] Margaret Cavendish, *Philosophical Letters, or, Modest Reflections upon Some Opinions in Natural Philosophy Maintained by Several Famous and Learned Authors of This Age, Expressed by Way of Letters* (London, 1664).

"necessity" forced her to return to England to "seek for relief." Learning that William Cavendish's forfeited estates were to be sold, the couple hoped that Margaret, as his wife, might be able to secure from parliament an "allowance" or "benefit" from the sale. Thus she traveled back to England with her brother-in-law, Charles Cavendish, aiming to secure some provision out of her husband's confiscated property.[44] Before leaving, she put her writing aside, locking it up in a trunk "as if it had been buried in a grave."[45] Once in London, she found that her petition for support failed—it was denied because her husband was regarded as a traitor to the English state, and, as she was informed, she had married him knowing that his estate had been confiscated. Disappointed—the Cavendishes were living on credit, and debts were mounting—she met her husband's grown children for the first time and reunited with members of her own family, including her surviving sisters, Elizabeth Lucas Walter, Anne Lucas, and Catherine Lucas Pye, with her brother John and his wife Anne, and with her brother Thomas Lucas's widow, Anne Byron Lucas. But her visits otherwise were few (she says they numbered only "some half score"), and her entertainments even fewer (two or three musical evenings). She left her lodgings only to "take the air" in Hyde Park with her sisters.

Anxious and deeply lonely, Cavendish turned once more to writing. As her stay in England dragged on, she gathered her new compositions, including "poetical fictions, moral instructions, philosophical opinions, dialogues, discourses, [and] poetical romances," into a volume to be published under the title of *Poems and Fancies*.[46] Even after sending her work to the printer, Cavendish continued writing, hoping to add additional material to the volume before it was published. Over the course of three weeks, she completed a series of philosophical essays on a wide range of topics, but as quickly as she wrote, it was not

---

[44] Cavendish describes her difficult and disappointing trip to England in *True Relation*, in Firth, ed., *Life of William Cavendish*, 166-70.

[45] Cavendish, "An Epistle to the Reader," *The Worlds Olio*, n. p. I have silently modernized the spelling and punctuation.

[46] Although she described her fruitless efforts to secure some kind of provision from parliament at length in her autobiography, Cavendish referred to her writing only briefly, noting that "part" of her time in England was spent in writing "a book of poems and a little book called my *Philosophical Fancies*." Cavendish, *True Relation*, in Firth, ed., *Life of William Cavendish*, 170. I have silently modernized the spelling and punctuation.

quick enough—the essays arrived too late to be included in *Poems and Fancies*, so they were published separately as *Philosophical Fancies*.[47]

Early in 1653, after eighteen months in England, Cavendish finally received a warrant allowing her to leave country and return to her husband in Antwerp—and to the work she had put aside and locked in a trunk. But, having given the material "a resurrection," she realized that it was not quite what she remembered. She looked over what she had written and "judged it not so well done." A "little more care" might have made the prose "smoother" and given "the sense a greater luster," but Cavendish decided to publish her work anyway: "I, being of a lazy disposition, did choose to let it go into the world with its defects rather than take the pains to refine it."[48] With the same kind of defensiveness she would later show when she published her collections of plays, Cavendish acknowledges what her critics might say even while she claims not to care. "I am so well armed with carelessness that their several censures can never enter to vex me with wounds of discontent," she writes; "I have my delight in writing and having it printed, and if any take a delight to read it, I will not thank them for it, for if anything please therein, they are to thank me for so much pleasure, and if it be naught, I had rather they had left it unread."[49]

She titled her collection *The World's Olio*, named after a Spanish stew, *olla podrida*, a highly spiced and rich mixture of meats and vegetables.[50] In a preface to this spicy mix, Cavendish raised the issue

---

[47] On the hectic pace of Cavendish's writing, see Whitaker, *Mad Madge*, 157-58. Interestingly, while *Poems, and Fancies* appeared in the folio format she favored, this second publication—written in just three weeks (Whitaker, *Mad Madge*, 157)—was published in a small, octavo format.

For an introduction to Cavendish's philosophical ideas, see *The Stanford Encyclopedia of Philosophy* (24 May 2012), s.v. "Margaret Lucas Cavendish," by David Cunning, http://plato.stanford.edu/archives/sum2012/entries/margaret-cavendish/.

For a detailed chronology of Cavendish's published work, see Appendix, 187-90.

[48] Cavendish, "An Epistle to the Reader," *The Worlds Olio*, n. p. I have silently modernized the spelling and punctuation.

[49] Cavendish, "An Epistle to the Reader," *The Worlds Olio*, n. p. I have silently modernized the spelling and punctuation.

[50] "A spiced meat and vegetable stew of Spanish and Portuguese origin. Hence: any dish containing a great variety of ingredients" (*Oxford English Dictionary* [online], www.oed.com, hereafter cited as *OED*). The *OED* also records Cavendish's use of the word here as the first example of "olio" in this figurative sense: "A collection of various artistic or literary pieces, a book containing miscellaneous items (such as engravings, or poems) on various subjects."

of the obvious disparity between the education women receive and that offered to men. She begins by acknowledging her deficiencies, explaining that she cannot be expected to write "so wisely or so wittily as men" because she is of "the effeminate sex." She then sets out to "give reason" why, as a woman, she "cannot be so wise as men," though first she begs "pardon" of her readers, female and male alike. She predicts that women will condemn her "out of partiality to themselves" and that men will condemn her either because they wish to curry favor with women or, for their own "comfort and ease," because they know that "women's tongues are like stings of bees." No man would knowingly rile up a "monarchy" of female bees to "swarm around [his] ears" and sting him to death.[51]

But the self-deprecation of Cavendish's opening apology quickly gives way to the kind of anger that, in Woolf's view, "disfigured" her work. Cavendish argues that men and women were "made equal by nature," but that men "from their first creation usurped a superiority to themselves" and then had unjustly maintained their "tyrannical government" of women ever since. Women "could never come to be free" and thus grew more and more "enslaved," treated by men "like children, fools, or subjects." Her conclusions about women's "slavery" are chilling: "we are become so stupid that beasts are but a degree below us, and men use us but a degree above beasts." Cavendish holds out a brief hope for women's education—"if we were bred in schools to mature our brains and to manure our understandings, . . . we might bring forth the fruits of knowledge." But at this point, almost as if she fears where her argument is leading her, Cavendish backs away. Although she refutes Adam's superiority to Eve in one of the essays printed *inside* the spicy stew of *The World's Olio*, the rest of her prefatory letter to her readers is an extended analysis not of men and women's equality but of men's superiority—they are stronger and their brains are better, "more clear to understand and to contrive than women's." Aside from giving birth, men perform virtually every useful function to society, from tilling fields to governing states.[52]

---

[51] Cavendish, "Preface to the Reader," *The Worlds Olio*, n. p. I have silently modernized the spelling and punctuation.

[52] Cavendish, "Preface to the Reader," *The Worlds Olio*, n. p. I have silently modernized the spelling and punctuation.

Her acceptance of male superiority leads her to conclude that women are properly ruled by men. Even so, Cavendish is a strong advocate for women's education. Just as barren ground, properly tilled and amply "manured" will produce "plentiful crops" and "diverse sorts of flowers," women's minds, enlarged by education, "may come to be far more knowing and learned." Cavendish doesn't offer women's intellectual inferiority and their proper subordination to men as any excuse for ignorance, however. In Cavendish's words, "being subject" to men is "no hindrance from thinking." Sounding much like Virginia Woolf some three centuries later, Cavendish insists "thoughts are free." Whatever women's physical circumstances, their minds "can never be enslaved."[53] Thus women are "not hindered from studying." Men may have their colleges and universities, but women, or at least women of a certain class, have their "closets" where they are free to read and to study.

Cavendish also wrote about the state of female education in a letter she addressed to the "famously learned" men of Oxford and Cambridge, included as a preface to her *Philosophical and Physical Opinions*, published in the same year as *The World's Olio*. She offers her philosophical work to "wise school-men and industrious, laborious students," not in the hope that they "should value it for any worth," but in the hope that they will "receive it without scorn, for the good encouragement of [her] sex." She is afraid that women "grow irrational as idiots" because of the "careless neglects and despisements of the masculine sex to the female, thinking it impossible [women] should have either learning or understanding, wit or judgment, as if [they] had not rational souls as well as men." And because such attitudes are customary, Cavendish fears that women, out of their "dejectedness," will come to "think so too" and be content occupying themselves with "low and petty employments." Without the encouragement to exercise their "higher capacities," women "are become like worms, that only live in the dull earth of ignorance, winding ourselves sometimes out by the help of some refreshing rain of good education, which seldom is given us, for we are kept like birds in cages, to hop up and down in our houses, not suffered to fly abroad." Women lack variety—"changes of

---

[53] As Woolf wrote, "Lock up your libraries if you like; but there is no gate, no lock, no bolt that you can set upon the freedom of my mind." Woolf, *A Room of One's Own*, 76.

fortune"—and experience; they lack "understanding and knowledge, and so, consequently, prudence." Thus deprived, they "are shut out of all power and authority": "we are never employed either in civil or martial affairs, our counsels are despised and laughed at," she writes, "the best of our actions are trodden down with scorn, by the overweening conceit men have of themselves and through a despisement of us."[54]

Cavendish's next work, *Nature's Pictures*, is a collection of "poetical" and "romancical" stories, told both in verse and in prose. Her goal in these narratives is not simply to amuse but to instruct; as she describes the "design" of her "feigned stories," the aim is "to present virtue" to her readers, "the muses leading her, and the graces attending on her, to defend innocence, help the distressed, lament the unfortunate, and show that vice is seldom crowned with good success." Here, too, she informs her reader about the drive that fuels her as a writer even as she acknowledges the constraints upon her as a woman: "That my ambition of extraordinary fame is restless and not ordinary I cannot deny, and since all heroic actions, public employments, as well civil as military, and eloquent pleadings are denied my sex in this age, I may be excused for writing so much, for that is the reason I have run, more busily than industriously, upon every subject I can think of."[55] The whole is conceived of as a frame-tale narrative, not unlike Chaucer's *Canterbury Tales*, with a small group of men and women deciding to entertain themselves by telling stories:

In winter cold a company was met,
Both men and women by the fire were set;
At last they did agree to pass the time
That everyone should tell a tale in rhyme;
The women said, "We no true measures know,
Nor do our rhymes in even numbers go";
"Why," said the men, "All women's tongues are free
To speak both out of time and foolishly,"

---

[54] Margaret Cavendish, "To the Two Universities," *Philosophical and Physical Opinions*, n. p. I have silently modernized the spelling and punctuation.

[55] Cavendish, "The Preface," *Natures Pictures*, n. p. I have silently modernized the spelling and punctuation.

And, drawing lots, the chance fell on a man,
Who having spit and blown his nose, began.[56]

The "feigned stories" in verse that follow in the first book include several she calls "mock tales" told by her husband. As she turns from verse narratives to prose—at which point she also abandons the framing narrative that had unified her first group of stories—she continues to include stories she attributes to her husband, notably one delightful piece titled "His Grace the Duke of Newcastle's Opinion, 'Whether a Cat Seeth in the Night, or No?'"[57] There are also several longer prose narratives in *Nature's Pictures*, in particular three that we might regard as *novellas*, "The Contract," "Assaulted and Pursued Chastity," and "The She Anchoret."[58] The volume concludes with her autobiography, *A True Relation of My Birth, Breeding, and Life*. As Cavendish's biographer Katie Whitaker notes, this collection was "exceptional": "Mary Wroth was the only woman to have published a work of original English fiction before Margaret, with disastrous results, and no woman had ever published—or probably even written—an autobiography like Margaret's."[59]

By this point, Margaret had also begun writing plays. She would later claim that her decision to write drama was inspired by her husband—he was writing plays and reading them aloud to her, carefully

[56] Cavendish, *Natures Pictures*, [2]. I have silently modernized the spelling and punctuation. Cavendish's use of the frame-tale narrative is interesting, since, in addition to Chaucer's use of the format in *The Canterbury Tales*, it is also a genre used by women writers. Cavendish herself may have known about Christine de Pizan's *Book of the City of Ladies*, composed in 1405; Cristina Malcolmson has argued that the Cavendishes acquired a lavishly illustrated manuscript collection of Pizan's work while they were in exile on the continent. Malcolmson, "Christine de Pizan's *City of Ladies* in Early Modern England," in *Debating Gender in Early Modern Europe, 1500-1700*, ed. Cristina Malcolmson and Mihoko Suzuki, Early Modern Cultural Studies (Palgrave Macmillan, 2002), 15-36. The frame-tale format was also used by Marguerite de Navarre (1492-1549), sister of Francis I of France, in her *Heptameron*, published posthumously in 1559, and by the Spanish writer Maria de Zayas y Sotomayor (1590-1661), who published two frame-tale narratives, *Amorous and Exemplary Novels*, in 1637, and *The Disenchantments of Love*, in 1647.

[57] Cavendish, *Natures Pictures*, 568-70.

[58] "The Contract" and "Assaulted and Pursued Chastity" are included in Margaret Cavendish, *The Blazing World and Other Writings*, ed. Kate Lilley (New York: Penguin Books, 1994), 1-118.

[59] Whitaker, *Mad Madge*, 197.

putting them aside, waiting "for a good time" when they might be performed. While her husband could afford to withhold his efforts from publication in the hope that English theaters might at some point be reopened and his plays staged, Margaret Cavendish knew that she could not keep her own plays "concealed in the hopes to have them first acted."[60] No woman had ever seen her play acted on a public stage in England. But the publication of her collection of plays was delayed by political events. In 1658, Oliver Cromwell, Lord Protector of England during the Commonwealth, died. He was succeeded briefly and unsuccessfully by his son, Richard. After seven months, the younger Cromwell was removed from office, and on 8 May 1660, Parliament decided that Charles II had been king since his father was executed in 1649. The Stuart monarch was recalled from exile and returned to England in May 1660. After sixteen long years, Margaret and William Cavendish were also able to return to England.

Although William Cavendish would ultimately be rewarded for his loyalty with the title of duke of Newcastle, he did not receive the kind of political appointment he had hoped for, nor was it a simple matter for him to recover his lost property.[61] By September, the Cavendishes left London for Welbeck Abbey, his estate near Nottingham.[62] The couple would spend the majority of their time together there in quiet retirement, devoting themselves to reading and writing. As Virginia Woolf would later describe their lives, with not a little degree of acerbity, "they lived together in the depths of the country in the greatest seclusion and perfect contentment, scribbling plays, poems, philosophies, greeting each other's works with raptures of delight, and

---

[60] "The Epistle Dedicatory," *Playes* (London, 1662), A3r. I have silently modernized the spelling and punctuation.

[61] William Cavendish received the title of "duke" in 1665. Margaret details carefully and at length all of the material losses her husband had suffered during the civil wars; on his "confused, entangled, and almost ruined estate," see Cavendish, *The Life of . . . William Cavendishe . . .* , in Firth, ed., *Life of William Cavendish*, 68-81.

[62] After the dissolution of the monasteries, begun by Thomas Cromwell during the reign of Henry VIII, the abbey was purchased by Richard Whalley in 1539; after Whalley's death in November 1583, Welbeck was purchased by Gilbert Talbot, earl of Shrewsbury. Talbot had been married to Elizabeth Cavendish, the daughter of Bess of Hardwick, in 1568, at the same time his father, George Talbot, married Bess (it was her fourth marriage). In 1607, Welbeck was sold to Bess of Hardwick's son, Charles Cavendish, William Cavendish's father. William Cavendish inherited Welbeck in 1617.

confabulating, doubtless, upon such marvels of the natural world as chance threw their way."[63] In splendid isolation and with her husband's devoted support, Margaret Cavendish could continue to write. And with some restoration of their finances, she could also employ a secretary to prepare her work for publication and to oversee proof copies. She could also dispense with booksellers, whom she had blamed for many of the problems with her earlier publications, instead choosing her own printers and financing her projects herself. As Katie Whitaker notes, this "arrangement gave her much greater control over production and resulted in more careful printing, without the numerous errors of her earlier works."[64]

Her first publication after the Restoration was *Plays*, which appeared early in 1662. Later in the year, in the fall, experimenting with yet another genre, she published *Orations of Divers Sorts*.[65] Cavendish also began to devote herself to the study of science; while in Antwerp, she had met the Dutch poet and diplomat Constantijn Huygens, who was himself very interested in the new science, and she had made him a present of her *Poems and Fancies* when it was published in 1653. (Unlike Hobbes and Descartes, he may have spoken *to* her, but he also spoke *about* her, writing to a correspondent—one of her husband's distant cousins—that he had received Cavendish's "wonderful book," but that reading about her "extravagant atoms kept me from sleeping a great part of last night in this my little solitude."[66]) The two had begun a

---

[63] Woolf, *The Common Reader*, 72.

[64] Whitaker, *Mad Madge*, 244.

[65] Margaret Cavendish, *Orations of Divers Sorts, Accommodated to Divers Places* (London, 1662).

[66] Constantijn Huygens to Utricia Ogle Swann, 15 September 1653, in J. A. Worp, ed., *Die Briefwisseling van Constantijn Huygens, 1608-1687*, vol. 5, *1649-1663* (The Hague: Martinus Nijhoff, 1916), 186-87. Utricia Ogle Swann was a member of the court of Mary Henrietta Stuart, Charles I's daughter, who had married William, prince of Orange. (Ogle was related to William Cavendish through his mother, Catherine Ogle). Constantijn Huygens (1596-1687) was a diplomat and had been knighted by James I of England in 1622, later filling a number of official roles for the princes of Orange. He was also the father of the noted Dutch mathematician and scientist Christiaan Huygens. It is hard to gauge the tone of his comment about Cavendish and her "extravagant atoms," but it is clearly different from that in his letters to Margaret Cavendish herself, two of which are included in William Cavendish's *Letters and Poems in Honour of the Incomparable Princess, Margaret, Dutchess of Newcastle* (London, 1676). In the first of these, dated 12 March 1657, Huygens expresses his gratitude for an afternoon's conversation and promises he will return soon to her "school" where

correspondence about science, one allowing Cavendish to express her scientific theories and even to attempt some scientific experiments, but as her biographer Douglas Grant observes, Cavendish's letters to Huygens demonstrate "the principal difficulties which hindered her as a natural philosopher": first, her lack of education, which she attempted to remedy, and second, the overwhelming opposition to women "dabbling" in science, which it was impossible for her to overcome. Grant concludes that "the few experiments she might conduct in Huygens's sympathetic company were a poor substitute" for formal training and careful experimentation.[67] Still, Cavendish carried on her correspondence with him, and if it did not lead to Cavendish herself becoming a key figure in the Scientific Revolution, it did result in her revision of earlier work. Dissatisfied with her *Philosophical and Physical Opinions*, originally published in 1655, she revised and expanded it, publishing a second edition in 1663. She also found a way into the discourse of philosophy and science in her *Philosophical Letters, or Modest Reflections upon Some Opinions in Natural Philosophy Maintained by Several Famous and Learned Authors of This Age, Expressed by Way of Letters.*[68]

The Cavendishes did leave Welbeck and travel to London on occasion, in 1665, for example, after William Cavendish received the title duke of Newcastle, and again in 1667. They attended court during their 1665 stay in London, and although they were still in debt and their finances shaky, they spent lavishly. This visit was brief, however. In 1666, while she was back in Welbeck, Cavendish's *Observations upon Experimental Philosophy, to Which is Added "The Description of a New Blazing World"* was published, the first of a series of works printed by her new

---

she will "once again be bountiful" to his "ignorance" (119-20); in the second, dated 28 November 1658, he records having presented a collection of her published work to the University of Leyden, as she had requested (1-2).

Several other letters from Huygens to Margaret Cavendish are in Worp's edition: from 20 March 1657, 27 March 1657, 30 March 1657, 12 October 1658, 11 January 1659 (all in vol. 5); from 12 August 1664 and 19 September 1671, in vol. 6, *1663-1687* (The Hague: Martinus Nijhoff, 1917). A facsimile of this multi-volume edition is reprinted, in its entirety, as *Correspondence of Constantijn Huygens 1608-1687* (Huygens Institute for the History of the Netherlands in The Hague, 2010), available online at http://resources.huygens.knaw.nl/briefwisselingconstantijnhuygens/en. The website also makes available facsimile copies of most of the letters.

[67] Grant, *Margaret the First*, 195-96.
[68] See above, 15.

printer, Anne Maxwell. By the time the Cavendishes returned to London in 1667, William Cavendish had at last recovered his town residence, Newcastle House, built in Clerkenwell Close on the grounds of a former nunnery.[69] There they entertained widely, and the king himself paid them the compliment of a visit. During their stay in London, the famously shy Margaret Cavendish became the talk of the city. For one thing, she was given to "masculine" conversation—that is, she was known to speak openly, confidently, and authoritatively on such topics as poetry, science, philosophy and theology. And then there was her manner of dress. In her autobiography, she had described her youthful love of clothing, especially those she "invented" for herself, taking "delight" in the "singularity" of her creations; now her "singular" costumes attracted a great deal of attention. In her public appearances, she sometimes affected male attire, or, rather, a hybrid mixture of male and female apparel, a fact noted by one observer who commented on her meeting with the duke of York. The somewhat bemused writer reported that Margaret's "behavior was very pleasant, but rather to be seen than told." She "was dressed in a vest," an item of masculine clothing, and rather than making an appropriate curtsey, she "made legs and bows to the ground with her hand at her head."[70]

The diarist Samuel Pepys tried repeatedly to see the duchess in London, his first efforts proving fruitless because of the crowds that gathered whenever and wherever she was rumored to make an appearance. When he finally did manage to get a glimpse of Cavendish, she was wearing a knee-length outer coat and a velvet cap, both garments inspired by fashionable male attire (the cap was a type favored by Christina of Sweden, also known for wearing male

---

[69] The property had formerly belonged to St. Mary's nunnery, suppressed in 1539. It was a fashionable neighborhood in the seventeenth century. After William Cavendish had acquired the property in the 1630s, the large mansion was renamed Newcastle House, and he spent considerable money in building and renovating. During his years in exile, the trustees for his sequestered property had sold it. On his return to England, it took William Cavendish several years, a court case, and the sale of other property in order to regain the house. On this see *Survey of London*, vol. 66: *South and East Clerkenwell*, ed. Phillip Temple (London: London County Council, 2008), 28-39, http://www.british-history.ac.uk/survey-london/vol46/pp28-39.

[70] Sir Charles Lyttelton (of Hagley Hall) to his cousin Sir Christopher Lyttleton (later viscount of Hatton), 7 August 1665. In *Correspondence of the Family of Hatton . . . 1607-1704*, ed. Edward M. Thompson, Camden Society n. s., vol. 22 (London: Camden Society, 1878), 1:47. I have silently modernized the spelling and punctuation.

clothing).[71] Her costumes attracted attention for other reasons as well. When she attended a public performance of a play written by her husband, one member of the audience reported that she herself "was all the pageant now discoursed on"; she was wearing "an antic dress" cut so low that her breasts were "all laid out to view," her nipples "scarlet trimmed."[72] But at least one contemporary seemed to enjoy Cavendish's appearance rather than pretending to be scandalized by it. On 18 April, Sir John Evelyn, who had known the couple since their exile in Paris, visited Newcastle House; he was received there "with great kindness," he writes, adding that he was "much pleased with the extraordinary fanciful habit, garb, and discourse of the duchess." He visited her at home again on 25 and on 27 April with his wife, whom Cavendish "received with a kind of transport, suitable to her

---

[71] Samuel Pepys, 26 April 1667, in *The Diary of Samuel Pepys . . .* , ed. Henry B. Wheatley (New York: Macmillan, 1895), 6:290. Pepys made repeated efforts to see Cavendish during her visit to London, recording his various attempts on 11 April, 1 May, and 10 May.

[72] Sir Charles North to his father, 13 April 1667, quoted in Susan Wiseman, *Drama and Politics in the English Civil War* (New York, Cambridge University Press, 1998), 93. I have silently modernized the spelling and punctuation. Some of Cavendish's modern critics assume that the word "antic," should be understood as "antique," thus referring to a dress in the classical style, but Sophie Tomlinson notes that "antic" in this context more likely refers to the costume's strangeness. Tomlinson, *Women on Stage in Stuart Drama* (New York: Cambridge University Press, 2005), 183. The *OED* records several contemporary uses of the adjective "antic" to describe "dress or attire": "Absurd from fantastic incongruity; grotesque, bizarre, uncouthly ludicrous" (*OED*).

The play Margaret Cavendish was attending was her husband's *The Humorous Lovers*. Pepys attended a performance of this play on 11 April 1667, although he believed the play was by Margaret Cavendish rather than her husband. Pepys thought the play was "the most ridiculous thing that ever was wrote" (*The Diary of Samuel Pepys*, ed. Wheatley, 6:269). His opinion might perhaps have been different had he known the play was by William Cavendish rather than his wife—but, then again, maybe not (see below, n. 134).

Pepys was not the only person to believe that *The Humorous Lovers* was by Margaret, and not William, Cavendish—her authorship was also assumed by Gervaise Jaquis, who in May 1667 noted that, "upon Monday last, the duchess of Newcastle's play was acted in the theater in Lincoln's Inn Field, the king and the grandees of the court being present, and so was her grace and the duke, her husband." Gervaise Jaquis to the earl of Huntington, May 1667, quoted in Nancy Cotton, *Women Playwrights in England, c. 1363-1750* (Lewisburg, PA: Bucknell University Press, 1980), 48-49.

extravagant humor and dress, which was very singular."[73] Mary Evelyn was less impressed than her husband. While she thought Cavendish's "habit" was "particular, fantastical, not unbecoming a good shape," she thought her conversation was as "airy, empty, whimsical, and rambling as her books, aiming at science, difficulties, high notions, terminating commonly in nonsense, oaths, and obscenity." She judged Cavendish to be "more than necessarily submissive," and while the duchess might affect humility, Mary Evelyn concludes, "Never did I see a woman so full of herself, so amazingly vain and ambitious."[74]

In yet another example of what Sophie Tomlinson has identified as Cavendish's "rhetoric of dress and behavior," Cavendish was honored by an invitation to the newly established Royal Society in London.[75] On 30 May 1667 she became the first woman to attend a meeting of the society (which didn't admit women as members until 1945). Pepys was present on the occasion of her visit, although he implies that he showed up at Arundel House not realizing that the Society's regular Tuesday meeting had been altered to Thursday—apparently it had taken some time for members to decide whether Cavendish would be invited. Pepys notes that there had been "much debate, pro and con," adding, "it seems many being against it."[76] Cavendish made an impressive entry, arriving "with her women attending her" and waited on by an eager "company" gathered in expectation of her arrival. On the occasion, Cavendish was treated to a series of scientific experiments, including a demonstration of Robert Boyle's air pump and of Robert Hooke's microscope. Cavendish had once imagined such an occasion, where she was the only woman honored among a group of illustrious men. In her fictional version of such a meeting, she had described herself as "extremely out of countenance," not sure "how to behave," and full of "bashfulness"; overwhelmed by the experience, she "made

---

[73] John Evelyn, 27 April 1667, in *The Diary of John Evelyn*, ed. William Bray (London: George Bell, 1889), 2:25-26. I have silently modernized the spelling and punctuation.

[74] Mary Evelyn to the Rev. Ralph Bohun, undated letter from 1667, in *The Diary and Correspondence of John Evelyn*, ed. William Bray (London: Henry Colburn, 1857), 4:8-9. I have silently modernized the spelling and punctuation.

[75] Tomlinson, *Women on Stage*, 183.

[76] Pepys, 30 May 1667, in *Diary of Samuel Pepys*, ed. Wheatley, 6:343. I have silently modernized the spelling and punctuation

the more haste to depart."[77] The real experience was much the same as her imagined version; as Pepys tells the story, after the various demonstrations, she "cried still she was full of admiration" and then promptly left. "I do not like her at all," he concludes, "nor did I hear her say anything that was worth hearing, but that she was full of admiration, all admiration."[78] In his account of Cavendish's visit to the Royal Society, Evelyn is more circumspect, noting in his diary that she arrived "in great pomp" and that he "conducted her to her coach" when the experiments were over.[79] But if he is indeed the author of the light-hearted verses composed on the occasion of her visit to the Royal Society, he may have shared his wife's rather less charitable view of Cavendish and her ambitions:

> But . . . her head gear was so pretty
> I ne'er saw anything so witty
> Though I was half afeared
> God bless us! When I first did see her
> She looked so like a cavalier
> But that she had no beard![80]

Just days after Cavendish's meeting with the Royal Society, London was in turmoil. In early June, the Dutch fleet sailed up the Thames and burned several war ships. The frightening event was reported by both Pepys and Evelyn—perhaps as fearful of English looters as the Dutch invaders. Pepys made his will and sent his wife, father, and money into the country, while Evelyn commented on the widespread panic that sent everyone "flying, none knew why or whither," and busied himself surveying the damage and lamenting the "dishonor."[81] Margaret Caven-

---

[77] Cavendish, Letter 199, *Sociable Letters*, 417-19. I have silently modernized the spelling and punctuation.

[78] Pepys, 30 May 1667, in *Diary of Samuel Pepys*, ed. Wheatley, 6:344. I have silently modernized the spelling and punctuation.

[79] John Evelyn, 30 May 1667, in *Diary of John Evelyn*, ed. Bray, 2:26. I have silently modernized the spelling and punctuation.

[80] Quoted in Jones, *A Glorious Fame*, 163. Jones indicates that the anonymous "scurrilous verses" were attributed to Evelyn.

[81] Pepys, in *Diary of Samuel Pepys*, ed. Wheatley, 6:354-71, and Evelyn, in *Diary of John Evelyn*, ed. Bray, 2:26-30. I have silently modernized the spelling and punctuation. The so-called raid on the Medway was part of the second Anglo-Dutch War and

dish and her husband, meanwhile, remained in London. They did not leave until after the crisis had passed and the Dutch were gone, quietly leaving for Welbeck in July. Their departure was unremarked by all of those who had paid such attention to them earlier.

Back in Welbeck, Margaret Cavendish resumed her fevered program of writing and publication. In the summer of 1667 she published her biography of her husband, *The Life of the Thrice Noble, High, Puissant Prince William Cavendish, Duke, Marquess, and Earl of Newcastle*, and then, in 1668, *Plays, Never before Printed*. She also published new editions of previously published work: a Latin translation by Walter Charleton of her biography of her husband; the *Grounds of Natural Philosophy*, a reissue, "much altered," of *Philosophical and Physical Opinions*; a second edition of *Observations upon Experimental Philosophy, to Which is Added 'The Description of a New Blazing World'*; a separate publication of *The Description of a New World, Called the Blazing-World*; *Poems, or Several Fancies in Verse, with the Animal Parliament, in Prose*, a third edition of *Poems and Fancies*; and a second edition of *Orations of Divers Sorts, Accommodated to Divers Places*. But then the hectic pace slowed. Two earlier works were reissued in 1671, *Nature's Pictures* and *The World's Olio*, both in second editions. But there was nothing new.

Constantijn Huygens visited London that fall, and although he wrote to Cavendish in September, he did not make the trip to Welbeck to see her. In July of 1672, she received a package from Mark Anthony Benoist, who had been a tutor to William Cavendish's sons, filled with books and pens. This was followed, a month later, by a letter from him, a reply to one of hers. She had sent him some "filings" of a lodestone along with the result of some experiments. He assured her he would show her letter to "several persons, to have their opinions whether it be right or no."[82] But a year later, in June of 1673, she still had not reimbursed Benoist for the books and pens he had sent. And then, on 15 December 1673, she suddenly died at Welbeck Abbey. She was fifty years old.

On 3 January 1674, her body left Welbeck for London. She lay in state for several days at Newcastle House before her burial in Westminster Abbey. As a tribute to his wife, her husband published the

---

occurred between 19 and 24 June 1667 (though Pepys and Evelyn both date their diary entries between 9 and 14 June in the Old Style).

[82] Quoted in Whitaker, *Mad Madge*, 236.

Letters and Poems in Honor of the Incomparable Princess, Margaret, Duchess of Newcastle in 1676.

Margaret Cavendish's literary career began in 1653, with the publication of her first poems and "philosophical fancies," and continued at a hectic pace for nearly two decades. She did not limit herself to genres "acceptable" for those few women who did publish in the early seventeenth century, lyric poems, devotional works, and personal letters, for example. Instead, she published two volumes of plays, philosophical and scientific works, a utopian romance that has often been called the first work of science fiction in English, a biography of her husband, and her own autobiography, *A True Relation of My Birth, Breeding, and Life.*

It can be hard to assess the significance of her publication today, but as her recent biographer, Katie Whitaker, reminds us, "In the first forty years of the [seventeenth] century fewer than eighty books by women had been published in England—making up only one-half of 1 percent of all books—and many of these had appeared only posthumously, or else in pirated editions, without their authors' consent."[83]

But for two short decades, Margaret Cavendish wrote and published as if she were trying to make up the difference all by herself.

Women, Performance, and Playwriting in Early-Modern England

When she attended the theater with her sisters, the young Margaret Lucas, as she was then, would not have seen women players on the stage. Women did not perform at the great London playhouses like Blackfriars, the Boar's Head, the Fortune, the Phoenix, and the Red Bull. Outside of the commercial playhouses, however, there was a history of female performance in England—from the Benedictine nuns of Barking Abbey, who played the roles of the three Marys in a series of Holy Week and Easter plays in the fourteenth century, to Moll Frith's infamous appearance on stage at the Fortune Theatre in 1611, when she "sat upon the stage in the public view of all the people there present in man's apparel and played upon her lute and sang a song"

---

[83] Whitaker, *Mad Madge*, xiii.

and "spoke immodest and lascivious speeches."[84] Women in towns and cities across England took part in civic pageants devised to honor visiting dignitaries, danced in parishes to raise money for charitable purposes, entertained guests in private houses, played the role of the May queen at May Day festivals, and, at least on occasion, performed in the communal and collaborative mystery plays that were popular well into the sixteenth century.[85] Itinerant troupes of performers— singers, acrobats, tumblers, and jugglers—played on makeshift stages on the street, in town squares and courtyards, at inns and ale houses, anywhere they could draw an audience. And aristocratic women regularly took part in court performances and masques—Anne Boleyn's first documented appearance at the Tudor court of Henry VIII was on 1 March 1522, when she participated in the *Chateau Vert* pageant in the role of Perseverance (her sister Mary was Kindness)— while Elizabeth Tudor's entire queenship has been described by many modern historians as an extended and consummate public per- formance.[86] The queen herself seemed to make that very point in her

---

[84] On the nuns of Barking, see Laurie A. Finke, *Women's Writing in English: Medieval England*, Women's Writing in English (New York: Longman, 1999), 110-11, and Katie Normington, *Gender and Medieval Drama*, Gender in the Middle Ages (Cambridge, UK: D. S. Brewer, 2004), 48-49. For more on the nuns at Barking Abbey, see below, 38- 39).

The case of Moll—or Mary—Frith has received considerable attention, but I recommend the account in Stephen Orgel's *Impersonations: The Performance of Gender in Shakespeare's England* (New York: Cambridge University Press, 1996), 139-53. The Consistory Court of London's Correction Book, with its account of Moll's appearance before the ecclesiastical court, is in S. P. Cerasano and Marion Wynne- Davies, eds., *Renaissance Drama by Women: Texts and Documents* (New York: Routledge, 1996), 172 (I have silently modernized the spelling and punctuation).

[85] See Normington, *Gender and Medieval Drama*, 48-52. Whether women performed in medieval drama is a vexed question, but Normington documents the performance of some "wyffs" of Chester in 1499 and 1539-40, and, while noting the ambiguity of this reference, points out the unambiguous participation of women in the Innocents play of Coventry, where they "sang before the slaughter of their children by Herod's soldiers" (40-41).

[86] For Anne Boleyn, see Eric Ives, *Anne Boleyn* (Cambridge, MA: Blackwell, 1988), 47. The literature on Queen Elizabeth's self-representation is large; see, for a start, Susan Frye, *Elizabeth I: The Competition for Representation* (New York: Oxford University Press, 1993); Carole Levin, *The Heart and Stomach of a King: Elizabeth I and the Politics of Sex and Power* (Philadelphia: University of Pennsylvania Press, 1994); and Helen Hackett, *Virgin Mother, Maiden Queen: Elizabeth I and the Cult of the Virgin Mary* (New York: St. Martin's Press, 1995).

1586 speech to parliament: "Princes, you know, stand upon stages so that their actions are viewed and beheld of all men."[87]

At the court of James I, Elizabeth's successor, Queen Anna of Denmark and her ladies performed in masques, including Samuel Daniel's *The Vision of the Twelve Goddesses*, on 8 January 1604, in which the queen took the role of Pallas Athena, and Ben Jonson's *The Masque of Blackness*, on 6 January 1605, with the queen as Euphoris, one of the twelve daughters of Niger, and Lady Mary Wroth—whose publication of *Urania* in 1621 drew such negative attention—as another, Baryte. The queen also appeared in Jonson's companion piece to *Blackness*, *The Masque of Beauty*, performed in on 10 January 1608, this time with sixteen women of the court participating. These performances were not without criticism; the Privy Council expressed reservations about the appropriateness of the queen's performance as well as concern about the expense of the productions.[88] For his part, the courtier Dudley Carleton disapproved of the queen's costume, if not her performance—in her appearance as Pallas Athena, he remarked that the queen's dress was too short, revealing her feet and legs—and he criticized the women's costumes in *The Masque of Blackness* as well—they were "too light and courtesan-like for such great ones."[89] It's important to note, however, that while royal and aristocratic women participated in Jacobean court masques, they were silent: they danced,

---

[87] Queen Elizabeth's First Reply to Parliament, 12 November 1586, in *Elizabeth I: Collected Works*, ed. Leah S. Marcus, Janel Mueller, and Mary Beth Rose (Chicago: University of Chicago Press, 2000), 189. This version of the queen's speech represents "a contemporary report of the speech, and probably close to the speech as the queen delivered it to the parliamentary delegates who waited on her with their petition at Richmond. Since she spoke impromptu, all MSS were created after the fact" (186n1). A second copy, this one published, phrases the metaphor somewhat differently: "for we princes, I tell you, are set on stages in the sight and view of all the world duly observed" (194).

[88] The Council to James I, December 1604, with its concern about the appropriateness of the queen's performance, is quoted in Tomlinson, *Women on Stage*, 2. On the Privy Council's concerns about the expense of the masques, see, for example, Leeds Barroll, "Inventing the Stuart Masque," in *The Politics of the Stuart Court Masque*, ed. David Bevington and Peter Holbrooke (New York: Cambridge University Press, 2006), 132.

[89] Dudley Carleton's criticism of Queen Anne's costume is quoted in Cerasano and Wynne-Davies, eds., *Renaissance Drama by Women*, 80; Carleton's criticism of the costumes in *The Masque of Blackness* is quoted in Tomlinson, *Women on Stage*, 25. In both cases I have silently modernized the spelling and punctuation.

but they did not speak. As queen, Anna performed in twelve court masques, including Daniel's *Tethys' Festival*, in 1610, which celebrated her son Henry's investiture as prince of Wales, but she stopped performing after Prince Henry's untimely death in 1612.

One noteworthy example of women's performance not *by* the queen but *for* her occurred in 1617, when the "young gentlewomen of the Ladies Hall in Deptford" performed Robert White's *Cupid's Banishment*.[90] These "young gentlewomen" were not part of the Stuart court, nor were they performing at Whitehall, but neither did they lack court connections; two of the queen's goddaughters attended the school, and the masque was dedicated to Lucy Russell, the countess of Bedford, who had regularly performed in court masques with the queen, including *The Vision of the Twelve Goddesses*, *The Masque of Blackness*, and *The Masque of Beauty*. But, while *Cupid's Banishment* may not have been performed at the king's court, it was performed at the *queen's* court, Greenwich Palace—and, most importantly, a young woman playing the role of Fortune spoke during the performance. In her analysis of this masque, Clare McManus claims that *Cupid's Banishment* is "a document of immense importance for the assessment of female performance" in early modern England: though the masque itself was "insubstantial" and "derivative," it marks the moment when "the female masquing voice was first heard."[91]

Anna of Denmark's daughter-in-law, Queen Henrietta Maria, not only continued the masquing tradition but was both patron of and performer in pastoral dramas presented at the Caroline court. In December of 1625, just months after her marriage to King Charles I, the queen began rehearsing her "troupe" for a performance of *Artenice*, a pastoral comedy based on Honorat de Bueil, sieur de Racan's *Les Bergeries* ("the sheepfold"). In February 1626, when Henrietta Maria herself played the lead role of Artenice, she shocked the audience by

---

[90] Robert White was the master of Ladies Hall, which Cerasano and Wynne-Davies describe as "a school located south of London in Deptford. . . . It seems to have been a sort of high-class private academy that offered both academic studies and training in social skills." Cerasano and Wynne-Davies, eds., *Renaissance Drama by Women*, 77.

[91] Clare McManus, *Women on the Renaissance Stage: Anna of Denmark and Female Masquing in the Stuart Court, 1590-1619* (Manchester, UK: Manchester University Press, 2002), 164-201. McManus's comment on the significance of *Cupid's Banishment* is found on p. 210.

performing a speaking role. The audience was also surprised by the spectacle of women playing the parts of men.[92] The Venetian ambassador to London appreciated the "rich scenery and dresses" of the queen and "her maidens," as well as the queen's "remarkable acting," but he also observed that "it did not give complete satisfaction because the English objected to the first part being declaimed by the queen." Another observer commented, "I have known the time when this would have seemed a strange sight, to see a queen act in a play," but he must have sighed as he added, "*tempora mutantur et nos*," or "times change, and so must we."[93] The queen's French retinue was rather quickly sent back home, but the royal performances continued. In 1633, Walter Montagu's masque, *The Shepherds' Paradise*, was staged, with women performing speaking roles—the queen played the role of Bellessa, and a majority of the female performers were cross-dressed, playing male roles. It is important to remember, however, that the queen's theatrical performances were private; as the Tuscan representative to the English court reported on one occasion, "The performance was conducted as privately as possible, inasmuch as it is an unusual thing in this country to see the queen upon a stage; the audience consequently was limited to a few of the nobility, expressly invited, no others being admitted."[94]

Nevertheless, the performance of women at the English royal court is widely regarded as in part prompting the anti-theatrical criticism of the London lawyer William Prynne's *Histriomastix*, published in 1633. Prynne condemns the appearance of "women actors on the stage to

---

[92] See Karen Britland, *Drama at the Courts of Henrietta Maria* (New York: Cambridge University Press, 2006), 35-52, and Melinda J. Gough, "Courtly *Comédiantes*: Henrietta Maria and Amateur Women's Stage Plays in France and England," in *Women Players in England, 1500-1660: Beyond the All-Male Stage*, ed. Pamela Allen Brown and Peter Parolin, Studies in Performance and Early Modern Drama (Burlington, VT: Ashgate Publishing, 2005), 193-215. The queen loved to attend the London playhouses as well; Tomlinson, *Women on Stage*, notes that the queen attended four performances at the Blackfriars in the 1630s and one special performance at the Phoenix (11).

[93] The letter of Zoane Pesaro, Venetia ambassador in England, 24 February 1626, and the note of John Chamberlain, 7 March 1626, are quoted in Cerasano and Wynne-Davies, eds, *Renaissance Drama by Women*, 169. I have quietly modernized the spelling and punctuation.

[94] Alessandro Antelminelli to the Grand Duke of Tuscany, 1625/6, quoted in Cerasano and Wynne-Davies, eds., *Renaissance Drama by Women*, 221. I have silently modernized the spelling and punctuation.

personate female parts"; in ancient times, he rails, such women were "all notorious impudent, prostituted strumpets." Prynne regards women players—even if they are acting "a female's part"—to be "evil" and "vicious," guilty of the "most abominable, unnatural sin of Sodom," just as full of "sodomitical wickedness" as the young male actor who might "put on a woman's apparel, person, and behavior, to act a female's part on the stage." "Both of them," he concludes, "are evil" and "extremely vicious." They are "abominable, both intolerable, neither of them laudatory or necessary, therefore both of them to be abandoned, neither of them to be henceforth tolerated among Christians." [95]

His condemnations of female actors point specifically to their public speech as a violation of Christian gender ideology:

Women . . . with a naked and an uncovered head, speak to the people without shame and usurp impudency to themselves with so great premeditation and infuse so great lasciviousness into the minds of hearers and spectators that all may seem, even with one consent, to extirpate all modesty out of their minds, to disgrace the female nature, and to satiate their lusts with pernicious pleasure. For all things that are done there are absolutely most obscene. For all things . . . (I say) are full of filthy wantonness.

The playhouse itself is a site for all kinds of sin: "whoredoms are there committed," "marriages are there defiled with adulteries," men "are there most unnaturally defiled," and "young men there are effeminate."[96]

Prynne's condemnation of "women actors" was also a response to the first documented appearance of professional actresses on the English stage. Continental women may have performed in England before the mid-seventeenth century—Italian acting companies traveled

---

[95] William Prynne, *Histrio-mastix: The Players Scourge, or, Actors Tragedie, Divided into Two Parts* . . . (London, 1633), [2]08-16. I have silently modernized the spelling and punctuation. Prynne's condemnation of the theater is massive, more than 1000 pages, followed by an extensive alphabetized "Table . . . of the Chiefest Passages in This Treatise."

[96] Prynne, *Histrio-mastix*, 414-15. I have silently modernized the spelling and punctuation.

in England during the reign of Queen Elizabeth, and, as Stephen Orgel notes, "Italian companies always included women."[97] And another hint that women may have performed in England comes from 1608. After traveling in Europe for some months, the Englishman Thomas Coryat reported at great length on the time he spent in Venice, including an account of his visit to a "playhouse," where he saw a comedy. Coryat thought the theater itself was "beggarly" when compared to the "stately playhouses in England." He didn't think the actors or their costumes or the music compared to those in English theaters either, but he admitted that he "observed there" in Venice something that he had never experienced before: "for I saw women act." Significantly, however, Coryat added that although *he* had never seen women actors, he had "heard that it [women acting on stage] hath been sometimes used in London." Coryat was impressed; although he had just said the Venetian actors could not compare to their English counterparts, he said the women performed "with as good a grace, action, gesture, and whatsoever convenient for a player as ever I saw any male actor."[98]

While these two references suggest at least the possibility that professional female actors *may* have performed in England late in the sixteenth or early in the seventeenth century, there is no doubt that women *did* perform in London in 1629. They were not *English* actors, however, but French players, who appeared at the Blackfriars Theatre. One Thomas Brande addressed an outraged letter to William Laud, bishop of London, reporting that "certain vagrant French players who had been expelled from their own country, *and those women*, did attempt . . . to act a certain lascivious and unchaste comedy in the French tongue at the Blackfriars." He continued, "Glad I am to say they were hissed, hooted, and pippin-pelted from the stage, so as I do not think they will soon be ready to try the same again." He was wrong about whether they would dare perform again in London, because the actors appeared twice more in commercial playhouses, at the Red Bull and at

---

[97] Orgel, *Impersonations*, 7.

[98] Thomas Coryat, *Coryats Crudities Hastily Gobbled up in Five Months Travels . . .* (London, 1611; rpt. Glasgow: James MacLehose, 1905), 1:386. I have silently modernized the spelling and punctuation. (Coryat also recorded at length his impressions of the "noble and famous courtesans" of the city who attended the performance, privileged to sit "in the best room of all the playhouse," 386-87.)

the Fortune.[99] William Prynne was aware of the same performance, and this was what he condemned in *Histriomastix*. There may well be "female players" in Italy and other "foreign parts," he wrote, but there were also "Frenchwomen actors in a play" who "not long since personated in Blackfriars Playhouse." Contrary to Brande's assertions, Prynne said the women actors were a great attraction, the cause of a "great resort" to the theatre.[100]

Despite outrage like Prynne's, court performances continued, even after the king and queen were forced out of London and relocated to Oxford, and despite the closure of the theaters by parliament in 1642, at the beginning of what would become the first English Civil War. Katie Whitaker indicates that "the court continued its prewar artistic life so far as conditions permitted." Actors, set adrift by the closure of the London theaters, "sometimes came into Oxford to perform plays for the court," and the queen herself "kept up the prewar tradition of producing masques for the court's entertainment." However, given the new economic realities, "the scale and grandeur of the proceedings were necessarily reduced." Once Henrietta Maria was forced to flee into France in 1643, she received a generous income, and "the full splendor and ceremony of court life resumed," at least for a time.[101] But after the execution of Charles I and the French civil wars of the *Fronde*, there was little occasion—or money—for such light-hearted entertainments. By 1654, the two Stuart princes, Charles and James, were forced to leave France, and they relocated in Cologne. The queen—now the dowager queen mother—retired to the convent of the Sisters of the Visitation of Holy Mary at Chaillot in Paris.[102]

---

[99] Thomas Brande's letter is quoted in Orgel, *Impersonations*, 7. Orgel's exploration of the question of why the professional stage in England was all-male—or, as he phrased the question, more provocatively, "Why did the English stage take boys for women?"—begins by noting that women were professional actors in France, Spain, and Italy beginning in the mid-sixteenth century. There was no public theater in the Netherlands (until the mid-seventeenth century) or in Protestant Germany, and so "the English situation is anomalous" (1-2).

[100] Prynne, *Histrio-mastix*, 415. I have silently modernized the spelling and punctuation.

[101] Whitaker, *Mad Madge*, 50, 58

[102] Henrietta Maria remained in the convent until after the Restoration; at her son Charles II's invitation, she briefly returned to England, but she went back to Paris and the convent in 1665 and died there in 1669. As an interesting aside, in his biography of Shakespeare, Sir Sidney Lee says that "from July 11 to 13, 1643, Queen

In England, meanwhile, despite the parliamentary ban of 1642 and two further ordinances, issued in 1647 and 1648, the "culture of female acting" did not disappear.[103] Rather, as Sophie Tomlinson argues, the "discontinuance of an all-male stage" seems to have "created new opportunities for women to perform." Women were able to "participate in private house theatricals"; they performed as part of "household entertainments," during country-house parties, and in schools. The playwright and entrepreneur William Davenant even staged a number of "musical entertainments" in London during the Interregnum, including ten days' of "declamations and music" at Rutland House, beginning on 23 May 1656 (though it was now his private residence, Davenant opened the performance at Rutland to a limited audience and charged admission). He also produced *The Siege of Rhodes*, generally considered the first English opera, at Rutland House later that year. Crucially, both works included performances by Catherine Coleman, the wife of the composer Edward Coleman. She performed as a member of the chorus in the earlier work but was a lead singer in *The Siege of Rhodes*. In 1658, she performed the same role when *The Siege of Rhodes* was staged at the Cockpit Theatre in Drury Lane.[104]

The history of female performance in England is thus complicated and uncertain. Did women participate in medieval mystery plays? Why were Englishwomen excluded from the professional stage? When did continental actresses first perform in England? What was the public reaction to their appearance on stage? The history of female play-writing, by contrast, is much easier to narrate.

Henrietta Maria, while journeying from Newark to Oxford" stayed in Stratford at New Place, Shakespeare's home, then in the possession of his daughter, Susanna. Lee, *A Life of William Shakespeare* (London: Smith, Elder, 1899), 281.

103 Ordinance for the suppression of Stage Plays and Interludes within the Cities of London and Westminster and the Counties of Middlesex and Surrey, 22 October 1647, and Ordinance for the suppression of Stage Plays and Interludes with the penalties prescribed for actors and spectators, 11 February 1647/8. In *Acts and Ordinances of the Interregnum, 1642-1660*, ed. Firth and Rait, 1027 and 1070-72.

104 On new performing opportunities for women and for the significance of Catherine Coleman, see Tomlinson, *Women on Stage*, 156-57. On William Davenant's "entertainments" staged during the Interregnum, see Dale B. J. Randall, *Winter Fruit: English Drama, 1642-1660* (Lexington: The University of Kentucky Press, 1995), 169-79.

The earliest Englishwoman known to have written a play is Katherine of Sutton, the abbess of Barking Abbey. Not much is known about her, except that she was abbess of the convent from 1363 to 1376. A prefatory note in the surviving manuscript of the Barking play says that it was "instituted" by the abbess in order to "dispel" the "sluggishness" of the "faithful." The play is a multi-part liturgical drama that focuses on significant events associated with the celebration of Easter: the *Depositio crucis*, a reenactment of the entombment of Christ performed on Good Friday, culminates in the removal of the cross and the host from the altar and their symbolic burial; the *Descensus Christi*, performed at Easter matins, dramatizes the descent of Christ into hell (the "harrowing" of hell), traditionally the time between Jesus's crucifixion and resurrection; the *Elevatio Christi* depicts the restoration of the cross and host to the altar; the *Visitatio sepulchri*, played directly after the *Descensus* and the *Elevatio*, reenacts the early-morning visit to the empty tomb of the "three Marys," Mary, the mother of Jesus, Mary Magdalene, and Mary Salome, a follower of Jesus, sometimes identified as the mother of two of the apostles, James and John. The play was written for performance by both friars and, as we have noted above, by nuns. Its audience included the nuns themselves (probably between thirty-five and forty women) as well as lay men and women who came to the convent's church for the celebration of Easter. The manuscript contains fairly extensive "stage" directions that give some sense of the performance.[105]

Nearly two centuries pass before we find another dramatic text written by a woman, a translation of Euripides' *Iphigenia* made by Lady Jane Lumley (c. 1537-1576), the daughter of Henry Fitzalan, earl of Arundel, and his wife, Katherine Grey.[106] Carefully educated by her father—she knew both Latin and Greek—Jane also had access to his

---

[105] On Katherine of Sutton, see Cotton, *Women Playwrights in England*, 27-28, and her earlier "Katherine of Sutton: The First English Woman Playwright," *Educational Theatre Journal* 30, no. 4 (1978): 475–81. See also Michael O'Connell, "Katherine of Sutton," in *Women's Works*, vol. 1: *900-1550*, ed. Donald W. Foster (New York: Wicked Good Books, 2013), 49-50. Following the brief essay on the abbess is "The Easter Play of the Nuns of Barking Convent," trans. Michael O'Connell, 51-53.

[106] Katherine Grey was the daughter of Thomas Grey, first marquis of Dorset; Katherine Grey's brother, Thomas Grey, second marquis of Dorset, was the grandfather of Lady Jane Grey, a formidable scholar and the so-called Nine Days' Queen.

extensive library; after her marriage to John, baron Lumley, she could employ the exceptional library at Lumley Castle. (Her father's library was later inherited by her husband.) It was after her 1550 marriage, at some point between 1553 and 1557, that Jane Lumley completed *The Tragedy of Euripides called Iphigeneia*, more likely working from a Greek-Latin translation by the Dutch scholar Desiderius Erasmus than from the Greek original.[107] While earlier generations of literary critics regarded Lumley's work as a purely academic exercise, one that enabled a teenage girl to show off her privileged education, Patricia Demars identifies it as a paraphrase rather than a close (and plodding) translation: "Here is Euripides filtered through the eyes of a widely read, capable, protected early modern young woman, whose domestic idiom, distinctive word choices, misconstruals, deliberate exclusions and sometimes softened, sometimes heightened tragic details convey the blended experience of the Greek and Latin texts."[108] And rather than a juvenile exercise, the play is surely intended as a complex political allegory. If the translation dates to 1553, it would have been completed after Jane Grey's brief "reign" as queen of England but before her execution—Lumley was related to Jane Grey through her mother, but Lumley's father played an important role in supporting Mary Tudor's claim to the throne, and he would sign the warrant for Jane Grey's execution in 1554. Iphigenia's willing and dignified self-sacrifice may thus represent Jane Grey's necessary death, which

---

[107] Diane Purkiss argues for a date of 1553, the year that her father acquired the confiscated library of Thomas Cranmer, which included two copies of the play by Euripides. On this see Purkiss, ed., *Three Tragedies by Renaissance Women: "The Tragedie of Iphigeneia," "The Tragedie of Antonie," "The Tragedie of Mariam,"* Penguin Dramatists (Harmondsworth, UK: Penguin Books, 1998), xxiv-xxv. Marion Wynne-Davies believes that the play was translated in 1557, when Lumley and her husband were at Nonsuch, the royal palace sold by Mary Tudor to Lumley's father in 1556. See Wynne-Davies, "The Good Lady Lumley's Desire: *Iphigeneia* and the Nonsuch Banqueting House," in *Heroines of the Golden StAge: Women and Drama in Spain and England 1500-1700*, ed. Rina Walthaus and Marguérite Corporaal (Kassel, Germany: Reichenberger, 2008), 111-128.

On Lumley, her education, and her play, see Marta Straznicky, *Privacy, Playreading, and Women's Closet Drama, 1550-1700* (New York: Cambridge University Press, 2004), 19-47.

[108] Demars, "On First Looking into Lumley's Euripides," *Renaissance and Reformation* n.s. 23, no. 1 (1999): 38.

preserved the security of England and the Catholic faith.[109] If the translation were completed in 1556 or 1557, after Elizabeth Tudor became queen, it might be read as a kind of exoneration of Arundel. In this context, as Marion Wynne-Davies argues, the play's "dramatic discourse allowed [Jane Lumley] to display the power and cultural sophistication of her father, while simultaneously presenting his actions as part of a wider necessity, perhaps even encouraging him to adopt such a stance as a new Protestant queen ascended the throne." Whatever the work's political context, Lumley "wisely chose to employ the cautious dramatic form of household theater" for her drama.[110] Her audience, while educated and privileged, is limited—a small group confined to her familial and social sphere.

Queen Elizabeth also produced a dramatic work, although a fragmentary one. The Tudor queen's translation, from a play by Seneca, was probably completed in 1589. The 123 lines from *Hercules on Oeta* come from a choral ode in the second act of the Latin original. The chorus of Aetolian women has just realized that the robe sent to Hercules by his wife is poisoned. Elizabeth's reworking of the chorus is "less a translation, strictly conceived, than an imitation," a version in which she omits the part of the original that focuses on unhappy wives, concentrating instead on "the chorus's reflections on the vulnerability of monarchs and other eminent persons to the treachery of fellow mortals and the vicissitudes of Fortune."[111] Once again we may see a woman using a dramatic text as a way of responding to political tragedy. Janel Mueller and Joshua Scodel read this speech, and the "exceptional volubility and freedom" with which Elizabeth approaches the original, as a means of "debating with herself over signing the

---

[109] See Demars, "On First Looking," *passim*.

[110] Wynne-Davies, "The Theater," *British Women's Writing*, 2:184. In addition to the Purkiss edition of Lumley's play, a significant portion of the play, in a modern English translation, is in *Women's Works*, vol. 2: *1550-1603*, ed. Donald W. Foster, (New York: Wicked Good Books, 2014), 24-30, the selection introduced and edited by Foster.

[111] Elizabeth I, *Translations, 1544-1589*, ed. Janel Mueller and Joshua Scodel (Chicago: University of Chicago Press, 2008), 442. Mueller and Scodel date Elizabeth's translation based on the publication of the edition of Seneca that seems to have been the queen's source, Lucius Annaeus Seneca, *Tragoediae* (London, 1589). In addition to the text in Mueller and Scodel, 439-56, Elizabeth's *Hercules Oetaeus* is in Cerasano and Wynne-Davies, eds., *Renaissance Drama by Women*, 7-12. A selection is also included in Foster, ed., *Women's Works*, 2:107.

warrant" for the execution of Mary Stuart, queen of Scotland. Even the recent victory over the Spanish Armada had not eliminated the threats to England, Elizabeth's continued anxiety perhaps triggering her reflection on the "agonizing dilemma" she had already faced and overcome as well as her "continuing apprehension" that England would once again face a Spanish invasion.[112]

Only two early-modern women, Mary Sidney Herbert and Elizabeth Cary, published their plays. In the case of Mary Sidney Herbert, countess of Pembroke (1561-1621), her elite status undoubtedly made publication possible, while her political ends made publication desirable. Sidney's 1592 *Antonius, A Tragoedie* was, at least ostensibly, a translation of the French poet Robert Garnier's *Marc-Antoine*, a Senecan tragedy written between 1574 and 1575 and included in his 1585 collected *Tragedies*.[113] As the 1592 title page describes Sidney's *Antonius*, the play was "done in English by the countess of Pembroke." And although public performances of professional actors like Pembroke's Men, under the patronage of her husband, Henry Herbert, in London playhouses like the Theatre, the Curtain, and the Swan, were now well established, Sidney's play was not written to be performed before large urban audiences in such theaters, but was instead, like Lumley's *Iphigeneia*, "intended" for private "staged readings" or household performance, and thus restricted to an exclusive coterie audience.

Publication, however, moved Sidney's play from the private realm into the public sphere. In her choice of a text and in her decision to publish, her motivations seem to have been political, a way to further the Protestant political program of the Sidney family, most notably of her brother, the poet and courtier Sir Philip Sidney; in Margaret Hannay's words, "When Mary Sidney made her decision to translate a work by Robert Garnier, a magistrate who used his drama to criticize

---

[112] Mueller and Scodel, eds., *Translations*, 444.

[113] Garnier's play was first published in 1578 then republished in *Les Tragédies* (Paris, 1585). Textual evidence indicates Sidney used the 1585 revised version of the play. On this see Barry Weller, "Mary Sidney, countess of Pembroke: *Antonius*," in *The Ashgate Research Companion to the Sidneys, 1500-1700*, vol. 2, *Literature*, ed. Margaret P. Hannay, Mary Ellen Lamb, and Michael G. Brennan (Burlington, VT: Ashgate Publishing, 2015), 199.

Sidney's play was first published in a volume that began with her *Discourse of Life and Death* . . . (London, 1592), the play appearing as second item in the book.

the state, she was making a political statement."[114] In her focus on the character of Cleopatra and in the powerful, extended speeches of the Egyptian queen, Sidney could promote a view of female heroism and fidelity even while demonstrating "the dangers of civil war, stressing the need for rulers to fulfil[l] their obligations to their subjects and not to allow passion to cloud their judgements."[115] Sidney's play proved popular—it appeared in two additional printings in 1595, under the revised title of *The Tragedie of Antonie*, with three more printings before 1607.[116] (By contrast, Jane Lumley's *Iphigeneia* was not published until 1909.[117])

Equally daring in her decision to publish was Elizabeth Tanfield Cary (1585-1639), the first Englishwoman known to have written an original play. Her *Tragedy of Mariam, the Fair Queen of Jewry* dramatized the story of Herod, the king of Judea, and his wife, Mariam. In his jealousy and rage, Herod has his wife murdered, prompting frequent comparisons between Cary's play and Shakespeare's *Othello*. Cary's source was Thomas Lodge's 1602 *Antiquities of the Jews*, his translation of the Jewish historian Titus Flavius Josephus's first-century history of the Jews; her play was probably completed between 1602, when, at the age of fifteen, she was married to Henry Cary, later Viscount Falkland, and 1604. (Shakespeare's *Othello* is dated to about the same period, its first recorded performance for King James's court at Whitehall on 1 November 1604.) As Cary's daughter would later write, Henry Cary left immediately after the wedding to continue his military career in the Low Countries, leaving Elizabeth, at first, with her own family. But his mother, Catherine Knevet Cary, soon insisted on "having" her son's

---

[114] Margaret Hannay, *Philip's Phoenix: Mary Sidney, Countess of Pembroke* (New York: Oxford University Press, 1990), 126-27.

[115] Cerasano and Wynne-Davies, eds., *Renaissance Drama by Women*, 17.

[116] Cerasano and Wynne-Davies, eds., *Renaissance Drama by Women*, 16. The text of *Antonie* is available in Purkiss, ed., *Three Tragedies by Renaissance Women*, and in Cerasano and Wynne-Davies, eds., *Renaissance Drama by Women*. The first modern publication of the play was by Alice H. Luce, *The Countess of Pembroke's "Antonie"* (Weimar: Emil Felber, 1897). One further Sidney dramatic piece may be noted here. Mary Sidney Herbert's pastoral "Dialogue between Two Shepherds, Thenot and Piers, in Praise of Astrea" was probably written for Elizabeth I's planned visit to Wilton in 1599. The visit did not take place, but the dialogue was printed in Francis Davison's *A Poetical Rapsody* (London, 1602).

[117] Jane Lumley, trans., *Iphigenia at Aulis*, ed. Harold H. Child (London: Malone Society, 1909).

wife in her custody, though Cary's daughter wrote that the young, newly married Elizabeth was "used" very "hardly" and confined "to her chamber" in her husband's family home. Cary seemed not to have minded too much, entertaining herself happily with reading, until her mother-in-law "took away all her books, with command to have no more brought her."[118] Undaunted, and deprived of books to read, the young woman began to write. Among her compositions seems to have been an earlier tragedy, now lost, set in Syracuse—in a poem written in praise of Cary, the English poet John Davies would later refer to Cary not only as his pupil but to her *two* plays "of state," one set in Syracuse, the other in Palestine, the setting of *Mariam*. When Cary published *Mariam* in 1613, she added a dedicatory sonnet, in which she alludes to her "first" play, set in Sicily and "consecrated to Apollo."[119]

When Cary published her work, she did not have the protection of the kind of title Mary Sidney had—Sidney presented herself in her publications not as Mary Sidney Herbert, but as "the countess of Pembroke." But Cary found other ways to protect her identity, first by insisting on the quality of her character ("written by that learned, virtuous, and truly noble lady"), then shielding herself by using only her initials ("E. C."). And the reasons for Cary's caution are clear— nowhere is the danger of women's public speech, and, by extension, publication, more starkly presented than in *Mariam*. In the first line of her opening soliloquy, Mariam acknowledges the fault of her "public voice," moving quickly to condemn her own speech as "too rash." "Unbridled speech is Mariam's worst disgrace," Herod's chief counselor observes. The chorus, too, comments on Mariam's public speech: even the most virtuous of women is not free from suspicion if she

---

[118] *The Lady Falkland: Her Life*, by "one of her daughters," in Elizabeth Cary, the lady Falkland, *The Tragedy of Mariam, the Fair Queen of Jewry, with "The Lady Falkland: Her Life" by One of Her Daughters*, ed. Barry Weller and Margaret W. Ferguson (Berkeley: University of California Press, 1994), 188-89.

[119] John Davies, *The Muses Sacrifice, or Divine Meditations* (London, 1612), in S. P. Cerasano and Marion Wynne-Davies, eds., *Readings in Renaissance Women's Drama: Criticism, History, and Performance, 1594-1998* (New York: Routledge, 1998), 13-14. Cary's sonnet is in *The Tragedie of Mariam, the Faire Queene of Jewry* (London, 1613), n. p. *The Tragedy of Mariam* was not published again until the early twentieth century: A. C. Dunstan, ed., *The Tragedy of Mariam, 1613*, Malone Society Reprints (Oxford: Oxford University Press, 1914). Cary's dedicatory sonnet and the play are in Weller and Hannay's edition; in Cerasano and Wynne-Davies, eds., *Renaissance Drama*; and in Purkiss, ed., *Three Tragedies by Renaissance Women*.

speaks openly and publicly. It's not enough to *be* chaste, the chorus warns, a woman must *behave* circumspectly, "by her proper self restrained." To speak openly is to "blot" her "glory": "That wife her hand against her fame doth rear, / That more than to her lord alone will give / A private word to any second ear." Though "most chaste," such a wife "wounds her honour." And then, the ultimate warning: "Her mind if not peculiar is not chaste, / For in a wife it is no worse to find, / A common body than a common mind." Or, as Herod puts it crudely before having Mariam killed, "She's unchaste; / Her mouth will open to every stranger's ear."[120] Even so, Cary did publish her play, perhaps encouraged by Davies's warning that if she gave her "works both birth and grave," those in "times to come" would not be able to "credit" the accomplishments of the "weaker sex"—nor would Cary's "wit and grace" have earned her "fame."[121] Marion Wynne-Davies writes that, among all these early women dramatists—Lumley, Sidney, even the queen herself—

it is Cary who most acknowledges the limitations that constrained a sixteenth-century Englishwoman writing a dramatic text, namely: that they could hardly hope for a performance of their work, that propriety and convention ensured that they would have no audience, and that they had no access to a public stage. . . . Elizabeth Cary . . . took the negation of voice, action, and space to its absurd conclusion, produc[ing] not only a stringent con-demnation of the repression of women, but also an early modern parable of tyranny, rebellion, and subjugation.[122]

After Elizabeth Cary, women in England seem to fall mostly silent, at least when it comes to writing drama. Mostly, but not entirely. Mary Sidney Herbert's niece, Mary Sidney Wroth (1587-1651?), has the distinction of being the first Englishwoman to write an original comedy, *Love's Victory*, probably composed about 1620, but it was not published. Her decision to write a dramatic work is understandable.

---

[120] Cary, *Mariam*, in Cerasano and Wynne-Davies, eds., *Renaissance Drama by Women*, 1.1, 6; 3.183-84, 219-50; 4.432-33.

[121] Davies, *The Muses Sacrifice*, in Cerasano and Wynne-Davies, eds., *Readings in Renaissance Women's Drama*, 14.

[122] Wynne-Davies, "The Theater," in *The History of British Women's Writing*, 2:193.

Not only had she performed in court masques, she had probably attended performances at public theaters.[123] But she had a more important precedent, her aunt's *Tragedie of Antonie*, and, also like her aunt, Wroth probably intended her play for readings with, and perhaps performance by, family and friends.

While many interpretations of Wroth's *Love's Victory* (and of her romance, *Urania*) focus on the way Wroth dramatizes the complex romantic relationships of the Sidney family, it may also be the case that the allegory of *Love's Victory* is, at the same time, political. Marion Wynne-Davies argues that the lovers Musella and Philisses represent *both* Wroth and her lover/cousin William Herbert *and* Elizabeth Stuart and her husband, Frederick of Bohemia. Despite Queen Anna of Denmark's opposition to the match, the young Stuart princess was married to the equally young prince palatine in a lavish ceremony at Whitehall in 1613, the play expressing the support of the Sidney family for the match. Akiko Kusonoki, however, argues that the play's "political import" might be slightly different, suggesting the play was written later, in 1619, when the young couple was being offered the crown of Bohemia. While King James opposed the offer, the play represented the support and encouragement of the Sidney-Herbert family circle, "an appeal in particular to female members to be active in promoting Protestant policy to help the couple" who were "wavering" about whether to accept the crown, given the English king's objections.[124] It is also possible that Wroth's play might have moved

---

[123] On Lady Mary Wroth's performance in Jacobean masques, see above, 32. Josephine Roberts concludes that Wroth had also attended performances in playhouses, "as suggested by her references to the theater in the *Urania*." Roberts, ed., *The Poems of Lady Mary Wroth*, 53. Wroth's *Love's Victory* is in Cerasano and Wynne-Davies, eds., *Renaissance Drama by Women*.

[124] On *Love's Victory* as historical allegory, in particular focused on Elizabeth Stuart's marriage, see Marion Wynne-Davies, *Women Writers and Familial Discourse in the English Renaissance: Relative Values*, Early Modern Literature in History (New York: Palgrave Macmillan, 2007), 102-3. For the view that the play encourages the young couple to accept the crown of Bohemia, see Akiko Kusonoki, "Wroth's *Love's Victory* as a Response to Shakespeare's Representation of Gender Distinctions: With Special Reference to *Romeo and Juliet*," in *Mary Wroth and Shakespeare*, Routledge Studies in Shakespeare, ed. Paul Salzman and Marion Wynne-Davies (New York: Routledge, 2015), 81.

Elizabeth Stuart and Frederick V, elector of Palatine, became king and queen of Bohemia for just one winter, Frederick crowned as king on 4 November 1619,

beyond the Sidney family circle, perhaps "staged" for amateur performances.[125] But *Love's Victory* was not published for more than two hundred years, and even then it was not published in its entirety— the great nineteenth-century scholar, antiquarian researcher, and editor James Halliwell[-Phillips] noted that he had discovered the play in manuscript, and while he had originally believed it to be "worth printing," he ultimately decided that it was not "of sufficient interest for publication, when a minute examination came to be made." Instead of the whole play, he concluded that only "brief extracts" were worthy of publication.[126]

Finally, and from our point of view much closer to home, is *The Concealed Fancies*, a play written by Elizabeth Cavendish Brackley and Jane Cavendish.[127] Elizabeth (1616-63) and Jane (1621-69, just two years older than Margaret Cavendish) were the children of William Cavendish's first marriage. While William Cavendish was serving as a general with the royalist forces during the first Civil War, his wife, Elizabeth Bassett, and their daughters (including a third daughter, Frances) remained behind at Welbeck Abbey, which served as a

---

Elizabeth as queen three days later. By November of the next year, their reign was over.

[125] A copy of *Love's Victory* is known to have belonged to Sir Edward Dering, an English politician and antiquarian who collected many play texts and arranged for amateur theatrical performances with his family and friends. The possibility that Dering, an "intimate friend" of Mary Sidney Wroth's brother, Robert Sidney, may have "staged" a performance of *Love's Victory* in the 1620s is suggested by Michael G. Brennan, ed., *Love's Victory* (London: The Roxburghe Club, 1988), 13-15. See also Cerasano and Wynne-Davies, eds., *Renaissance Drama by Women*, 93. The possibility of a performance staged by Dering is also discussed by Stephanie Hodgson-Wright, "Beauty, Chastity, and Wit: Feminising the Centre-Stage," in *Women and Dramatic Production, 1550-1700*, Longman Medieval and Renaissance Library, ed. Alison Findlay, Stephanie Hodgson-Wright, and Gweno Williams (New York: Routledge, 2000), 59.

[126] "Extracts" from "an unpublished MS. Drama of the Seventeenth Century, entitled *Love's Victorie*" were included in James O. Halliwell, ed., *A Brief Description of the Ancient and Modern Manuscripts Preserved in the Public Library, Plymouth, to Which Are Added, Some Fragments of Early Literature, Hitherto Unprinted* (London, 1853), 212-36. The comments are from p. 212. It's also interesting to note that Halliwell concludes his extract by saying that the dramatist James Shirley had written a play "now perished" with the title *Love's Victory*, but "the internal evidence would scarcely lead us to believe that this is one of his productions" (236).

[127] Elizabeth Cavendish Brackley and Jane Cavendish, *The Concealed Fancies*, is in Cerasano and Wynne-Davies, eds., *Renaissance Drama by Women*.

garrison for the army loyal to the king. After Elizabeth Bassett died in 1643, William Cavendish's daughters remained at Welbeck, offering what help they could to the royalist cause—Jane, in particular, seems to have acted as a kind of agent for the king, sending whatever information she could come by to him. Welbeck was surrendered to the parliamentary army in August of 1644, but the young women remained there, under the protection of the commander of the garrison; after the abbey's surrender, the victorious earl of Manchester wrote that he had "engaged" himself "for their quiet abode."[128] Welbeck was briefly recaptured by the king in 1645, but was finally turned over to the parliamentary forces for good in November of 1645.

William Cavendish's daughters seem to have written *The Concealed Fancies* during the time they were under siege in their family home. The play's main plot involves two young women, Luceny and Tattiney, the daughters of Lord Calsindow. These two well-educated and witty young women refuse to marry their suitors until the young men have been effectively "tamed." In the play's subplot, three young women are under siege in the castle of Bellamo, where they must endure their "captivity," separated from their lovers, the sons of Lord Calsindow. While they are in Bellamo, they pass the time by acting out plays, including one about Cleopatra "when she was in her captivity," though their plays are not presented as plays-within-the-play—we only hear about these entertainments, we don't see them. The three young women are finally released from Bellamo when the siege is lifted, and they are reunited with their lovers; Luceny and Tattiney, too, end the play as married women.

Even without the play-within-a-play device, *The Concealed Fancies* embeds one story within another, with the Cavendish sisters, under siege in Welbeck, writing a play about young women under siege— Elizabeth and Jane give their besieged heroines the happy ending that they haven't yet achieved for themselves. They might also have been writing in response to their father's relationship to the young Margaret Lucas. S. P. Cerasano and Marion Wynne-Davies suggest that the duke's daughters satirize their future stepmother in the character of Lady Tranquility, a vain old woman who is in love with Lord

---

[128] Edward Montagu, earl of Manchester, letter of August 1644, quoted in Nathan Comfort Starr, "*The Concealed Fansyes*: A Play by Lady Jane Cavendish and Lady Elizabeth Brackley," *PMLA* 46, no. 3 (1931): 813.

Calsindow but who, at the play's end, is married off to Corpolent, a suitor whom Luceny has rejected.[129] But, while Lady Tranquility might be old, Margaret Lucas was not—and she didn't get passed off to a fat boob, either.[130]

This, then, is the context for Margaret Cavendish as she began writing her plays in the 1650s: between 1558, about the time Jane Lumley translated *Iphigeneia*, and 1642, when the theaters were closed (and about the time Jane and Elizabeth Cavendish wrote *Love's Victory*), some 2,000 to 3,000 plays were written and performed by Englishmen. Of this number, about 650 plays survive.[131] But, in contrast to the thousands of plays written by men, only a handful of dramatic texts are known to have been written by women, including Elizabeth Tudor's fragment. And only two plays written by women had been published. Understanding this context is essential to assessing the enormity of Margaret Cavendish's accomplishment in writing and publishing two collections of plays.

Whether Cavendish might have had access to Mary Sidney's *Tragedie of Antonie* or Elizabeth Cary's *Tragedy of Mariam* is unknown. Aside from her reading of Shakespeare and her youthful experience of seeing plays in London, she does not write much about her familiarity with dramatic performance, at least not in her autobiography. Cavendish may have seen plays or masques performed for Henrietta Maria when she was with the queen in Oxford or in Paris, but she does not write about them. She mentions only her painful shyness: "I neither heeded what was said or practiced but just what belonged to my loyal duty and my own honest reputation."[132] But in marrying William Cavendish, she

---

[129] Cerasano and Wynne-Davies, eds. *Renaissance Drama by Women*, 129.

[130] The Cavendish sisters' play was not published until Nathan Comfort Starr's 1931 transcription in "*The Concealed Fansyes*: A Play by Lady Jane Cavendish and Lady Elizabeth Brackley," 802-38.

[131] For this number see W. W. Greg, ed., *Henslowe's Diary* (London, 1904-8), 2:146, cited also by G. K. Hunter, *English Drama 1586-1642: The Age of Shakespeare*, vol. 6 of *The Oxford History of English Literature* (Oxford: Clarendon Press, 1997), 3n6. The records for one London company—the Admiral's Men—show that between 1594 and 1602 "some 230 plays [were] paid for and (usually) performed"; during the same period, the Chamberlain's/King's men paid for 289 plays (Hunter, 362-63).

[132] Cavendish, *True Relation*, in Firth, ed., *Life of William Cavendish*, 160. I have silently modernized the spelling and punctuation.

found a husband who was interested in plays, performance, and playwriting. Before the Civil Wars sent him into exile on the continent, he had staged household performances, including two for Charles I and Henrietta Maria, one at Welbeck Abbey, the other at Bolsover Castle.[133] He is also well known for his financial support of the playwrights Ben Jonson and James Shirley, who made have had a hand in William Cavendish's *The Country Captain*, performed by the King's Men at the Blackfriars Theatre between 1639 and 1642. This play was published in 1649 along with a second, *The Varietie*, both attributed on the title page to "a person of honor."[134] Another play by William Cavendish, *The Humorous Lovers*, was first performed in 1667, although, as we have seen, when Samuel Pepys saw the play he thought it was by *Margaret* Cavendish.[135] A fourth play, *The Triumphant Widow*, was published in 1677; it was performed in 1674 by the King's Men—in the words of the title page, "acted by His Royal Highness's Servants"—its authorship attributed to "His Grace, the duke of Newcastle."[136] One further play, *Sir Martin Mar-all*, was also attributed to William Cavendish; when the play was entered in the Stationer's Register in 1666, his

---

[133] Margaret Cavendish, *Life of . . . William Cavendishe . . .* , in Firth, ed., *Life of William Cavendish*, 103-4. See also Julie Crawford, "'Pleaders, Atturneys, Petitioners and the like': Margaret Cavendish and the Dramatic Petition," in *Women Players in England*, ed. Brown and Parolin, 243.

[134] *The Country Captain and The Varietie, Two Comedies* (London, 1649). Samuel Pepys saw *The Country Captain* when it was revived in London after the Restoration. About the 26 October 1661 performance by the King's Company, he wrote that it was "the first time it hath been acted this twenty-five years, . . . but so silly a play as in all my life I never saw, and the first that ever I was weary of in my life." I have silently modernized the spelling and punctuation. Wearied or not, he saw the play again on 25 November 1661, on 14 August 1667, and on 14 May 1668. His view of the play did not change. For these references see Samuel Pepys, in *The Diary of Samuel Pepys . . .* , ed. Henry B. Wheatley (New York: Macmillan, 1893), 2:118, 2:134; and *The Diary of Samuel Pepys . . .* , ed., Henry B. Wheatley (New York: Macmillan, 1896), 7:67-68 and 8:16.

[135] *The Humorous Lovers, a Comedy* (London, 1677). For Pepys's view of this play, see above, n. 72.

[136] *The Triumphant Widow, or the Medley of Humours, A Comedy* (London, 1677). Although attributed to William Cavendish, the playwright Thomas Shadwell seems to have collaborated on *The Triumphant Widow*.

On William Cavendish's plays, see also Lynn Hulse, ed., *William Cavendish: Dramatic Works*, Malone Society Reprints 158 (Oxford: Oxford University Press, 1996). Hulse publishes twenty-three previously unpublished "dramatic pieces," including fragments, scenes, a masque, and several play songs.

authorship was noted. Performed at the Duke of York's Playhouse and at court for some thirty performances in 1668 and 1669, it was an enormous success. The play was published anonymously in 1668 and in a 1678 second edition, but the 1691 third edition listed the author as John Dryden; Cavendish's "authorship" of this play may have rested on his translation of *L'Étourdi* by Molière, on which *Sir Martin Mar-all* was based.[137]

In 1646, when Henrietta Maria was in Paris, Prince Charles, later Charles II, joined his mother; while there, he maintained a group of actors. In her biography of Margaret Cavendish, Katie Whitaker indicates that William Cavendish "was among those who wrote pieces for them." Reports about his writing for such frivolous purposes reached England and were commented on in *The Kingdom's Weekly Intelligencer: Sent Abroad to Prevent Misinformation*, a parliamentary newspaper. That William Cavendish would participate in such an activity "showed in him either an admirable temper and settledness of mind," the writer sniffed, "or else an infinite and vain affection unto poetry, that in the ruins of his country and himself he can be at leisure to make prologues and epilogues for players."[138] Margaret may also have seen theatrical performances at the Palais Royal during the Cavendishes' Parisian exile—when she came to write her own plays she would embed in one of them a criticism of Italian and French plays, or at least of Italian and French actors. In *The Female Academy*, a woman asks one of the Academy's speakers her opinion of "Italian and French plays." The "lady speaker" doesn't think much of them, though her criticisms seem to focus on the performers rather than the plays, perhaps because (like Margaret herself), she spoke neither language: "the truth is, in their discourse or rehearsals they do not only raise their voice a note or two too high, but many notes too high, and in their actions they are so forced as the spectators might very easily believe the actors would break their sinew strings." And, she adds, "in their speech they fetch their breath so short and thick and in such painful fetches and throes as those spectators that are strangers might verily believe that they were gasping for life." The lady speaker offers one final

---

[137] The indefatigable Pepys saw this play numerous times as well and enjoyed it immensely.

[138] Quoted in Whitaker, *Mad Madge*, 88. I have silently modernized the spelling and punctuation.

judgment: "for the actors, their best grace is to play or act in the traces or paths of nature."[139]

After the Cavendishes left Paris in 1648, they moved on briefly to Rotterdam. William Cavendish may already have been at work preparing *The Country Captain* and *The Variety* for publication; Margaret would later write about her appreciation of her husband's plays and his "performance" of them for her, as his audience. She also believed her husband to be "the best lyric and dramatic poet of his age."[140] After relocating to Antwerp, the couple visited the duchess of Lorraine at Beersel Castle, where there were theaters catering to English exiles and where they could also see plays and masques performed by the duchess's courtiers.[141] In Antwerp, William Cavendish staged a number of entertainments, including pastorals, at Rubens House, where the couple lived from late in 1648 until their return to England in 1660.[142] There Cavendish began writing her series of "sociable letters." In one of her early letters, she—or, rather, the "Margaret Cavendish" who addresses the letter to an unnamed woman—professes not to care much about attending plays. While emphasizing her love of "retirement," a life of "calm silence" where she can live "free from disturbance" and in peace, "Cavendish" names attending plays as one of the activities she avoids. "I do not go personally to masques, balls, and plays," she writes, "yet my thoughts entertain my mind with such pleasures, for some of my thoughts make plays, and others act those plays on the stage of imagination, where my mind sits as a spectator."[143] Perhaps her playwriting began with these pleasant thoughts, for she suggests as much in her verse dedication to the 1662 *Plays*:

---

[139] Cavendish, *Playes*, 671. I have silently modernized the spelling and punctuation.

[140] Cavendish, *Life of . . . William Cavendishe . . .* , in Firth, ed., *Life of William Cavendish*, 108-9.

[141] Whitaker, *Mad Madge*, 119-21.

[142] Designed by Peter Paul Rubens, it had been the artist's home; the Cavendishes rented it from his widow. For a description of the house and grounds, see Grant, *Margaret the First*, 133-35; Jones, *A Glorious Fame*, 71-73; and Whitaker, *Mad Madge*, 108-109. The Grant and Whitaker biographies include courtyard views of the house, but Jones reproduces multiple images, including interiors and grounds.

[143] Cavendish, Letter 29, *Sociable Letters*, 56-57. I have silently modernized the spelling and punctuation. Cavendish did not publish her *Sociable Letters* until 1664, after the Cavendishes returned to England, but they were written while she was living in Antwerp.

To those that do delight in scenes and wit
I dedicate my book, for those I writ,
Next to my own delight, for I did take
Much pleasure and delight these plays to make,
For all the time my plays a-making were,
My brain the stage, my thoughts were acting there.[144]

But the letter-writer is not completely uninterested in public performance, however, as she spends a considerable amount of time in a later letter describing the variety of "sights and shows" that could be seen in Antwerp: "dancers on the ropes," tumblers, jugglers, "private stage-players," mountebanks, "monsters," and beasts among them. She is quick to add, however, that she doesn't "take the pains to see them," except for a few. Among those "few" she admits to making an effort to see is one of the "monsters" she mentions, a woman at a carnival whom Cavendish describes as "like a shag-dog, not in shape but hair, as grown all over her body."[145] Cavendish is disturbed by the "strangeness" of this "dog-like creature." "It troubled my mind a long time," she writes.[146]

She also describes watching an Italian mountebank, attended with several actors who performed upon an "open stage." "Cavendish" notes that the mountebank drew lots of people around to "hear him tell the virtues, or rather lies, of his drugs, cures, and skill," clearly hoping to "persuade them to buy and to be cozened and deceived, both in words, drugs, and money," but she is more interested in the

[144] Cavendish, "Dedication," *Playes*, A2r. I have silently modernized the spelling and punctuation.

[145] "Having shaggy hair. Formerly sometimes hyphened, as *shag-dog*" (OED).

[146] M. A. Katritzky suggests Margaret Cavendish may have seen the harpsichordist Barbara Urslerin, "the only sufferer of hypertrichosis born in seventeenth-century Europe known to have survived into adulthood," whose "Bavarian parents showed her around European fairgrounds for money from earliest infanthood." She continued touring in adulthood with her husband/manager. Katrizky, "'A Wonderfull Monster Borne in Germany': Hairy Girls in Medieval and Early Modern German Book, Court and Performance Culture," *German Life and Letters* 67, no. 4 (2014), http://www.ncbi.nlm.nih.gov/pmc/articles/PMC4296693/. See also Katritzky, "Introduction: 'Mountebanks, Monsters, and Several Beasts': Margaret Cavendish at the Antwerp Carnival Fair," *Women, Medicine and Theatre, 1500-1850: Literary Mountebanks and Performing Quacks*, Studies in Performance and Early Modern Drama (Burlington, VT: Ashgate, 2007), 1-22.

performers accompanying him—in particular a fool and "two handsome women actors, both sisters," one the wife of the mountebank, one the wife of the actor playing the fool. Cavendish writes that the fool's wife "was the best female actor that ever I saw." The women were clearly cross-dressed and playing men's roles. Cavendish adds, "for acting a man's part, she did it so naturally as if she had been of that sex, and yet she was of a neat, slender shape, but being in her doublet and breeches, and a sword hanging by her side, one would have believed she never had worn a petticoat and had been more used to handle a sword than a distaff." So pleased was Cavendish with this performance, that she hired a room in a house "and went every day to see them" until they were forced to leave town, to her "great grief." And then, "they being gone, I was troubled for the loss of that pastime which I took in seeing them act; wherefore to please me, my fancy set up a stage in my brain."[147]

While Cavendish may profess a preference for imagined performances over the reality of performance—at least most of the time—she did write at some length about Shakespeare in one of her letters. Her observations are not shallow; indeed, from the number of characters she mentions, it is clear that she has great familiarity with the body of Shakespeare's work. But it is also clear that she is not so much interested in Shakespeare on stage as she is Shakespeare on the page—"there is not any person he hath described in his book, but his readers might think they were well acquainted with them," she writes. And, again, while arguing that those who "dispraised his plays" were envious rather than offering valid criticism, she adds, "for those that could read his plays could not be so foolish to condemn them."[148] Notably, for all the ridicule and criticism she received in her lifetime, Cavendish is today credited for having published the first critical essay on Shakespeare and his work—"she anticipates Dryden in being the first to give a general prose assessment of Shakespeare as a dramatist."[149]

---

[147] Cavendish, Letter 195, *Sociable Letters*, 405-8. I have silently modernized the spelling and punctuation.

[148] Cavendish, Letter 123, *Sociable Letters*, 246-7. I have silently modernized the spelling and punctuation.

[149] G. Blakemore Evans *et al*, eds., *The Riverside Shakespeare* (Princeton, NJ: Houghton Mifflin, 1974), "Early Critical Comment on the Plays and Poems," 1847. See also Ann Thompson and Sasha Roberts, eds., *Women Reading Shakespeare, 1660-1900: An Anthology of Criticism* (Manchester, UK: Manchester University Press, 2013), 11-14.

Margaret Cavendish and the Folio Tradition

In 1662, when Margaret Cavendish decided to publish a collection of her plays, she was participating in a genre not particularly welcoming to women, as we have seen; at the same time, she also decided to present her dramatic work in a format that had only recently been adopted for plays written by men—men who had dominated the Elizabethan and Jacobean stages, the "Triumvirate of Wit," Ben Jonson, William Shakespeare, and the collaborative writing partners Francis Beaumont and John Fletcher.[150] As a woman writer, Cavendish had few precedents for the publication of her dramatic work. Mary Sidney Herbert had been the first woman to publish a play, and when *Antonius* appeared in 1592, in the same volume as her translation of Philippe de Mornay's *Discourse of Life and Death*, the play was printed in a quarto volume; when it was published as a separate text in 1595, it was printed in the smaller octavo format. Elizabeth Cary's 1613 *Mariam* was also a quarto volume. When Cavendish's husband published two plays, *The Country Captain* and *The Variety*, in a single volume in 1649, they were printed in an even smaller format, the duodecimo.[151]

The quarto and octavo formats were the standard for individual plays in early-modern publishing. Even for collections of plays, there were other precedents besides the folio format Cavendish would ultimately choose. In 1632, for example, the London publisher Edward Blount produced a collection of plays by John Lyly, *Six Court Comedies*, in a duodecimo volume, while in 1651, the poet and dramatist William Cartwright published a multi-genre collection, *Comedies, Tragicomedies, with Other Poems*, in an octavo volume. The Caroline dramatist Richard Brome published two collections of plays, both titled, confusingly, *Five New Plays*, the first in 1653 and the second in 1659, both in octavo

---

[150] About Cavendish's "unusual, grandiloquent format," William Poole notes that she "liked her books to look as imposing as they would sound." Poole, "Margaret Cavendish's Books in New College, and around Oxford," *New College Notes* 6 (2015): 2, http://www.new.ox.ac.uk/ncnotes.

[151] On the sizes of folios, quartos, and octavos, see above, n. 12. To produce a duodecimo volume, a single sheet of paper is folded into twelve leaves, producing twenty-four pages. William Cavendish's *The Humorous Lover* and *The Triumphant Widow*, published in 1677, were each produced in quarto volumes.

format.[152] James Shirley's *Six New Plays* was also published in 1653, in an octavo volume.[153] In 1662, the year Cavendish published her *Plays*, another collection of plays appeared, in a duodecimo size, the *Gratiae Theatrales*.[154]

However, Cavendish did not choose one of these smaller-sized volumes. When she published her plays, she decided to present them in the large folio format she had used for her earlier publications. This was not a casual or accidental decision. In her analysis of Cavendish's printing choices, Rebecca Bullard notes, the "prestigious, folio format creates an impression of monumentality that reflects Cavendish's desire to speak to posterity."[155] The folio is also the format William Cavendish used, not when he published his plays, but for his masterwork on horses and horsemanship, *La Méthode et invention nouvelle de dresser les chevaux*, published in 1658. As Katie Whitaker describes it, this lavish volume "was a luxury item" and one that, with its large-scale format, was not a book William Cavendish could afford to produce himself— he needed financial backers. Margaret Cavendish's decision to collect her *plays* and publish them in this format was guaranteed not only to draw attention to them but also to align her collection with those of Jonson, Shakespeare, and Beaumont and Fletcher.[156] Indeed, it is a comparison she invites as she draws explicit connections between her plays and theirs, at once praising her male predecessors even while suggesting that her plays are, in some sense, *better* than the works of these great literary forefathers.

Jonson's 1616 *Works* established a precedent for the folio collections of plays that were to follow: a frontispiece and elaborate title

---

[152] The 1653 *Five New Plays* contained *A Mad Couple Well-Match'd*, *The Novella*, *The Court Beggar*, *The City Wit*, and *The Demoiselle*; the 1659 *Five New Plays* contained *The English Moor*, *The Lovesick Court*, *The Weeding of Covent Garden*, *The New Academy*, and *The Queen and Concubine*.

[153] Shirley's collection contained *The Brothers*, *Sisters*, *The Doubtfull Heir*, *The Imposture*, *The Cardinall*, and *The Court Secret*.

[154] *Gratiae Theatrales, or, a Choice Ternary of English Plays Composed upon Especial Occasions by Several Ingenious Persons* (London, 1662). The volume's plays included *Thorny-Abbey, or The London-maid* "by T. W.," *The marriage-broker, or The pander* "by M. W. M.A.," and *Grim the collier of Croydon, or The devil and his dame* "by I. T."

[155] Bullard, "Gatherings in Exile: Interpreting the Bibliographical Structure of *Nature's Pictures Drawn by Fancies Pencil to the Life* (1656)," *English Studies* 92, no. 7 (2011): 803.

[156] See above, 3-5.

page, a series of commendatory verses addressed to the playwright by fellow poets, then the individual play texts. This arrangement was echoed in the Shakespeare First Folio of 1623, with the addition of a verse written by Ben Jonson and addressed "To the Reader," a dedication of the volume to two noble patrons, William Herbert, earl of Pembroke, and his brother Philip Herbert, earl of Montgomery, and an epistle "To the Great Variety of Readers," written by the collection's editors, John Heminge and Philip Condell.[157] Like Heminge and Condell's *Mr. William Shakespeare's Comedies, Histories, and Tragedies*, the 1647 Beaumont and Fletcher folio was produced after the dramatists' deaths—Beaumont had died in 1616, Fletcher in 1625, the collection produced by the publishers Humphrey Robinson and Humphrey Moseley. Following the Jonson and Shakespeare precedents, the folio opened with a portrait, though, oddly of Fletcher alone (in his preface to the reader Moseley comments, "I was very ambitious to have got Mr. Beaumont's picture, but could not possibly, though I spared no inquiry"), the facing title page emphasizing that the plays within the volume were "never printed before."[158] Thirty-seven commendatory poems follow, many of them stressing male friendship, not only the bonds between Beaumont and Fletcher but also the bonds of friendship between the various writers of the praise addressed to the two writing partners.[159] The volume also includes a dedicatory epistle from surviving actors of the King's Company addressed to Philip Herbert, now earl of Pembroke and the sole surviving brother of the Heminge and Condell dedication, and a preface addressed "To the Reader," written by the playwright John Shirley.

In her 1662 *Plays*, Cavendish demonstrates her awareness of all of this—and her anxieties are evident. Even while following, or attempting to follow, what Jeffrey Masten identifies as the "patriarchal model" established by Jonson's 1616 *Works*, Cavendish has to make adjust-

---

[157] William Herbert and his brother were the sons of Mary Sidney Herbert, countess of Pembroke.

[158] Humphrey Moseley, "The Stationer to the Reader," quoted in Masten, *Textual Intercourse*, 123. Masten notes (p. 147) that Moseley had tried to publish the collection earlier, but that the King's Men had "blocked" him from doing so—however, the plays "had lost all utility for them with the closing of the theatres in 1642," making their publication possible.

[159] On this "strange unimitable intercourse," the intimate relationship established between the writers in this volume, see Masten, *Textual Intercourse*, 132-38.

ments.[160] In one respect, of course, she could emulate the model her predecessors offered, not only in the size of her volume but also in the richness and extensiveness of their prefatory materials. At the same time, however, it is a model with which she struggled: she had no playwriting colleagues to produce commendatory verses addressed to her on the occasion of the folio's publication. Instead of opening her volume with page after page of poems full of praise, she carefully enclosed her fourteen comedies and tragedies within a protective frame, a series of explanations, justifications, defenses, and apologies.

The large folio volume begins with an impressive but contradictory two-page spread.[161] On the left is an engraved frontispiece featuring a portrait of Cavendish, not a simple bust, as in her predecessors' folios, but a full-length image of the author displayed as a classical sculpture.[162] Her flowing robes conceal much of her figure but not her rounded breasts. Despite the multiple folds of the ermine-lined robe, which she lifts up provocatively, we can see that she is posed *contrapposto*, standing with her weight on her left foot, her right leg bent, her shoulders and torso slightly turned to face forward. This is a pose we find often in Renaissance sculpture—we see it in Michelangelo's *David*, for example, and Cavendish's pose in the classically inspired setting looks almost like a mirror image of that famous sculpture. Her figure is placed within an arched niche and, as if the arch is just a bit too low to accommodate her, the small coronet she is wearing is askew, sliding down the back of her head. She is flanked by two classical gods: on her right is Athena, the virgin-goddess of wisdom and the arts, wearing a helmet and carry-

---

[160] Masten, *Textual Intercourse*, 123.

[161] The dimensions of surviving copies of *Playes* vary, depending on how the pages have been cropped and the books bound. British Library 79.I.14 measures 30.2 cm by 18.5 cm (approximately 11.9 inches by 7.3 inches), with the interior pages measuring 28.2 cm by 17.5 cm (approximately 11.1 inches by 6.9 inches). By comparison (for generations of students who have hauled it around), the dimensions of *The Riverside Shakespeare* are 10.1 inches by 8.2 inches, though at 2.6 inches thick (some 2000 pages), it is twice as thick as Cavendish's volume, which measures 3.3 cm (1.3 inches).

[162] See Figure 1. The frontispiece was engraved by the Flemish engraver Pieter van Schuppen from a design by the Dutch artist Abraham van Diepenbeke, and it was first used several years earlier, in the 1655 *Worlds Olio*. The Cavendish frontispieces (there are three) have intrigued her biographers; Jones, *A Glorious Fame*, includes only one, but Grant reproduces all three in *Margaret the First*, as does Whitaker in *Mad Madge*.

ing a staff and shield, on which is the head of her disgraced priestess, Medusa; on Cavendish's left is Apollo, god of music and prophecy, holding a lyre and a scepter topped with a rayed sun. The gods ignore Cavendish, however, preferring to stare at each other from their respective pedestals. Cavendish pays them no mind. Instead of gazing serenely away from the viewer, as Michelangelo's David does, Cavendish is looking out of her image on the page and directly at us, inviting, if not welcoming, our gaze.[163]

In the engraving, Cavendish stands on a plinth inscribed with an untitled twelve-line poem, startling in its echoing of the verses that open the Shakespeare First Folio. There, however, Jonson's poem is not part of the engraved bust of the author but faces the title page, with the opening lines pointing to and commenting on the portrait of Shakespeare: "This figure that thou here seest put / It was for gentle Shakespeare cut." Jonson laments the inability of the engraver to capture the poet's wit as well as his image, the final couplet addressed directly to the reader: "But since he cannot, reader, look / Not on his picture but his book." The verses inscribed on Cavendish's plinth are much the same—but not quite. The author of the verses—who is speaking?—immediately issues us a command, not a gentle invitation to look: "Here on this figure cast a glance." But even as we are ordered to view the image, we are warned not to stare too long or too intently. We should look casually, "as if it were by chance," and then only briefly. Our eyes "must not stay." The figure of Cavendish is meant to be seen but not studied. Moreover, we are instructed that "this" representation, though beautiful, is a mere shadow. We will not find her true beauty in the artist's portrait, however well it might capture the "lovely lines" of her face and form, but in her writing; only there will

---

[163] Theodora Jankowski describes Cavendish's pose in this image—"with her right hand on her hip and her elbow pointed toward, and looking over her right shoulder at the viewer"—as a "regal stance," comparing it to Anthony van Dyck's portrait of Charles I "in hunting dress." The English king does not wear a crown, but the painter depicts "Charles with his left hand on his hip, elbow bent and pointed toward the viewer, looking superciliously over his shoulder at his audience." Jankowski claims the pose in the Cavendish frontispiece "was obviously copied by van Scuppen": "Cavendish appears to tread upon sovereign turf here in her chosen pose." Jankowski, "Critiquing the Sexual Economies of Marriage," in *The History of British Women's Writing*, vol. 3, *1610-1690*, ed. Mihoko Suzuki (New York: Palgrave Macmillan, 2911), 234.

we discover "her soul's picture." At the verse's end, we are issued a final order: "read those lines which she hath writ."[164] This ambiguous image, both demanding that we look even as it redirects our attention, faces a title page that is entirely unambiguous. It boldly announces the volume's contents, "PLAYES," and Cavendish's authorship: "written by the thrice noble, illustrious and excellent princess, the Lady Marchioness of Newcastle."[165] While the title of her book is set in large capital letters, her name extends over eight lines of increasingly emphatic type.

Following this impressive double-page spread is an array of prefatory material, superficially not unlike that in the folio volumes of her male predecessors. Cavendish begins with a six-line verse dedication of her book to "those that do delight in scenes and wit." These brief lines are followed by "The Epistle Dedicatory," although it is not addressed to a noble patron of her work but to her husband, William Cavendish, whom she greets as "my lord." A sequence of nine epistles, each one individually titled "To the Readers," follows. Most of these addresses are relatively brief, just a paragraph in length, but a few are longer, with one extending to two full pages of closely printed prose. There is a tenth such "letter," tacked on and lacking the embellished printer's ornament, large title heading, and salutation that carefully mark out each of the preceding nine. Although printed on its own page, this last seems more like a hastily written postscript than a final dedicatory epistle, beginning, without a preamble, "I must trouble my noble readers to write of one thing more." And yet this "one more thing" is not the last thing we encounter.

Still turning the pages and looking for her plays, we encounter yet another dedication, this one a poem "upon her plays," written by her husband. This is the single commendatory poem included in her collection. It is followed by Cavendish's 104-line "General Prologue to All My Plays" in rhymed couplets. It is here that Cavendish draws an

---

[164] The notion that the best portrait of the artist is found in his work is also seen in the Beaumont and Fletcher folio, where Humphrey Moseley explains his failure to include a portrait of Beaumont: "the best pictures and those most like him you'll find in this volume." Moseley, "The Stationer to the Reader," quoted in Masten, *Textual Intercourse*, 124.

[165] In this title, the adverb "thrice" is used as an intensifier, to mean "very" or "extremely" (*OED*).

explicit link between her folios and those of Jonson, Shakespeare, and Beaumont and Fletcher. She begins with a reference to Jonson, though one that immediately warns readers that her plays will *not* be like his: "Noble spectators, do not think to see such plays that's like Ben Jonson's." His plays were "masterpieces, and were wrought by wit's invention"; they were enhanced by his reading of "several authors," those sources contributing a great deal to the success of Jonson's own work. Cavendish's "praise" of Jonson's plays is followed by her lengthy dispraise of her own "poor plays," that are, by contrast, lacking wit, quickly written, and not the result of serious study but of "play" and idleness. By implication, she aligns herself as a writer to "gentle Shakespeare" and his "fluent wit"; he had "less learning" than Jonson, yet his plays, written solely through "nature's light," give his "readers and spectators sight." Then she once again excuses her own efforts even while suggesting they are, in some crucial sense, superior to those of her male predecessors:

> But, noble readers, do not think my plays
> Are such as have been writ in former days,
> As Jonson, Shakespeare, Beaumont, Fletcher writ—
> Mine want their learning, reading, language, wit,
> The Latin phrases I could never tell,
> But Jonson could, which made him write so well;
> Greek, Latin poets, I could never read,
> Nor their historians, but our English speed,
> I could not steal their wit, nor plots out take,
> All my plays' plots my own brain did make.

Cavendish thus makes it clear that she does *not* "steal" her language, plots, and themes from any sources. Unlike the plays of Jonson, Shakespeare, and Beaumont and Fletcher, her work is *entirely* her own: "All the materials in my head did grow, / All is my own, and nothing do I owe."[166]

---

[166] Cavendish, "A General Prologue," *Playes*, A7r-AA7r. I have silently modernized the spelling and punctuation.

After this prologue, we turn the page to discover "An Intro-duction," written in the form of a dramatic scene.[167] The two-page play opens, immediately, without any setting or stage direction other than "Enter three gentlemen." One of these gentlemen abruptly confronts his companion. "Come, Tom," he asks, "will you go to a play?" Tom's answer is simple and direct: "No." But this clear response doesn't satisfy the first gentleman. When pressed about why he won't go, Tom again replies simply and directly: "Because there is so many words and so little wit, as the words tire me more than the wit delights me." And besides, he adds, the actors are bad, as are the plays in which they appear. Neither Tom nor the third gentleman, who does not seem much of a fan of plays himself, is convinced by the first gentleman's eagerness, and as the scene progresses, Tom is compelled to reiterate the reasons for his refusal: plays are full of "empty words, dull speeches, long parts, tedious acts, ill actors." As if that isn't enough, he adds that "there is not enough variety in old plays" to please him.

Only at this point does the first and most enthusiastic gentleman tell his companions that he wants them to go with him to see a *new* play—even more surprising, this new play is written by a woman. Tom is shocked: "A woman write a play! Out upon it, out upon it, for it cannot be good. Besides, you say she is a lady, which is the likelier to make the play worse. A woman and a lady to write a play? Fie, fie." After further debate about whether a woman can write a play at all, much less a good one—accompanied by the worry that, if a woman *were* to write a good play, it would mean that men would lose their "preeminence"—Tom grudgingly agrees to go along with his companions, although it's not clear whether he has finally been convinced to give the female-authored play a chance or whether he decides to go simply because he doesn't want to be left behind. In the end, Tom will only say that he is "contented to cast away so much time for the sake of the sex" despite the fact that he has "no faith" in the "authoress's wit." But "Who knows?" asks the third gentleman in the last line of this "Introduction," at the very bottom of page. Since many sinners convert and repent after hearing a "good sermon," Tom might

---

[167] Cavendish, "An Introduction," *Playes*, 1-2. I have silently modernized the spelling and punctuation. Interestingly, like the rest of the plays in the volume, "An Introduction" is numbered, and the play that follows immediately, *Loves Adventures*, begins on p. 3.

change his mind after "seeing this play." On the next page, *Love's Adventure*, subtitled *Play*, begins.

The question of whether Tom changes his mind about the play written by a "lady" remains unanswered. As the readers to whom Cavendish's many epistles are addressed, we might regard the fourteen comedies and tragedies in *Plays* as the definitive proof of a woman's ability to write a good play or, more specifically, of the marchioness of Newcastle's ability to do so.[168] But, while "An Introduction" is a witty dramatization of the anxieties of authorship that are revealed throughout the prefatory materials in the 1662 *Plays*, there is no return to this group of three gentlemen at the end of the volume, no response to "An Introduction" in a final scene titled "A Conclusion," a little play at the end of the collection showing Tom's conversion and repentance. Instead, Cavendish completes the frame around her plays with one more letter addressed to her "noble readers."

In this final epistle, Cavendish apologizes if some of us have had more than "enough" of her plays "to cloy" our "gusto." Perhaps the plays haven't "whet" our "appetites" but have instead managed to make us a little sick to our stomachs. Considering this possibility, Cavendish suggests that maybe we should just read *one* of the plays she has written (interesting advice, here at the end of the collection), and if this one play proves to be "unpleasant or hard of digestion," then we shouldn't bother to read any more. We may not enjoy the taste of her "poetical dishes"; she is, after all, just a "plain" English cook who can't make fancy food to tempt the appetites of those of us who might prefer rich dishes. "You may turn me away, which is to put my works out of your studies," she writes, adding, "I only desire I may not depart with your displeasures, but as an honest, poor servant that rather wanted art and skill in my works than will or endeavor to make or dress them to every palate." In any case, she is still hard at work writing, with more to come soon. She acknowledges having promised her readers that she "would not trouble" them with "any more" of her works even

---

[168] It is somewhat difficult to number Cavendish's plays in this volume. Today the contents are usually tallied at fourteen, but six of the plays are in two parts. If these were counted separately, the number of plays in the collection would number twenty. In the letter to her readers at the end of *Playes*, however, Cavendish says she's completed twenty-one plays—perhaps she has already written one of the plays that will be published in *Plays, Never before Printed* (London, 1668).

as she offers a preview of her next project.[169] Then, after nearly seven hundred pages, she is done: "And so farewell."[170]

Rather than acting as a welcome to the readers she addresses so fulsomely in *Plays*, all of this—the initial dedication, the long series of letters, William Cavendish's praise of his wife and her work, the prologue, the introduction, and the farewell address—seems instead to pose a challenge, if not an obstacle, to her readers. Cavendish protects her plays behind a wall of words. She erects a formidable, almost impenetrable, barrier of complaints and apologies, self-praise and self-criticism, modesty and boastfulness, at once normalizing her act of playwriting even while proclaiming her unique status as a writer of plays.

Six years later, Cavendish published *Plays, Never before Printed*. In contrast to the earlier collection, this volume contains only four plays, including *The Convent of Pleasure*. Even so, the folio anthology is more than four hundred pages long.[171] Cavendish once again uses the

---

[169] Cavendish indicates that she's already completed "above threescore letters" and hopes "to make them up a hundred"; Cavendish exceeded her goals, publishing *CCXI Sociable Letters, Written by the Thrice Noble, Illustrious, and Excellent Princess, the Lady Marchioness of Newcastle* in 1664.

[170] Cavendish's final epistle follows *The Female Academy*, in *Playes*, 653-79. A single page headed "errata" follows in some but not all surviving copies of *Playes*. Cavendish notes that the list contains only the most serious of the "errors of the press," those that might cause misunderstanding. Less serious errors, "too numerous to be here set down," remain, but she is sure that "every common reader" will be able to see and correct them.

[171] The dimensions of surviving copies of *Plays, Never before Printed* may vary, depending on how the pages have been cropped and the books bound. British Library 79.I.15 measures 30.2 cm by 18.5 cm (approximately 11.9 inches by 7.3 inches), its pages measuring 29.8 cm by 18.9 (approximately 11.7 inches by 7.4 inches).

Again, although the volume is customarily said to contain four plays, there are difficulties with this number. The volume's second play is *The Presence, A Comedy*, but following its 92 pages is *Scenes*, which Cavendish introduces with the following note: "These scenes were designed to be put into *The Presence*, but by reason I found they would make that play too long, I thought it requisite to print them by themselves." (I have silently modernized the spelling and punctuation.) Although each play in the collection is numbered separately, the numbers from *The Presence* continue in *Scenes* (93-155), and the list of *dramatis personae* for *The Presence* follows both (on an unnumbered page). And *The Convent of Pleasure, A Comedy* follows immediately after *The Bridals, A Comedy*, which examines two marriages, that of Lady Virtue and Lady Coy, who, after her marriage, becomes Lady Amorous. Both of these characters

elaborate frontispiece that had opened her earlier collection of plays. The title page that faces the frontispiece is no less impressive. Underneath the title, with "PLAYS" printed in large capitals that dwarf the much smaller "Never before Printed," Cavendish again proudly proclaims her authorship: "written by the thrice noble, illustrious, and excellent princess, the duchess of Newcastle." The title for this new collection is interesting. In his analysis of Cavendish's collections of plays, Jeffrey Masten suggests that the title for this second volume "speaks resonantly" in its "recollection" of the 1647 Beaumont and Fletcher folio, with its emphasis that the plays were "never printed before." While acknowledging this parallel, Shannon Miller observes the strong connection between Cavendish's subtitle and the phrase that appeared on the title page of the third Shakespeare folio, printed just four years earlier, in 1664: *Mr. William Shakespear's Comedies, Tragedies, and Histories . . . unto This Impression is Added Seven Plays, Never Before Printed in Folio.*[172] The point is made either way—once again Cavendish is explicitly linking her collection to those of her male predecessors.

---

appear in *The Convent of Pleasure*, along with several of the male characters from *The Bridals*. Most significantly, Madam Mediator mediates herself between the two plays, and *The Bridals'* fool, Mimic, makes a crucial appearance in the final scene of *The Convent of Pleasure*. About the relationship between the two plays, Anne Shaver observes that, while they are clearly "not a single play in two parts," it is a "challenge" to figure out just how the plays are related. Margaret Cavendish, *The Convent of Pleasure and Other Plays*, ed. Shaver (Baltimore: Johns Hopkins University Press, 1999), 12. About the relationship, Theodora Jankowski concludes, "I view *The Convent of Pleasure* not so much as a 'second part' in terms of plot, but rather a continuous—if more pointed—examination of the nature of early modern marriage as well as women's place within the estate." Jankowski, "Critiquing the Sexual Economies of Marriage," in *The History of British Women's Writing*, 3:232.

While *The Convent of Pleasure* may seem to be the last play in the volume, even that is in some doubt. Immediately following is *A Piece of a Play*, prefaced with an "Advertisement to the Reader," in which the reader is "desired to take notice" that the "following fragments" are part of a play that Cavendish "did intend" for her "*Blazing World*, and had planned to print with it." But, she says, before she finished the second act, she discovered that "all her genius did not tend that way," and so she "left the design." She writes that since she is "now putting some other comedies to the press, I suffer this piece of one to be published with them." The "play" is still incomplete, the "piece" comprising just two acts, each act composed of two scenes.

[172] For the title's echoing of Beaumont and Fletcher's 1647 folios, see Masten, *Textual Intercourse*, 156. On the link with Shakespeare Third Folio (London, 1664), see Miller, "'Thou art a Moniment," in *Cavendish and Shakespeare*, ed. Romack and Fitzmaurice, 22.

Figure 1.

Frontispiece, *Playes* (1662) and *Plays, Never Before Printed* (1668)

Used by Permission of the National Portrait Gallery (London)

Figure 2.

Title page, *Plays, Never before Printed* (1668)

Used by Permission of the Folger Shakespeare Library

Although the title page of the 1668 collection looks very similar to the one in the 1662 *Plays*, there is a subtle difference. Unlike the title page in the first collection, all of the elements here—the volume's title, the author's name, the ornamental title vignette, and the place of publication, printer, and year—have been enclosed in a double-ruled border, each element contained within its own box.[173] Not surprisingly, the box noting Cavendish's authorship is the biggest of the four on the page, though it is much more modest than the sprawling "written by" in the earlier book.[174] While such a double-ruled border on a title page is in no way unique in the seventeenth century, its use here is visually striking.[175] It seems, in fact, to reproduce something of the effect of the protective barrier of framing texts in the 1662 *Plays*. Again, the Cavendish figure staring out at us from the frontispiece opens herself and her book to us, but the extra-strength frame around the facing page seems designed to guard her work and her name from us. They are closed off and sealed in. Since Cavendish is so careful about the printing of her books, paying close attention to their appearance if not always to the "errors of the press" frequently found inside, this protective frame seems deliberate. As Rebecca Bullard argues, the physical characteristics of Cavendish's publications offer crucial

---

[173] See Figure 2.

[174] The 1662 *Playes* was printed by Alice Warren, the widow of the bookseller and printer Thomas Warren; Alice Warren seems to have been active as a printer from her husband's death in 1661 through 1662, after which the business was passed to her sons, Thomas and Francis Warren. The business was destroyed in the Great Fire of 1666. For her 1668 *Plays, Never before Printed*, Cavendish used the printer Anne Maxwell, also a printer's widow, but one who successfully ran her business for ten years, from 1665 until 1675. Further information about both these printers is in Henry R. Plomer's *A Dictionary of the Booksellers and Printers Who Were at Work in England, Scotland and Ireland from 1641 to 1667* (London: The Bibliographical Society, 1907), 125 and 188.

For a complete list of Cavendish's printers, see Cameron Kroetsch, "Margaret Cavendish's Texts, Printers, and Booksellers (1653-1675), *Digital Cavendish Project* (2013), http://www.digitalcavendish.org/texts-printers-booksellers/.

[175] The title page of John Milton's *Paradise Lost* (London, 1667) has such a double-ruled border, as only one contemporary example of this very common feature of printed books. And, for comparison, a number of title pages with the same kind of border, all of them printed by women, can be seen at online: Alison Connor, "The Feminine Touch: Women and the Work of the Book," online exhibition, J. Willard Marriott Library, University of Utah (2011), http://www.lib.utah.edu/collections/rarebooks/exhibits/past/feminine-touch.php.

evidence about their "intellectual contents": their "physical structure" reveals "a material articulation of Cavendish's life that speaks to and speaks beyond the words that it contains."[176] Cavendish may not have known "the precise mechanisms involved in printing books," but "she paid attention to their physical appearance and sought to use it to influence the reader's experience of her texts."[177] And so, while the number of anxious prefatory materials *inside* the second collection may have been reduced, Cavendish's defenses seem not to have been lowered.

The contradictory effect of the paired frontispiece and title page is mirrored in the single dedicatory epistle in *Plays, Newly Printed.* Titled "To the Readers"—there is no greeting—the letter occupies only a page and a half, but this brief text is a poignant testament to Cavendish's continuing difficulties as a woman writer, particularly as a writer of plays. The letter begins with an indirect reference to the criticism her work has received: "It is most certain that those that perform public actions expose themselves to public censures, and so do writers, live they never so privately and retired, as soon as they commit their works to the press." But once she's made this bold declaration—*it is most certain*—she hedges: "I do not say that this is so, but if it be, I can truly say that I am sorry of it, merely for the age's sake and not in relation to myself or my books, which I write and disperse abroad only for my own pleasure and not to please others." She is—or so she asserts—"very indifferent" as to whether anyone reads her books and, if they are read, she does not care "how they are esteemed." But, since only the "most worthy and most meritorious persons" attract "envious detractors," it would be "a presumptuous opinion" for her to think she is in danger of attracting any criticism. And in any case, she avers, "malice cannot hinder me from writing, wherein consists my chiefest delight and greatest pastime."[178] The pattern of contradictions is clear. Cavendish states a certainty, then retracts it. She writes for her own pleasure, but she has her work printed for publication. And she titles her work *Plays*, even though, she admits, "I do not believe to have

---

[176] Bullard, "Gatherings in Exile," 796.

[177] Bullard, "Gatherings in Exile," 801.

[178] Cavendish, *Plays, Never before Printed*, n.p. The page is unnumbered, but it is the first page following the title page. I have silently modernized the spelling and punctuation.

given it a very proper title." Her "works" have acts and scenes and dialogue, but they are not plays. Yet, having told us they are not plays, she says that she "will venture, in spite of the critics, to call them plays." If *we* accept them as plays, then she is happy. If not, she shrugs and bids us "farewell."[179]

Margaret Cavendish's *The Convent of Pleasure* (1668)

Margaret Cavendish's *The Convent of Pleasure, A Comedy* is the last complete play in the 1668 *Plays, Never before Printed*. It is thematically linked to the play that precedes it in the volume, *The Bridals*, continuing the earlier play's examination of the institution of marriage. In addition to this thematic connection, several of the characters from *The Bridals* suddenly appear, unheralded and uninvited, at various spots in *The Convent of Pleasure*. But, while the focus of *The Bridals* is on the *making* of marriages, *The Convent of Pleasure* offers the dazzling possibility of *unmaking* marriage, at least in its first four acts. The play's protagonist, Lady Happy, has decided to establish the Convent of Pleasure as a refuge for herself and for the few select women who are privileged to shelter with her behind its protective walls. Lady Happy's convent is a thoughtfully designed intentional community, offering its inhabitants not only shelter and protection but, more importantly, freedom. Its female occupants are free *to* determine the course of their own lives only because they are free *from* the restrictions of marriage. The women who enter into Lady Happy's eponymous convent have decided to separate themselves from men, and they have no intention of ever returning to them.

While linked to *The Bridals* in the 1668 *Plays, Never before Printed*, *The Convent of Pleasure* is also linked to two plays in Cavendish's 1662 *Plays*. In the two-part *Bell in Campo*, Lady Victoria creates an all-female army, leads her company of "female heroics" into battle, and emerges victorious. In *The Female Academy*, two "grave matrons" create an all-female school, into which "a company of young ladies" withdraws—

---

[179] Cavendish, *Plays, Never before Printed*, n.p. The page is unnumbered, but the paragraph beginning "When I call this new one *Plays*" begins on the reverse of the preceding page, and faces the list of characters in the collection's first play, *The Sociable Companions, or, The Female Wits: A Comedy*, 1-95. I have silently modernized the spelling and punctuation.

separated from men, who can hardly stand it, the enclosed women dedicate themselves to education.[180]

Cavendish also draws on familiar genres and modes in *The Convent of Pleasure*, incorporating elements from both courtly masque and pastoral comedy into her play and delighting in the transgressive cross-dressing that was a feature not only of court entertainments but also of popular comedies on the commercial London stage: the women who enter into the Convent of Pleasure amuse themselves by dressing and performing as men. Cavendish exploits the erotic possibilities of these cross-dressed women as well, though with one significant difference. In comedies with so-called transvestite heroines, like Shakespeare's *As You Like It* and *Twelfth Night*, the audience is aware that Rosalind and Viola have assumed male identities, and that, while the attractions of Audrey and Olivia for Ganymede and Cesario can be explored and exploited—for laughs—Rosalind and Viola will be restored to their "appropriate" clothing and partners before the play ends. We have no such assurances in *The Convent of Pleasure*, however, when Lady Happy finds her soul's mate in a princess rather than a prince.

As the play begins, Cavendish focuses our attention on the contemporary marketplace of marriage—like Shakespeare's Petruchio, the young men we see in the opening scene of *The Convent of Pleasure* hope to "wive it wealthily"—and "if wealthily," then "happily." We don't see any women at all onstage; rather, we see three young gentlemen meeting up at a critical juncture in their individual lives and in the larger life of their social world. The first of these young men asks the second why he is looking "so sadly." The second, Tom, responds that he has been at the funeral of Lord Fortunate. He's not grieved by the death of Lord Fortunate, however, but at the fact that the man's money will pass to his only heir, a daughter. Lady Happy will be "very rich." A wealthy heiress might seem to offer a wonderful prize for three unmarried gentlemen, but Cavendish quickly shows us why an heiress represents a threat to men, despite their wealth or social status: when wealth escapes patrilineal lines of descent and comes into women's hands, it endangers men. According to the first young man, an heiress

---

[180] Portions of the analysis of *The Convent of Pleasure* that follows are adapted from Sharon L. Jansen, *Reading Women's Worlds from Christine de Pizan to Doris Lessing: A Guide to Six Centuries of Women Writers Imagining Rooms of Their Own* (New York: Palgrave Macmillan), 71-100.

like Lady Happy represents a financial loss: "If she be so rich, it will make us all . . . spend all our wealth in fine clothes, coaches, and lackeys to set out our wooing hopes." The third young man is a younger brother, and he has no wealth to lay out in the hope of acquiring a wealthy heiress. But, as this unfortunate young man makes clear, even men with no money to spare will risk the little they have or the little that they can get their hands on. They will "undo" themselves "upon bare hopes, without probability."

Tom describes Lady Happy as "handsome, young, rich, and virtuous," but the only "virtue" that really seems to matter to these young men is her wealth. As the young men exit the scene, Lady Happy and one of her attendants enter. In addition to being rich, Lady Happy immediately shows herself to be witty and determined as well, but these qualities seem to have little or no value in the marriage market. Madam Mediator, making her entrance, is afraid that Lady Happy will remove herself as a commodity from the marriage exchange. "Surely, madam, you do but talk," she protests, adding, "surely you will not encloister yourself, as you say."[181]

But the rumors that Madam Mediator has heard are true—taking herself out of circulation is exactly what Lady Happy has in mind. It is clear that she has thought a great deal about the institution of marriage and what it means for women. Her conclusions are a thorough indictment of "traditional marriage," at least as it affects women. Even

---

[181] The convent life is something Margaret Cavendish had considered at some length, probably before she wrote *The Convent of Pleasure*. Her essay on "The Monastical Life" was included in *The Worlds Olio* (1655); there she had argued that those who withdrew from the world into monasteries and convents were not "an idle, lazy and unprofitable people," as many had argued (they were criticized as places where women, enough to "populate whole nations," were "kept barren"). But rather than arguing their spiritual benefit, she argues that "monastical lives" are "profitable for the Commonwealth" because they provide alternatives to an "overstocked" economy—taking in younger sons, preventing overpopulation, and, most interesting, providing entertainment:

it [the church] Amuses the Common people and busies their mindes, and it is as it were a recreation: and pastime to them, as Saints dayes and the like; nay they take pleasure, and make a recreation to have fasting dayes, so as they have much to think on, and imploy their time in, as fasting-dayes, processions of saints, confessions, penance, absolutions, and the like, as Mass and Musick, and shewes, as at Christmas, Easter, our Lady day, & on many dayes of the yeers, and these affording one and the same, but varieties in all." (28-31)

if a woman manages to marry "the best of men," she will find "more crosses and sorrows than pleasure, freedom, or happiness." For a good woman, even one who is fortunate enough to marry a good man, marriage is still "a greater restraint than a monastery." But if a woman isn't lucky enough to find a good husband and turns to admirers for solace, she will experience no gain; in exchange for empty words and appreciative stares, she will lose her reputation. And if a woman should dare to take a lover, instead of pleasure she will find only more torment—"jealous" rivals will only make trouble with their dis-agreements and fights. Lady Happy has come to the logical conclusion that, "since there is so much folly, vanity, and falsehood in men," women simply shouldn't endanger themselves by marrying one of them.

Since men are "the only troublers of women," Lady Happy is determined to live without them. In fact, if a woman can afford to remain single, Lady Happy asserts, she would be "mad to live with men, who make the female sex their slaves." Lady Happy vows that she "will not be so enslaved." Not all women are so fortunate, however—Lady Happy seems almost callous in leaving "poor" women to their fate. Unfortunately, it seems, such women are "fit for men" because they are lacking the "means to buy delights and maintain pleasures." But, while Lady Happy is "resolved to live a single life and vow virginity," she has no intention of devoting herself to a life of prayer and penance. Her convent will not be "a cloister of restraint but a place for freedom," a place where all the senses will be "pleased."

Lady Happy has also decided to invite a few "noble persons" of her sex to join her in the Convent of Pleasure, but only as many as she can afford to maintain "plentifully" and only those "whose births are greater than their fortunes." In the world she is determined to leave behind, a young woman must have money in order to buy herself a "good" husband; in the brave new world Lady Happy is creating, a young woman will not have to buy herself a place. Lady Happy has inherited so much money that she can afford to invite into her convent a few women whose birth is greater than their assets. Lady Happy will be offering full scholarships to the twenty young women who fulfill the requirements for admission to the Convent of Pleasure. On the one hand, these arrangements seem harsh—she chooses to save a handful of elite women, leaving those less fortunate to suffer the pains of marriage. On the other, we learn that her retreat will accommodate many more women than just the chosen few.

In order to ensure that no men will ever be needed in her convent, Lady Happy has arranged for women to function as "physicians, surgeons, and apothecaries," and she has reserved the role of priest and confessor for herself. In addition to her twenty companions and these female professionals, women will undertake "every office and employment" necessary for the efficient functioning of the convent. To that end, a "numerous company of female servants" will also be included, ensuring that there will be "no occasion for men" in any capacity whatsoever. These women may have to work, but they too will be sheltered from the dangers of men and marriage. Meanwhile, outside the convent, it is a different story. The unhappy men first consider a few desperate ways of breaking up this all-female refuge, like setting it on fire, for instance (2.4). The "foolish" women in their "retirement" have so "vexed" the young men left outside that they even contemplate the drastic measure of disguising themselves as women, hoping to get into the convent that way, although they quickly conclude that such efforts would be fruitless—even dressed as women, their behavior and their voices would give them away. One of the frustrated young men thinks they could pass for women if they dressed themselves as "strong, lusty country wenches" and worked as cooks, dairy maids, or laundresses, but the men realize that even if they disguised themselves in the appropriate outfits, their inability to cook, milk cows, or starch women's collars would still give them away.

Lady Happy has taken care not only of the design and staffing of the convent but also of the comfortable interior space. She describes, in great detail, the lavish appointments of the interiors, the sumptuous fabrics, the exotic fragrances, and the beautiful accessories, all of which will change with the seasons (2.2). She has also designed the convent's extensive grounds, providing in every way for its maintenance. It is interesting to note here that, in imagining her perfect retreat as a "convent," Cavendish may be drawing on her own life experiences, not as a woman familiar with the rigorous ascetic life of a religious institution, but as a woman whose comfortable family home, St. John's Abbey, had been a Benedictine monastery before it was suppressed during the reign of Henry VIII. William Cavendish's Welbeck Abbey was a former Premonstratensian monastery, while Newcastle House, in

London, was constructed on the grounds of St. Mary's Abbey, formerly a house of Augustinian canonesses.[182]

We soon learn that Lady Happy has admitted one more woman into this carefully planned community (2.3). According to Madam Mediator—who, as her name suggests is somehow allowed to pass between the women's world inside the convent and the men's world outside—a "great foreign princess," "a princely brave woman truly, of a masculine presence," has arrived and has been admitted into Lady Happy's retreat. Inside their pleasure palace, and in order to entertain themselves, the women have decided to divide themselves into couples—some of the young women have adopted "masculine habits" in order to facilitate a masquerade in which they "act lovers' parts." The princess and Lady Happy make up one of these happy couples and swear themselves to friendship (3.1). In the language of Renaissance love

---

[182] Julie Crawford argues that the Convent of the Visitation of St. Mary at Chaillot (Paris), founded in 1651 by Henrietta Maria, is also a source of inspiration for Cavendish's Convent of Pleasure. Crawford, "Convents and Pleasures: Margaret Cavendish and the Drama of Property," *Renaissance Drama*, n. s., 32 (2003): 177-223, especially pp. 178, 202-4. (In addition, Crawford argues "the convent that Lady Happy plans in *The Convent of Pleasure*" represents Cavendish's way of "restor[ing] royalists' losses of property and privilege to their former glory," p. 179.)

In "Margaret Cavendish, the Antwerp Carmel, and *The Convent of Pleasure*," J. P. Vander Motten and Katien Daemen-de Gelder note that Margaret Cavendish was connected to the English Carmelite convent at Antwerp and argue that these "hitherto unsuspected ties" may also have contributed to Cavendish's imagined convent. Vander Motten and Daemen-de Gelder, "Margaret Cavendish," *Archiv für das Studium der neueren Sprachen und Literaturen* 251, no. 1 (2014): 134-45.

Cavendish herself commented on the Suppression of the Monasteries in *The Worlds Olio*, her thoughts titled "Of pulling down of the Monasteries in Henry the Eighths time":

> Some wonder that Henry the Eighth did pull down and destroy so many Monasteries as were in England, which had stood so long, without Opposition: but it was likely that the Opposition could not be great; for first, the People were perswaded in some part, by the Doctrine of Luther, to dislike the Tyrannie of the Pope; for first, it eased their Purses and their Persons, the one from Peter-pence, and the like, and the other from hard Penance; the next, the Gentry and the Nobles thought of the gaining of the Houses, and Lands, and Liberty; the King for the bulk of their Wealth; so the King, Nobility, and Commons, and all had ends in it; and where the King follows the Commons, an Innovation is easy; or I may say, an Innovation is easy where the King follows the People. (127)

poetry, the princess asks Lady Happy to be her "mistress" while she, dressed as a young man, will "act the part" of Lady Happy's "loving servant." Lady Happy is so pleased at the prospect that she bursts into a couplet: "More innocent lovers never can there be, / Than my most princely lover that's a she." The women enclosed in the Convent of Pleasure have organized themselves into same-sex pairs—even while one member of each pair has dressed herself as a man so that the couples *look like* opposite-sex couples.

Cavendish has just shown us a group of young men who are forced to admit that they can't disguise themselves as women—she juxtaposes that scene with one showing us a group of young women who can successfully perform as men. What we *see* on Cavendish's stage are happy "male"-female pairs who settle themselves down to be entertained by a play-within-a-play. Along with this audience, we see a sequence of nine scenes, of varying length, each one illustrating the hardships of marriage from a woman's point of view (3.2-3.10). Cavendish shows us poor women whose alcoholic husbands beat them, middle-class women whose husbands ignore their businesses and waste their time and money in taverns, and well-born ladies whose husbands spend their money on gambling and whores. We see one woman pregnant and sick, one woman groaning with the pangs of childbirth, one woman who labors for three days to give birth to a stillborn baby, and another whose child has died. We see an old lady whose son has abandoned her, and a "fair young lady" who is threatened with rape. This "entertainment" has an admonitory function, and the women inside the Convent of Pleasure are quick to learn its lesson: "Marriage is a curse we find, / Especially to womankind; / From the cobbler's wife, we see, / To ladies, they unhappy be" (3.10)

This seventeenth-century play-within-a-play thus vividly depicts women's sufferings in marriage. Regardless of their social class, of their age, or of their marital status, all women are united in their common experiences as women. At the same time, the scenes remind us that the women who have retired into the Convent of Pleasure have devised a way to avoid the dangers of marriage, childbirth, and motherhood. And in their refuge inside an all-female world, they have not only avoided pain, they have found pleasure. More significantly Cavendish dares to imagine a radical alternative to marriage: since men and marriage cause only pain and suffering, perhaps a woman can fill her emotional and sexual needs with another woman.

Lady Happy finds herself drawn to the princess and poses a critical question to herself and to us: "But why may not I love a woman with the same affection I could a man?" (4.1). At first, believing "nature is nature and still will be," Lady Happy resists her attraction to the princess. She sees her desire for another woman as unnatural: nature "will punish me for loving you more than I ought to love you," she warns the princess. But the princess, although she is still dressed as a man, ignores questions of sex and gender. "Can lovers love too much?" she asks Lady Happy—"Can any love be more virtuous, innocent, and harmless than ours?" Once Lady Happy replies that she hopes not, the princess suggests that they "please" themselves as lovers always have, by embracing and kissing. Although the princess says that their kisses will "mingle souls together," what we see, according to Cavendish's stage directions, is a physical joining of two women, one of them dressed as a man, holding "each other in their arms" and kissing. This isn't just a quick peck on the check, either. After side-stepping issues of sex and gender, the princess reintroduces them here: "These my embraces, though of a female kind, / May be as fervent as a masculine mind."

Lady Happy and the princess then act out a pastoral frolic, dancing around a maypole—Cavendish isn't always a very subtle writer. At the end of their celebration, having been crowned as king and queen of the shepherds, the princess says she wants to live out her life in Lady Happy's favor: to "be possessed" of Lady Happy's "love and person" is the "height" of her ambition. Lady Happy responds that she can "deny" her beloved neither her "love nor person." They then bind themselves into a same-sex alternative to heterosexual marriage. "We shall more constant be," Lady Happy asserts, and "in a married life better agree" than opposite-sex lovers. "We shall agree," the princess responds, "for we true love inherit, / Join as one body and soul or heavenly spirit." But at this critical moment their happy idyll is rudely and abruptly interrupted—Cavendish breaks off her play and turns her pen over to her husband.

Instead of further action, a consummation of the love between the princess and Lady Happy, a joining of their bodies as well as their souls, we find instead a pause in the action and the intrusion of the male voice into this female-authored play (and into the all-female world of the Convent of Pleasure). Inserted into Cavendish's play are two poems, each one labeled with a pasted-in strip that reads "written by my Lord Duke." According to the stage directions, both of these lyrics are sung by "shepherds," but clearly these shepherds are female inhabitants of the convent still wearing male clothing. In the first of these songs, the singer addresses the princess and Lady Happy, as the newly crowned king and queen of the shepherds, promising to obey "all their commands." In the second, "another shepherd" reminds everyone, characters and audience alike, that "couples" must be "draw[n] by holy Hymen's law." The stage directions indicate that the "scene"—the pastoral scene and our newly joined lovers—"vanishes," and we see the "princess," no longer with her beloved but alone on stage. In a soliloquy, the princess berates herself for wearing a petticoat and for abandoning "her" kingdom for a "beautiful mistress." Before we can entirely make sense of the princess's words, we see another extravagant production inside the Convent of Pleasure, this one a courtly masque featuring the princess dressed as Neptune and Lady Happy as a sea goddess. In a hint of what is to come, "Neptune" proclaims, "I am the king of all the seas" and then, just in case we missed it the first time, "I am sole monarch of the sea, / And all therein belongs to me."

In the first scene of Act 5, Lady Happy is reunited with her princess, still "in man's apparel," but Lady Happy remains completely silent when the "princess" suddenly reveals that "she" is really a he, not a princess but a prince who has come to get himself a wife to take back with him to his kingdom. And he intends to have Lady Happy, no matter what—if the "councilors of the state" (who must include the very men Lady Happy had hoped to avoid) won't give him their permission to marry her, he will "have her by force of arms." Madam Mediator is shocked and titillated at the same time—"O, the lord!" she cries out, "I hope you will not bring an army to take away all the women, will you?" No, he assures her—whatever happens, they will leave Madam Mediator behind. But Lady Happy, so adamantly outspoken about her opposition to marriage in Act 1 of the play, says nothing. Her female lover has just revealed "herself" to be a man who has gained Lady Happy's love through trickery and disguise and who threatens her with violence, but Lady Happy remains silent.

The next scene (5.2), which takes place outside the convent, is again prefaced with a pasted-in strip indicating it is "written by my Lord Duke." In it, Madam Mediator, "lamenting and crying," encounters two young men who spar with her, meeting her fears and wonder with their "witty" jests and delivering to her—and us—the news that "the state" has agreed to Lady Happy's marriage to the prince(ss), accounting it "an honor" and something more. The "state" is not only "willing" to act in the matter but also sees the possibility that it will "reap much advantage by the match." As the play's final scene begins (5.3), the prince(ss) enters costumed "as a bridegroom" and immediately begins to make wedding plans—evidently the joining of body and soul acted out with Lady Happy when *he* was a *she* isn't sufficient now, when he is a he.

Lady Happy, once so active in deciding, organizing, and taking charge, is passive and acquiescent. She speaks only once more in the rest of the play, four brief and inconsequential lines, all of them to or about a new arrival, the fool Mimic. In addition to losing her voice, she also loses her identity—she is no longer "Lady Happy" but "the princess"—she has not only become the prince's wife but, in some eerie way, she is erased entirely. She literally *assumes* the role the prince had played. Meanwhile, the prince is busy dismantling the Convent of Pleasure. Once Lady Happy's to order and run as she saw fit, it is now his, and he divides it into two parts, designating one part for virgins, the other for widows, deciding that he will in the future fund what is now *his* institution out of his own "bounty." He gives the last word in the play not to the former Lady Happy but to Mimic, who has arrived just in time to speak the epilogue.

What has happened? What are we to make of the strip attributing the authorship of *something* to William Cavendish? More specifically, are we to understand that William Cavendish's authorship is limited to the single scene (5.2) that immediately follows the pasted-in label, or does he finish the play? In other words, has Cavendish turned over her pen to the duke, her husband, only briefly, for one scene, or even part of one scene, or does the duke take over entirely and complete the play that Cavendish had begun? When it comes to the two lyrics inserted at the end of Act 4 and identified as "written by my Lord Duke," the limits of his authorship are fairly clear. But in the fifth act, the extent of William Cavendish's contribution is less clear. In fact, in her edition of

The Convent of Pleasure, Anne Shaver argues that "since no terminus is given, it seems that he is the author of the final two scenes and the epilogue."[183]

The end of the play does present a shocking reversal to the plot and theme of Margaret Cavendish's play, but I don't think we need to conclude that her husband is responsible for the ending of *The Convent of Pleasure*. No terminus is given for the end of his contributions in Act 4, either, and Shaver does not argue that William Cavendish wrote everything after his first intrusion into the text there. I would argue that, despite his contributions to 5.2, the reversal of the play's direction is not due to William Cavendish's authorship of the play's conclusion. Rather, the reversal is not out of character for Margaret Cavendish at all—she does the same thing in two earlier plays that focus on all-female institutions, *Bell in Campo* and *The Female Academy*. She writes her female characters into radical new positions—victorious and independent in *Bell in Campo*, educated and independent in *The Female Academy*, happily partnered and utterly free of men in *The Convent of Pleasure*—only to reverse course and return them to the *status quo ante* at the very last moment. And, it is worth emphasizing here, neither Mimic nor William Cavendish, *if* he did complete his wife's play, has the last word. In reality it is Margaret Cavendish who has the final say, and the list of the *dramatis personae* that follows the epilogue of *The Convent of*

---

[183] *The Convent of Pleasure and Other Plays*, ed. Shaver, 238n. There is a great deal written about Margaret Cavendish's corrections to her printed books, about the Cavendishes' "collaborative authorship," and about what exactly happens at this point in the play. For a brief survey of the literature, see James Fitzmaurice, "Margaret Cavendish on Her Own Writing: Evidence from Revision and Handmade Correction," *The Papers of the Bibliographical Society of America* 85, no. 3 (1991): 297-307; Jeffrey Masten, "Material Cavendish: Paper, Performance, 'Sociable Virginity,'" *Modern Language Quarterly*, 65, no. 1 (2004): 49-68; Tanya Wood, "Margaret Cavendish, Duchess of Newcastle, *The Convent of Pleasure* (1668), Ending Revised by Her Husband, the Duke of Newcastle," in *Reading Early Modern Women: An Anthology of Texts in Manuscript and Print, 1550-1700*, ed. Helen Ostovich and Elizabeth Sauer (New York: Routledge, 2004), 435-37; Amy Greenstadt, "Margaret's Beard," *Early Modern Women: An Interdisciplinary Journal* 5 (2010): 171-82; and Valerie Billing, "'Treble marriage': Margaret Cavendish, William Newcastle, and Collaborative Authorship Author(s)," *Journal for Early Modern Cultural Studies* 11, no. 2 (2011): 94-122.

Pleasure does not name "the prince" among the play's characters but, emphatically, "the princess."[184]

The ending of this play (and of *Bell in Campo* and *The Female Academy*) can be disappointing to a twenty-first century reader—Cavendish offers Lady Happy and her companions a taste of freedom and independence only to deny them. I have often read this play with student readers who simply refuse to accept the princess's final "transformation," arguing that the real performance here is when "she" assumes the guise of a "prince." They become extraordinarily close readers, emphasizing Madam Mediator's description of the princess as "a princely brave woman *truly*" (2.3, emphasis added). They point to stage directions that continue to use female pronouns when referring to the "prince," even as "she" seems to reveal herself as a "he."[185] And they come back again and again to Cavendish's list of the play's characters at the end of the play—where the "prince" is returned once more to "his" true identity as "the princess." But I would like to suggest that one of Margaret Cavendish's "sociable letters" offers us a yet another way of understanding what happens not only to Lady Victoria, the women of the Female Academy, and Lady Happy but also to Cavendish herself.

In *The Sociable Letters*, late in the collection, Cavendish the letter-writer describes her experience of seeing ice skaters for the first time while she is living Antwerp. She leaves her warm fireside only at her husband's insistence, and she passes through the safe and familiar city to a strange new world outside the city walls. There, she is taken "to see men slide upon the frozen moat, or river, which runs, or rather stands about the city walls." To her surprise, she enjoys the experience. And then her perspective shifts. More than just the delight she experiences while watching the skaters, she comes to envy them: "I wished I could and might slide as they did." She is afraid she doesn't have the skill to skate, "the agility, art, courage, nor liberty," but she cannot quite put aside the wish.

---

[184] The list of characters is on an unnumbered page following *The Convent of Pleasure*. While the list of *dramatis personae* precedes the first play in the collection, *The Sociable Companions*, the lists follow the plays in the cases of *The Presence* (and its additional scenes) and *The Bridals*.

[185] See, for example, the stage directions in 4.1 (below, 155 and 158).

Even after returning home, once more safely inside the walled city, once more beside her fireside, and once more "alone," she is no longer the same:

I found I had a river, lake, or moat frozen in my brain into smooth, glassy ice, whereupon diverse of my thoughts were sliding, of which some slid fearfully, others as if they had been drunk, having much ado to keep on their incorporeal legs, and some slid quite off their feet and fell on the cold, hard ice, whereon some sliding upon imaginary shoes, with the imaginary fall, were tossed up into the air of my brain, yet most of my thoughts slid with a good grace and agility, as with swift and flying motion. But after I had sat by the fireside some time, the imaginary ice began to melt, and my thoughts prudently retired or removed, for fear of drowning in the imaginary river in my brain.[186]

I love the way Cavendish's description of this exhilarating but brief experience corresponds to what happens in her plays. In withdrawing from a world dominated by men, the women in *The Convent of Pleasure* escape their reality for a brief period of time. Like the ice skaters on the frozen river outside the city walls of Antwerp, they are suddenly free. So free that they almost fly. We want them to continue gliding over the ice, gracefully and swiftly and happily, but in the end, the ice melts, and they wind up right back where they started. In the same way, Margaret Cavendish, sometimes sliding fearfully, sometimes falling, sometimes "tossed up" into the air, finds herself soaring "as with swift and flying motion." Ambitious for herself and boosted by a loving and supportive husband, she tries over and over again to break free from social restrictions that limit her access to the intellectual, political, and social world controlled by men. She addresses herself to men in her many dedicatory prefaces and letters, almost demanding, rather than soliciting, their attention. She analyzes their books in her own, thus creating a dialogue with them, whether they choose to engage with her or not. She shocks the crowds by her gender-bending apparel, she manages to insert herself into the all-male ranks of the Royal Society,

---

[186] Cavendish, Letter 192, *Sociable Letters*, 399-401. I have silently modernized the spelling and punctuation.

and she creates and recreates alternative worlds where women are in charge of their own lives, freed from restrictions and limitations. But despite all her efforts, Cavendish never gets the respect, acceptance, and audience she seeks. In the end, like Lady Happy, Margaret Cavendish is fearful of drowning "in the imaginary river" of her mind. Her retreat to her fireside may have been done "prudently," but after all that she—and Lady Happy—have attempted, after their near escape from the ties that bind them, their retreat is also disappointing.

The Legacy of Margaret Cavendish and Her Work

By the time *Plays, Never before Printed* was published in 1668, an Englishwoman had acted for the first time on stage in a London playhouse.[187] And, notably, a play written by an Englishwoman—or, at least, translated by an Englishwoman—had also been performed on the public stage. In February of 1663, Katherine Philips's *Pompey*, a translation of the French playwright Pierre Corneille's 1643 tragedy *La Mort de Pompée*, was performed at the Theatre Royal in Dublin; by summer, the play had been staged in a London production. Following this success, Philips began translating Corneille's *Horace*, but she died before she could finish the project. The translation was completed by John Denham and performed at court in 1668, then in London at the Theatre Royal in 1669.[188] Later that same year, Frances Boothby's *Marcelina, or The Treacherous Friend*, a tragicomedy, was performed by the King's Company. It was the first original play by an Englishwoman produced on the English stage. By 1670, Aphra Behn's first play was staged by the Duke's Company—and by the end of the seventeenth century, Elizabeth Polwhele, "Ephelia," "Ariadne," Catherine Trotter,

---

[187] While either Margaret Hughes or Anne Marshall is generally credited as being the first Englishwoman to have acted on the public stage, Randall, *Winter Fruit*, notes that Catherine Coleman's performance in the 1656 production of *The Siege of Rhodes* is "the first appearance of an actress on a public stage in England" (171). For Coleman, see above, 38.

[188] Interestingly, when Katherine Philips's *Pompey* was printed (London, 1663), it appeared in quarto. When a collection of her work was published in 1669, two years after Philips's death and a year after Cavendish's *Plays, Never before Printed*, it was published in a folio format, though one that was not exclusively a collection of plays: *Poems . . . , to which is added . . . Corneille's "Pompey" and "Horace," tragedies. With several other translations out of French* (London, 1669).

Delariviere Manley, Mary Pix, and Susan Centlivre were all writing for the public stage.

Whatever inspiration Margaret Cavendish's two collections of plays might have offered for the female dramatists who emerged in the late 1660s, her reputation as a writer was ambiguous. As we have seen, her behavior and clothing received a great deal of public attention when she was in London—her writing, less so. One of the most frequently cited critical assessments of Cavendish's work is Dorothy Osborne's rather horrified comment, preserved in the letters she wrote to the man who would become her husband, Sir William Temple. Their correspondence was a clandestine one; both families opposed the match, and the letters dated to the last two years of their separation. Osborne was interested in literature, and her letters frequently referred to what she was reading, for example Madeleine de Scudéry's wildly popular *Artamène, ou le Grand Cyrus* (ten volumes, published between 1648 and 1653) and the heroic romance *Cléopâtre*, by Gauthier de Costes, seigneur de la Calprenède (published in 1648), both of which Osborne read in French. Osborne also mentions "Reine Marguerite," a volume Temple had sent to her and that she returned to him, probably an edition of Marguerite of Navarre's *Memoirs*, published posthumously in 1628. Early in May 1653, writing to Temple in London, Osborne asks if he has "seen a book of poems newly come out by my Lady Newcastle." "For God's sake, if you meet with it, send it me," she exclaims, adding, "they say 'tis ten times more extravagant than her dress." And then, not having read Cavendish's poems, Osborne concludes, "Sure the poor woman is a little distracted; she could never be so ridiculous else as to venture at writing books, and in verse too. If I should not sleep this fortnight, I should not come to that."[189] Virginia Woolf used this comment as a way to illustrate her claim that "the crazy Duchess became a bogey to frighten clever girls with."[190] But as

---

[189] Dorothy Osborne to Sir William Temple, 1(?) May 1653, *The Letters of Dorothy Osborne to Sir William Temple*, ed. Edward A. Parry (New York: E. P. Dutton, 1914), 81-82. I have silently modernized the spelling and punctuation. Within a few weeks, Osborne had satisfied her curiosity. "You need not send me my Lady Newcastle's book at all," she wrote to Temple, "for I have seen it, and am satisfied that there are many soberer people in Bedlam. I'll swear her friends are much to blame to let her go abroad." Dorothy Osborne to Sir William Temple, 12 June (?) 1653, *Letters of Dorothy Osborne*, ed. Parry, 100.

[190] Woolf, *A Room of One's Own*, 62.

the letter makes clear, Osborne's opinions were formed without having read a single word of Cavendish's *Poems and Fancies*—she didn't have a copy of the book. And, most important, perhaps, Osborne's views were expressed in her private correspondence, not publicly offered.

In the same way, when Mary Evelyn offered up her views of Cavendish's writing, it is not altogether clear she had actually read any of it. Nevertheless, she judges Cavendish's conversation to be "as airy, empty, whimsical, and rambling as her books." "I hope," she concludes in her letter, "as she is an original, she may never have a copy."[191] Evelyn also reports, with more than a little skepticism, on the opinions of some of those who had presumably been sent copies of Cavendish's work and who vied with one another to praise her. At one of the gatherings where Evelyn met Cavendish, she claims to have overheard the physician and natural philosopher Walter Charleton "complimenting [Cavendish's] wit and learning in a high manner." For her part, Cavendish does not seem to have taken Charleton's compliments too seriously, since Evelyn reports that the duchess "swore if the schools did not banish Aristotle and read Margaret, duchess of Newcastle, they did her wrong and deserved to be abolished." Evelyn, however, seems to think Cavendish accepted Charleton's excessive praise at face value, receiving it as "so much her due." Evelyn adds that when "a new admirer" approached Cavendish at the gathering, she rewarded him with her views of her faith and religion and even began to "cite her own pieces, line and page in such a book."[192]

Even if Margaret Cavendish were serious in her comments that her work should replace Aristotle's as a subject of study, Mary Evelyn's prejudices about Cavendish's aspirations are clear, revealed in a letter sent to the same correspondent several years later: "Women were not born to read authors and censure the learned, to compare lives and judge of virtues, to give rules of morality and sacrifice to the muses." Further, "all time borrowed from family duties is misspent. The care of children's education, observing a husband's commands, assisting the

---

[191] Mary Evelyn to the Rev. Ralph Bohun, undated letter from 1667, in *The Diary and Correspondence of John Evelyn*, ed. Bray, 4:8-9. I have silently modernized the spelling and punctuation.

[192] Mary Evelyn to the Rev. Ralph Bohun, undated letter from 1667, in *The Diary and Correspondence of John Evelyn*, ed. Bray, 4:9. I have silently modernized the spelling and punctuation.

sick, relieving the poor, and being serviceable to our friends are of sufficient weight to employ the most improved capacities among us." And then one further damning observation: "if sometimes it happens by accident that one of a thousand aspires a little higher, her fate commonly exposes her to wonder but adds little of esteem."[193] Again, however, it is important to note that, while Mary Evelyn's views on Cavendish and her work are frequently cited by modern critics and biographers, her opinions were, like Dorothy Osborne's, privately shared in personal letters.

Clearly with the aim of a gaining a readership for her work, Margaret Cavendish sent copies of her publications to friends and intellectuals, among them the diplomat and philosopher Sir Kenelm Digby; the renowned philosopher Thomas Hobbes, to whom she claimed to have "spoken" only a few words; the Cambridge philosopher Henry More; Walter Charleton, the man whom Mary Evelyn overheard complimenting Cavendish on her "wit and learning"; and the playwright Thomas Shadwell. In 1657, Digby wrote to express his appreciation to Cavendish for the "worthy present" of books she had sent, a gift that had inspired in him "new admiration of your goodness and knowledge." But perhaps the praise is a little equivocal—he notes that "every page" in her "excellent book" affords "abundant matter," but that doesn't seem to be saying much. Writing a few years later, in a letter from 1661, Hobbes was a bit more specific, probably having received a copy of *Nature's Pictures*. He tells Cavendish, "I have already read so much of it . . . as to give your excellence an account of it thus far"; her book is "filled throughout with more and truer ideas of virtue and honor than any book of morality I have read." Henry More, while privately mocking Cavendish's philosophical pretensions, sent a note to her expressing his surprise that "so illustrious a person" would send him such "noble volumes as an intended testimony" of her respect— he thought at first the books must have been sent as a gift to his college library, but the duchess's "messenger" had insisted they were for him personally. He wrote in haste to thank her before he had time to "compute the value" of her "most elegant and ingenious writings." Walter Charleton wrote at some length to Cavendish about her work in

---

[193] Mary Evelyn to the Rev. Ralph Bohun, 4 January 1672, in *The Diary and Correspondence of John Evelyn*, ed. Bray, 4:31-32. I have silently modernized the spelling and punctuation.

1667, clearly having spent time with her books, and he carefully details his responses to her natural philosophy, her moral philosophy, and her poetry. In 1671, Shadwell turned the tables, sending Cavendish the gift of a play, *The Humorists*, which he hoped to dedicate to her, while apologizing that his request was, perhaps, "too great a presumption for me to hope that your grace (that makes so good use of your time with your own pen) can have so much to throw away as once to read this little offspring of mine." Her response was to send him a present, probably of her work: "to reward my crime [the "presumption" of his dedication] is beyond expression generous," he replied.[194]

Cavendish also presented copies of her books to the colleges of Oxford and Cambridge; today over one hundred presentation copies of her books are still in the Oxford libraries to which she donated them.[195] In his survey of these Cavendish volumes in Oxford, William Poole observes that her books seem to have been sent to every college library: "Of the colleges and halls then extant, all received copies, and most still hold anywhere between two and nine of her early editions; and although not all these books came from Margaret herself, most did." And "In Cambridge, the picture is the same: the older college libraries

---

[194] Kenelm Digby to Margaret Cavendish, 9 June 1657, in *Letters and Poems*, ed. William Cavendish, 65; Thomas Hobbes to Margaret Cavendish, 9 February 1661, in *Letters and Poems*, ed. William Cavendish, 67-68 (Hobbes refers to stage comedies in the letter—"if some comic writer, by conversation with ill people, ha[s] been able to present vices upon the stage more ridiculously and immodestly, by which they take their rabble, I reckon that among your praises, for that which most pleases lewd spectators is nothing but subtle cheating or filth"—leading Grant, *Margaret the First*, 221, to conclude Cavendish had sent him her *Playes*); Henry More to Margaret Cavendish, [1664], in *Letters and Poems*, ed. William Cavendish, 90-91 (meanwhile, in a March 1664/5 letter to Anne Finch Conway, More belittled Cavendish's *Philosophical Letters*, writing that he trusted Conway would "smile" at the "conceit" of Cavendish's attempts to "confute" his work in her "large book"; in a second letter, written in early May, he informed Conway that Cavendish had "sent two more folios of hers" to him, again "intended to confute" his writing, adding "I believe she may be secure from any one giving her the trouble of a reply"; *The Conway Letters: The Correspondence of Anne, Viscountess Conway, Henry More, and Their Friends, 1642-1684*, rev. ed. Marjorie Hope Nicholson and Sarah Hutton [New York: Oxford University Press, 1992], 234, 237); Walter Charleton to Margaret Cavendish, 7 May 1667, in *Letters and Poems*, ed. William Cavendish, 108-19; and Thomas Shadwell to Margaret Cavendish, 25 May 1671, in *Letters and Poems*, ed. William Cavendish, 130. I have silently modernized the spelling and punctuation.

[195] Poole, "Margaret Cavendish's Books," 2.

are awash with Cavendish, perhaps even more so than their Oxonian cousins."[196] Her gifts produced many flattering and effusive letters of thanks in return—the flattery and effusion are not at all unusual in letters from beneficiaries to wealthy and noble patrons, which clearly the Cavendishes were—but very few of the letters that William Cavendish collected and published in his wife's honor after her death suggest the recipients read her books.[197] It would be interesting to know what Cavendish herself made of the extravagant praises the letters of thanks contained. Some of the letters sent from the colleges, thanking her for her gifts, were accompanied by Latin versions in addition to the English, which must have been a source of some discomfort to Cavendish, aware, as she was, of her deficient education, in particular of the language of universal scholarship. Cavendish also disseminated her volumes beyond the English universities—a letter to her from Constantijn Huygens, dated 28 November 1658, informs Margaret that, "according to your excellency's command," he presented her *Philosophical and Physical Opinions* to Leiden University.[198] (She responded by sending the university all of her books along with a specially prepared Latin index.[199])

The writer, philosopher, and clergyman Joseph Glanvill presented Cavendish with a copy of his book on witchcraft, and she thanked him by returning the favor, sending him what he described as her own "ingenious works." He did her the honor not only of writing to thank her for the present but also of replying in some detail to criticisms she has offered of his work. He then asked her a favor "on public account": Bath had just "erected" a library, and as Glanvill notes, "there are in it several worthy authors, but it wants the great honor and

---

[196] Poole, "Margaret Cavendish's books," 3.

[197] After his wife's death, William Cavendish included dozens of such letters from Oxford and Cambridge in *Letters and Poems*.

[198] Constantijn Huygens to Margaret Cavendish, 28 November 1658, in *Letters and Poems*, ed. William Cavendish, 102. I have silently modernized the spelling and punctuation. This is followed by a Latin letter of thanks addressed to "Illustrissima Domina," from the academic rector of the university. Margaret Cavendish's undated letter to Constantijn Huygens, accompanying her present of books, is in *Die Briefwisseling van Constantijn Huygens*, ed. Worp, 5:312.

[199] Constantijn Huygens to Margaret Cavendish, 2/12 August 1664, in *Die Briefwisseling van Constantijn Huygens*, ed. Worp, 6:88-89. I have silently modernized the spelling and punctuation.

ornament of the illustrious duchess of Newcastle's works." As a "humble solicitor," Glanvill hoped that she would favor the library at Bath just as she favored the many "considerable libraries of England," clearly those at Oxford and Cambridge.[200] She also received letters of thanks for gifts of her "*oeuvres*" from the philosopher Samuel de Sorbière and from the Scottish physician William Davison, who signed himself "D. Avissone," both writing in French. Did these letters too remind her of her linguistic deficiencies? Robert Creighton, a royalist exile living in Utrecht, also received a gift of books from Cavendish, or, rather, in his words, she "was pleased to appear" to him in "another dress, under the veil of books." Undoubtedly his praise is excessive: "Were those ancients now alive who first discoursed of atoms, matter, form, and other ingredients of the world's fabric, they would hang their heads, confounded to see a lady of most honorable extraction, in prime of youth, amidst a thousand fasheries [troubles, vexations] of greatness, say more of their own mysteries than they," he rhapsodizes. But he offered her one true nugget of thoughtfulness and comfort in response to her apologies for her own lack of any language other than English. "Those old philosophers too knew only their own tongue, Greek," he reminds her.[201]

While she was alive, Cavendish published no commendatory verses from colleagues in her folio collections of plays because she had no colleagues, aside from her husband, and no commendatory verses were written. One bit of verse, sent to her from Trinity College, Cambridge in 1668, might have served, a few lines intended as an "honorable monument" to her:

To Margaret the First,
Princess of Philosophers,
Who hath dispelled errors,

---

[200] Joseph Glanvill to Margaret Cavendish, 22 December [1666?], n. d., and 25 August [1667?], in *Letters and Poems*, ed. William Cavendish, 85, 98-100, 103-4. Glanvill was rector of the Abbey Church in Bath from 1666 to 1680; his *Philosophical Considerations Touching the Being of Witches and Witchcraft* was published in 1666. Presumably his letters to Cavendish, one undated and two not fully dated, were written between 1666 and 1667. I have silently modernized the spelling and punctuation.

[201] Robert Creighton to Margaret Cavendish, 1653, in *Letters and Poems*, ed. William Cavendish, 85-87. I have silently modernized the spelling and punctuation.

Appeased the differences of opinions,
And restored peace
To learning's commonwealth.[202]

She did not publish these lines, however flattering. But poems full of praise did come, at last, solicited or not, after her death, and they filled the last thirty pages of the book William Cavendish dedicated to his wife's memory. Poems in English and Latin, poems signed and unsigned, poems "to" her, poems about her, even one addressed to her "closet," described as a "sacred cell / Where holy hermits anciently did dwell." Poems comparing her to the Faerie Queene, to Dido, to Helen, poems that claim she broke the glass ceiling—or, rather, she "scaled the walls of fame, / And made a breach where never female came"— and that she was the tenth muse. Praises, elegies, epitaphs. And one, perhaps unconsciously reflecting Cavendish's gender-bending in *The Convent of Pleasure*, observing that as long as she was alive, "wit was hermaphrodite," but "now 'tis only masculine again."[203] And yet, even in death, Cavendish was a target of ridicule. This mock epitaph was copied by John Stainsby, a law clerk, and sent on to his friend, the antiquarian Elias Ashmole:

"Here lies wise, chaste, hospitable, humble—"
I had gone on, but Nick [the devil] began to grumble:
"Write, write," says he, "upon her tomb of marble
These words, which out I and my friends will warble:
'Shame of her sex, Welbeck's illustrious whore,
The true man's hate and grief, plague of the poor,
The great atheistical philosophraster,
That owns no God, no devil, lord, nor master,
Vice's epitome and virtue's foe,
Here lies her body, but her soul's below."[204]

---

[202] Trinity College to Margaret Cavendish, 5 October 1668, in *Letters and Poems*, ed. William Cavendish, 152. I have silently modernized the spelling and punctuation.

[203] The poems are in *Poems and Letters*, ed. William Cavendish, 153-82. I have silently modernized the spelling and punctuation

[204] Quoted in Grant, *Margaret the First*, 199, and in Whitaker, *Mad Madge*, 348. I have silently modernized the spelling and punctuation.

Still, there were a few readers who took Cavendish seriously and published their response to her work. The earliest of such responses to Margaret Cavendish's work came in 1657, notable because it was a public notice rather than a private note, and notable because the critic was a woman, Suzanne du Verger. Du Verger was a writer and translator who had published a collection of "histories" carefully edited from Jean-Pierre Camus's *Les Événements singuliers* and printed under the title *Admirable Events . . . together with Moral Relations* in 1639, a volume dedicated to Queen Henrietta Maria. In *Du Verger's Humble Reflections upon Some Passages of the Right Honorable the Lady Marchioness of Newcastle's Olio*, du Verger addressed Cavendish directly.[205] As her title suggests, she took issue with some of Cavendish's views, which she regarded as "misinformed." In a dedicatory epistle, Du Verger praised Cavendish's "delicious and exquisite" *Olio*, elaborating on the literal meaning of the Spanish word for spicy stew and contrasting Cavendish's dainty dish, "delicately dressed, seasoned, and set out" with her "noble hand" to her own more humble and "ordinary, poor fare." But after "greedily" eating the delicacies Cavendish had prepared, du Verger says that she unexpectedly "met with morsels so willowish [ill-tasting] and un-sound," even "wholly corrupted," that she became nauseated and began to "loathe" what had formerly tasted so good. Du Verger's par-ticular objection was to Cavendish's essay "On the Monastical Life."[206] In her *Humble Reflections*, Du Verger identified points of contention, summarized Cavendish's views, and then responded to each point, in turn, addressing a series of "paragraphs," reflections, and objections directly to Cavendish herself. The aim was to "correct" the inaccuracies and misrepresentations in Cavendish's essay with her own views of monasticism. Clearly Du Verger had not only *read* Cavendish, she took her seriously, responding to the two-and-a-half folio pages of Cavendish's original essay in a hundred and sixty-eight octavo pages of her own.

And in 1673, the year of Cavendish's death, the early feminist Bathsua Makin published *An Essay to Revive the Ancient Education of Gentlewomen*, in which she praises Cavendish as a woman who, "by her

[205] *Du Vergers Humble Reflections upon some Passages of the right Honorable the Lady Marchionesse of Newcastles OLIO, or an Appeale from her Mes-informed, to her owne better informed judgement* (London, 1657).

[206] Cavendish, *The Worlds Olio*, 28-31. On this essay, see above, n. 181.

own genius, rather than any timely instruction, overtops many grave gown-men." Makin listed Cavendish, along with such female notables as the humanist scholar Olympia Morata, Elizabeth Tudor, Jane Grey, and Christina of Sweden, among others, as women who were "educated in arts and tongues" and recognized as "eminent in them."[207] And two years later, there was another note of recognition when the critic and author Edward Phillips included Margaret Cavendish in his *Theatrum Poetarum Anglicanorum*, a comphrensive survey of English poets, describing her as "a very obliging lady to the world" who had "largely and copiously impart[ed] to public view her studious endeavors in the arts and ingenuities."[208] Interestingly, however, Phillips notes only "three ample volumes in print": "one of orations, the other of philosophical notions and discourses, the third of dramatic and other kinds of poetry." From these very general descriptions of Cavendish's "ample volumes," it's hard to tell which of her books he may have had in mind, or whether he was actually familiar with any of them.

As the seventeenth century drew to a close, the biographer and critic of stage drama Gerard Langbaine included Margaret Cavendish (as well as her husband) in his *Account of the English Dramatic Poets.*[209] Langbaine had more than a passing familiarity with Cavendish's work. He writes that, "her soul sympathizing" with her husband's "in all things, especially in dramatic poetry," she published "twenty-six plays besides several loose scenes" in two collections. However, Langbaine declines to pass judgment on her writing even as he points out that "some have but a mean opinion of her plays." In Cavendish's defense

---

[207] *An Essay to Revive the Antient Education of Gentlewomen in Religion, Manners, Arts, & Tongues* . . . (London, 1673), in *First Feminist: British Women Writers, 1578-1799*, ed. Moira Ferguson (Bloomington: Indiana University Press, 1985), 132. I have silently modernized the spelling and punctuation.

[208] Edward Phillips, *Theatrum poetarum anglicanorum, or a Compleat Collection of the Poets* . . . (London, 1675), 2:48. The book contains two "volumes," and only the second "volume" is paginated. Here, Cavendish and other female writers are separated from male poets and placed in a list headed "Women." I have silently modernized the spelling and punctuation.

[209] Gerard Langbaine, *An Account of the English Dramatick Poets, or, Some Observations and Remarks on the Lives and Writings of all those that have Published either Comedies, Tragi-Comedies, Pastorals, Masques, Interludes, Farces, or Opera's in the English Tongue* (Oxford, 1691), 390-94. I have included the full title to show the comprehensive nature of Langbaine's effort. In quoting from his work, I have silently modernized the spelling and punctuation.

Langbaine notes, "if it be considered that both the language and the plots of them are all her own, I think she ought with justice be preferred to others of her sex, which have built their fame on other people's foundations." To illustrate her originality, he quotes from the "General Prologue" to her 1662 *Plays*, where Cavendish contrasted her plays to those of Jonson, Shakespeare, and Beaumont and Fletcher, who relied on sources for their plots. Langbaine's entry on Cavendish includes an alphabetized list of her plays, describing each title's genre and frequently adding some additional descriptive information, such as "this play consists of three and twenty scenes but is not divided into acts" (about *Apocryphal Ladies*) and "His Grace writ the epilogue to the first part" (about the two-part comedy *The Play Called Wit's Cabal*). Langbaine's entry on Cavendish ends with a brief bibliography of her non-dramatic work.

In the eighteenth century, the legal writer and would-be poet Giles Jacob (who, unfortunately for him, figured as one of the dunces in Alexander Pope's *Dunciad*) included an entry on Margaret Cavendish in his two-volume *Poetical Register*, describing her as "the most voluminous dramatic writer of our female poets."[210] Although Jacob judges Cavendish to have "a more than ordinary propensity to dramatic poetry," for the rest of his entry he simply reproduces Langbaine's list of plays, noting his source and adding "all the language and plots of her plays, Mr. Langbaine tells us, were her own." He rearranges Langbaine's list, however—in Jacob's list, the plays are neither alphabetically nor chronologically arranged, and he reduces the number to nineteen rather than Langbaine's twenty-six. Like Langbaine, Jacob follows his discussion of the plays with brief comments about additional work published by Cavendish, but where Langbaine included eight titles in total, Jacob reduces the number to three: a book of poems (the title of which he did not give), her biography of her husband, and her own autobiography. Aside from his claims that Cavendish was the "most voluminous" female dramatist and that she had a natural inclination to the writing of drama, there was nothing new in Jacob's discussion of

---

[210] Giles Jacob, *The Poetical Register: or, the Lives and Characters of All the English Poets, with an Account of their Writings* (London, 1723), 2:190-92. I have silently modernized the spelling and punctuation.

Cavendish and no indication that he was actually familiar with any of her plays.

When the historian George Ballard came to write a profile of Cavendish some thirty years later, in his 1752 *Memoirs of Several Ladies of Great Britain Who Have Been Celebrated for Their Writings or Skill in the Learned Language and Sciences*, he relied for much of his information on Langbaine and Jacob.[211] Ballard's focus was principally on biography, not criticism, and in writing about Margaret Cavendish, he tamed the story of her life. In Ballard's retelling, the young Margaret Lucas's rather limited education becomes a "remarkably careful . . . education." He also asserts that the young woman was taught "the French tongue," which, as we have seen, Cavendish did not know. (Though Ballard did lament that Cavendish did not have training in the "learned languages," Greek and Latin.) Interestingly, however, while Ballard relied on Langbaine and Jacob for a critical assessment of Cavendish's work, he seems to have searched out her volumes himself, since he describes drawing up a "catalogue of all her works which have come to my knowledge"; living in Oxford, he may well have been able to locate many of the volumes Cavendish had donated to the various colleges. The list he annotates is fascinating: about *The World's Olio*, he writes, "which I have not seen yet"; about *Observations upon Experimental Philosophy*," he notes, "Mr. James Bristow began to translate some of those philosophical discourses into the Latin tongue."[212] Ballard includes her 1662 *Plays* in his Cavendish bibliography, but about the 1668 *Plays, Never before Printed*, he writes, "this book I have not seen." He relied on Langbaine for his information about her dramatic works, however, simply listing her plays "in the same order that gentleman placed them." Indeed, by the time Ballard was searching out information about Cavendish, it wasn't even clear when she had died—the date wasn't on her monument in Westminster Abbey, and Ballard could only find it by consulting one "Mr. Fuhrman, in the fifteenth

---

[211] George Ballard, *Memoirs of Several Ladies of Great Britain* (Oxford, 1752), 299-306. In quoting from Ballard, I have silently modernized the spelling and punctuation.

[212] James Bristow, a scholar from Christ Church, had been "commissioned to Latinize Margaret's philosophy," but "abandoned the project 'finding great difficulties therein, through the confusedness of the matter.'" Quoted in Whitaker, *Mad Madge*, 256.

volume of his manuscript collections in Corpus Christi College archives."

A year later, the actor and playwright Theophilus Cibber (son of the much more famous playwright and poet-laureate Colley Cibber) published *Lives of the Poets of Great Britain and Ireland, to the Time of Dean Swift.* Cibber cites Langbaine and Jacob for much of his information about Cavendish, but he also expands biographical details he must have found in Ballard, adding that Cavendish's mother "was remarkably assiduous" in her children's education, for example, and that "her trouble in cultivating this daughter's mind was not in vain, for she discovered early an inclination to learning." Cibber also adds to the story of the Cavendish-Lucas courtship an anecdote about Margaret's brother. In Cibber's telling, Charles Lucas had told William "he was not solicitous about his own affairs, for he knew the worst could be but suffering either death or exile in the royal cause, but his chief solicitude was for his sister, on whom he could bestow no fortune and whose beauty exposed her to danger." This "raised the marquis's curiosity to see her and from that circumstance arose the marquis's affection to this lady." Cibber has little to say about Cavendish's writing, simply noting that, after the Restoration, "she dedicated her time to writing poems, philosophical discourses, orations, and plays," and adding that "though she was very beautiful, she died without issue." He quotes Jacob on her productivity and "propensity," and Langbaine on the originality of her plots, and although he quotes, almost verbatim, Ballard's search for the date of her death (down to the reference to Fuhrman and his fifteenth volume) and reproduces almost exactly Ballard's bibliography of Cavendish's works, he does not name Ballard as a source.[213]

Just a few years later, Cavendish made a brief appearance in Horace Walpole's *Catalogue of the Royal and Noble Authors of England, Scotland, and Ireland,* first published in 1758.[214] A well-known playwright, historian, and novelist, the author mostly famously of the gothic *Castle of Otranto,*

---

[213] Theophilus Cibber, *The Lives of the Poets of Great Britain and Ireland* (London, 1753), 2:162-69. Cibber clearly relied on Ballard elsewhere; in the biography of Katherine Philips, for example, which immediately precedes Cavendish's, Cibber adds a footnote citing "Ballard's *Memoirs*"). I have silently modernized the spelling and punctuation.

[214] Horace Walpole, *Catalogue of the Royal and Noble Authors of England, Scotland, and Ireland,* ed. Thomas Park (London, 1806), 145-56.

Walpole includes an entry for Margaret Cavendish among his "royal and noble authors," first listing her works and then concluding this bibliography with a bit of an insult: "Whoever has a mind to know more of this fertile pedant will find a detail of her works in Ballard's *Memoirs*, from whence I have taken this account." Walpole follows this with a few biographical and critical comments, including a long extract from "The Pastime and Recreation of the Queen of Fairies in Fairyland, the Center of the Earth" (from *Poems and Fancies*) as an example of "her grace's happier efforts," and then a passage from "Epistle to My Brain" (from *Philosophical Fancies*), which, he says, "may be cited as an aggregate of much metrical obscurity." A few pages later, Walpole sets out to write about William Cavendish, but he can't quite draw himself away from the duke's wife and offers a few remarks about the "fantastic couple," the duke and his "faithful duchess"—Walpole regards many of Margaret's judgments in her biography of her husband to be "amusing," and he is quick to observe that, "though she had written philosophy, it seems she had read none." She had an "unbounded passion for scribbling." (Though, to be fair, he also regarded William Cavendish as "a man in whose character ridicule would find more materials than satire.") About the couple, he concludes, "What a picture of foolish nobility was this stately poetic couple, retired to their own little domain, and intoxicating one another with circumstantial flattery, on what was of consequence to no mortal but themselves!"[215] Aside from his jibes, Walpole offers little new information in his account of Cavendish, drawing liberally not only on Ballard but also on Langbaine, Jacob, and Cibber, all of whom he cites.

With the exception of her biography of her husband, none of Cavendish's books had been—or would be—republished after her death, but a small selection of her poetry was included in the 1755 anthology *Poems by Eminent Ladies* edited by George Colman, an essayist and dramatist, and Bonnell Thornton, a poet and essayist.[216] The two repeat the mistake first made by Ballard that Margaret was the youngest child of *Charles* Lucas; according to their brief biographical note, "it is plain, from the uncommon turn of her compositions, that she possessed a wild native genius." They lament the fact that this "native

215 Walpole, *Catalogue*, 189-205

216 George Colman and Bonnell Thornton, eds., *Poems by Eminent Ladies* (London, 1755), 2:197-212. I have silently modernized the spelling and punctuation.

genius" clearly had not been "duly cultivated," thus preventing Cavendish's poetry from "show[ing] itself to advantage in the higher sorts of poetry." *Poems by Eminent Ladies* contains two Cavendish dialogues, "Melancholy and Mirth" and "Peace and War"; a poem about death, headed "Nature's Cook"; and a poem titled "Wit." The two longest selections in the anthology focus on fairies: "The Pastime and Recreation of the Queen of the Fairies in Fairyland, the Center of the Earth" and "The Pastime of the Queen of the Fairies, When She First Comes upon Earth out of the Center." All of these are from Cavendish's 1653 *Poems and Fancies*, although, as Katie Whitaker notes, Colman and Thornton carefully trimmed Cavendish's poems by "omitting those sections that offended against the editors' sense of decency," and omitting, too, any "comment whatsoever to tell the readers what they had done." In the "Pastime and Recreation," for example, "the two editors cut out the grotesquerie of Margaret's description of the fairies' diet—including ants' eggs, flies, and dormouse milk—and of the mischief they practiced on humans."[217] And while Colman produced plays and managed the Covent Garden Theatre, there is no reference in this anthology to any of Cavendish's plays.

Cavendish's name continued to appear in biographical encyclopedias as well. The *Biographium Faemineum: The Female Worthies*, a collection of "memoirs of the most illustrious ladies of all ages and nations" published in 1766, contained an entry for "Newcastle, Margaret (duchess of)," though all of the information is recycled, almost verbatim, from Langbaine and Jacob. But along the way, all criticism of Cavendish has been excised, leaving her as a perfect paragon: "In her person she was noble and graceful; in her temper, shy and reserved; in her studies, contemplations, and writings, indefatigable." She was, in sum, "pious, generous, and charitable," an "excellent economist," "kind to her servants," and a "perfect pattern of conjugal love and duty."[218] Margaret Cavendish was not included in Alexander Chalmers's eleven-volume *New and General Biographical*

[217] Whitaker, *Mad Madge*, 352.
[218] *Biographium Faemineum: The Female Worthies*, or, Memoirs of the Most Illustrious Ladies, of All Ages and Nations . . . (London, 1766), 149-51

Dictionary, although her husband was.[219] Nor did she rate an entry in the wonderfully title *Eccentric Biography, or Memoirs of Remarkable Female Characters Ancient and Modern, Including Actresses, Adventurers, Authoresses, Fortunetellers, Gypsies, Dwarfs, Swindlers and Vagrants* published in 1803. Given the pervasive skeptical views of Cavendish, it's probably just as well.

As the nineteenth century began, Cavendish was included in one of the rare biographical encyclopedias compiled by a woman, *Memoirs of Celebrated Female Characters*, published in 1804 by the poet and novelist Mary Pilkington.[220] The entry reproduces earlier errors, for example the claim that Cavendish was the daughter of Charles Lucas, and Pilkington adds this about Cavendish's mother: "Few women were more capable of the task of education than lady Lucas, and her daughters were allowed to be the most accomplished females of the age." Nothing in Cavendish's autobiography suggests anything of the sort about Elizabeth Lucas's capacities for (or interest in) educating her daughters. But Pilkington was more than charitable to Cavendish and her work, perhaps sympathetic to the hostility a woman like the duchess experienced. "Though their biographers have ridiculed the scribbling mania which seized them," she writes about William and Margaret Cavendish, "it afforded them a degree of happiness which very few attain." Pilkington does not add a detailed bibliography of works by Margaret Cavendish, however, noting that to "specify the various performances of this fertile author, would give a work so concise as this, the appearance of a bookseller's catalogue of sale," adding, in a sad note, "as they scarcely outlived the memory of their illustrious composer, the account would not be likely to entertain." Of the wealth of Cavendish's literary production, Pilkington includes only seventeen lines from "Dialogue between Melancholy and Mirth," a

---

219 Chalmers's eleven-volume dictionary was enlarged and republished as the *General Biographical Dictionary*, published in thirty-two volumes between 1812 and 1817. The entry on William Cavendish focuses mainly on his role during the English Civil Wars; about his writing, the entry says, "Of his grace's literary labours, it is less possible to entertain a high opinion."

220 Mrs. [Mary] Pilkington, *Memoirs of Celebrated Female Characters, Who Have Distinguished Themselves by Their Talents and Virtues in Every Age and Nation* (London: Albion Press, 1804), 272-73.

poem from *Nature's Pictures* that extends over some five pages in the original.

Just a few years later, the first edited collection of Margaret Cavendish's poetry appeared. In 1813, Egerton Brydges published *Select Poems of Margaret Cavendish, Duchess of Newcastle*, a slim volume only twenty pages long.[221] Like Colman and Thornton, Brydges ignores Cavendish's philosophy and science writing, her essays, her epistles, and her plays, restricting himself to publishing a selection of her poetry. In the "advertisement" prefacing the poems, Brydges defends Cavendish, "whose genius has been decried and ridiculed," even while admitting that there are "many absurd passages in many of Her grace's compositions." But, while defending Cavendish's genius and granting that she had an "active, thinking, and original mind," as well as an imagination that was "quick, copious, and sometimes even beautiful," he condemns her "taste." It was "not only uncultivated, but perhaps originally defective." "Nothing that I have read of hers, [sic] is touched by pathos," he sniffs, adding, "we are too frequently shocked by expressions and images of extraordinary coarseness; and more extraordinary as flowing from a female of high rank, brought up in courts." He can't publish her poetry without offering, in his notes, his own commentary and suggestions about the ways it could be improved. About a line in "A Dialogue between Melancholy and Mirth," for instance, he writes, "This and the nineteen following lines are highly spirited and beautiful, and prove the Duchess to have felt at times the inspiration of real genius, which only wanted the pruning hand of a more correct judgment." And a few lines later: "In these days it seems a little wonderful that a lady of rank so high, and mind so cultivated, could use language so coarse and disgusting as is seen here." Still, and uniquely, this volume contained two brief lyrics from *The Convent of Pleasure*, titled by Brydges "Song of the Princess, in the Character of a Shepherd: Answered by Lady Happy" and "Song of the Lady Happy."[222]

---

[221] Egerton Brydges, ed., *Select Poems of Margaret Cavendish, Duchess of Newcastle* (Kent, UK: Lee Priory Press, 1813). At the end of his prefatory "Advertisement" (n.p.), Brydges notes "From her the Editor of these Poems is proud to record his descent."

[222] The two lyrics from *The Convent of Pleasure* are in Brydges, *Select Poems*, 10-12 and 16-17. (In the play itself, these lyrics appear in 4.1 and 1.2.)

One intriguing reference to Cavendish—elusive in its vagueness and unusual in its appreciation—is found in Charles Lamb's *Essays of Elia*, published in 1823, though the essays themselves first began appearing in *The London Magazine* in 1820. In these essays, Lamb presented himself as Elia, his sister Mary as Cousin Bridget. In "Mackery End, in Hertfordshire," Lamb/Elia writes that he and his "housekeeper," Bridget, live "generally in harmony" with only "occasional bickerings— as it should be among near relatives." One of their points of difference lies in their literary tastes: "I can pardon her blindness to the beautiful obliquities of the *Religion Medici*, but she must apologize to me for certain disrespectful insinuations which she has been pleased to throw out latterly touching the intellectuals of a dear favorite of mine of the last century but one, the thrice noble, chaste, and virtuous, but again somewhat fantastical and original-brained, generous Margaret New- castle."[223] This is the most intriguing of several allusions to Cavendish in Lamb's essays. Earlier, in "The Two Races of Men," Lamb embarked on a bit of a rant about "those who borrow" and "those who lend," directing his anger especially at those who borrowed books and failed to return them. In the essay, he imagines addressing one of those borrowers who offended him: "But what moved thee, wayward, spiteful K., to be so importunate to carry off with thee, in spite of tears and adjurations to thee to forbear, the *Letters* of that princely woman, the thrice-noble Margaret Newcastle, knowing at the time, and knowing that I knew also, thou most assuredly wouldst never turn over one leaf of the illustrious folio?" Even worse, K. had taken the book to France![224] In "The Complaint of the Decay of Beggars in the Metropolis," Cavendish is just an aside, where Elia refers to the "poets and romancical writers," adding "(as dear Margaret Newcastle would call them)."[225] When Lamb published a second series of essays ten years later, the *Last Essays of Elia*, Cavendish was still with him. In "Detached Thoughts on Books and Reading," Lamb makes it a point to scoff at bad books that have been beautifully bound, and when he turns to Cavendish, you might cringe, thinking that he is about to poke fun at

---

[223] Charles Lamb, *Essays of Elia* (1823; New York: D. Appleton, 1879), 121-22. I have silently modernized the punctuation. *Religio Medici* (*The Religion of a Doctor*) is Sir Thomas Browne's long religious testament, first published in 1643.

[224] Lamb, *Essays of Elia*, 45. I have silently modernized the punctuation.

[225] Lamb, *Essays of Elia*, 184.

the duchess's lavish folio volumes. Instead, he uses Cavendish's biography of her husband as an example of a book that is both "good and rare." For such a volume, he says, "no casket is rich enough, no casing sufficiently durable, to honour and keep safe such a jewel."[226] His fascination with and appreciation for Cavendish seem genuine and enduring. Lamb is also said to have entertained his guests one evening by posing a topic for discussion: "persons one would wish to have seen." While his companions suggest John Locke and Isaac Newton, Shakespeare, Chaucer, Petrarch, and Dante, Henry Fielding and Samuel Richardson, among many other famous men, "Lamb impatiently declared for the duchess of Newcastle."[227]

Margaret Cavendish is also noted in Robert Watt's four-volume *Bibliotheca Britannica*, published in 1824.[228] There is little detail about her, except for her place of birth, the year of her death, and the description "a useful literary character." As with all of the other 40,000 entries in this massive series, what follows that brief note is a list of the titles of her works and their dates of publication.

In addition to biographical and bibliographical catalogues, at least a bit of Cavendish's poetry continued to appear in edited collections throughout the century. In his 1825 *Specimens of British Poetesses*, Alexander Dyce published not just an extract from but the complete "Pastime and Recreation of the Queen of the Fairies," adding in a note that previously published versions were "considerably curtailed" from the original.[229] He includes the complete poem, only to add that "it would be difficult to point out a composition, which contains a more extraordinary mixture of imagination and coarse absurdity." Aside from six lines on "the theme of love" and eight lines of "The Funeral of Calamity" (from *Poems and Fancies*) the only other poem in Dyce's

---

[226] Lamb, *The Essays of Elia*, ed. Alfred Ainger (New York: A. C. Armstrong & Son, 1888), 220.

[227] This account of an evening's conversation in 1814 is by William Hazlitt, quoted in Edward V. Lucas, *The Life of Charles Lamb*, 4th ed. (London: Methuen, 1907), 287. (The entire conversation is summarized on pp. 280-87).

[228] Robert Watt, *Bibliotheca Britannica, or, a General Index on the Literature of Great Britain and Ireland Ancient and Modern including Such Foreign Books as have been translated into English or printed in the British Dominions* . . . (Edinburgh: Archibald Constable, 1824), 1:204-5.

[229] Alexander Dyce, *Specimens of British Poetesses*, 2nd ed. (London: T. Rodd, 1827), 88-98.

anthology is one we have seen repeatedly, an extract from the "Dialogue of Melancholy and Mirth." In 1848, the American preacher George Washington Bethune published three brief selections in *The British Female Poets with Biographical and Critical Notes*, extracts from "The Pastime and Recreation of the Queen of Fairies" and the dialogue "Melancholy and Mirth," just sixty-two lines in total from all the poetry Cavendish had published over the course of her writing career. In the biographical note, in which he cites Brydges as his source, Bethune observes, "Certainly nothing can exceed her or his [William Cavendish's] vanity, except the flattery they bestowed upon one another."[230] A year later, Frederick Rowton includes a few lyrics by Cavendish in his landmark anthology, *Female Poets of Great Britain*. In a brief headnote, he observes that Cavendish's husband "assisted her in her literary labours" and judges that, while she was ambitious, none of her "plays, poems, orations, and essays" was remarkable "for wit or genius."[231]

Meanwhile, for Louisa Stuart Costello, who published the multi-volume *Memoirs of Eminent Englishwomen*, Margaret Cavendish is the perfect example of a woman who had "some talent and no genius," one of those women who "contrive to bring themselves into notice by dint of resolute scribbling, and manage to attain a certain reputation by means of frequent assurances to the world that they deserve a high place in public estimation."[232] Costello dismisses Cavendish as a nuisance, as vain, and as ignorant (suggesting that Cavendish was too dim to realize she was being ridiculed), and as a woman foolishly "pluming" herself on her husband's literary reputation—but, since Costello includes many disparaging comments about William Cavendish as a writer, it's hard to see exactly how Margaret could have been "pluming" herself on his reputation. In compiling her bibliography of Margaret's work, Costello cites Walpole and Brydges, quoting their comments about Cavendish at some length, but she does seem to add her own views about selections from *The World's Olio, The*

---

[230] George W. Bethune, *The British Female Poets with Biographical and Critical Notes* (1848; Philadelphia: Lindsay and Blakiston, 1856), 35-38.

[231] Frederick Rowton, *The Female Poets of Great Britain* (Philadelphia: Carey and Hart, 1849), 79-82.

[232] Louisa Stuart Costello, *Memoirs of Eminent Englishwomen* (London: Richard Bentley, 1844), 3:211-35.

Blazing World, and Cavendish's autobiographical *True Relation*, so it may well be that she had actually read some Cavendish rather than contenting herself with recapitulating previous treatments of the work. However, aside from a few lines Cavendish wrote about poetry, Costello reproduces only a small passage from Cavendish's poem on wit, a selection from "The Pastime and Recreation of the Queen of the Fairies," and a part of the "Dialogue between Melancholy and Mirth."

The first really significant publication of material from Cavendish's work is Edward Jenkins's *A Cavalier and His Lady: Selections from the First Duke and Duchess of Newcastle*.[233] In his introductory essay, Jenkins stresses his unique efforts: "I warrant," he writes, "few have ever seen one of her folios, and hardly any one ever reads them. Many of them are rarer than gold. . . . Perhaps I have read them more and oftener than any other curious bookworm of these days, and amongst sad heaps of rubbish it has seemed to me there are a few treasures well worth disinterment." Jenkins seems to have owned at least one of Cavendish's books—he recalls that, after reading Lamb's praise of Cavendish's life of her husband, "I had that first-mentioned jewel lying in a dirty buff casket on my shelf." He also sought out and read *Poems and Fancies*, *The World's Olio*, *Philosophical and Physical Opinions*, *Nature's Pictures*, and the *CCXI Sociable Letters*. He calls his efforts "discouraging," noting in particular all the prefaces ("numerous, apologetic, remonstrative, defensive, discursive, grotesque"), regards some of her "philosophical opinions" as "madder than those of an Alexandrian gnostic or a medieval dreamer," and sums it all up as a great "chaos" of work. "Nevertheless," he concludes, "wherever one reads in the Duchess's books, he finds the tokens of a lively, vigorous, exuberant fancy and an ingenious wit," "here and there good strokes of dry sarcastic humour," "often thoughts of great force and beauty," and "many felicitous thoughts and expressions." But Jenkins can't end his preface on an entirely positive note: "In every page there are things offensive to a fastidious or even an ordinarily healthy taste." Her images too frequently display "extreme coarseness." And Jenkins condemns the "absurd and audacious" poems addressed to her after her death, collected, and published by William Cavendish. Though she

---

[233] Edward Jenkins, ed., *A Cavalier and His Lady: Selections from the First Duke and Duchess of Newcastle* (London: Macmillan, 1872).

had been dubbed "the mad duchess," Jenkins concludes that Cavendish was "harmless," perhaps the most dismissive charge of all. But rather than simply reprinting the same two poems we have seen so many times before, he publishes her autobiography in its entirety, sixty pages of her poetry, Lady Happy's speech about men from the second scene of *The Convent of Pleasure*, sixty pages of "allegories, essays and aphorisms," and twenty-two of her "sociable letters." Indeed, despite the subtitle of the volume, the anthology is far more Margaret Cavendish's than it is her husband's—fewer than forty pages of the "selections" come from William Cavendish's poetry, nothing at all from his masterwork on horsemanship.

About nineteenth-century attitudes toward Cavendish, Katie Whitaker writes that, as "critics crew increasingly aware of Margaret's deviations from contemporary taste, she came to be seen as a woman of bizarre character." She became "an inspired, but utterly fantastic figure."[234] Such a view of Cavendish—he even uses the word *bizarrerie* to describe her "mode of working"—is reflected in Eric Robertson's *English Poetesses: A Series of Critical Biographies*, published as the nineteenth century drew to an end.[235] Robertson begins his discussion of Cavendish by comparing her to Aphra Behn—in contrast to Behn, he writes, Cavendish has been "treated" to the "sneer of the dissolute" at her "pretensions to innocence," which Robertson seems to suggest is unfair. Nevertheless, he regards the "frankness of her disclosures with respect to herself" as "embarrassing," though he grudgingly admits that her "artless candour" and her conceit combine to disarm criticisms. In detailing the many failings of her writing, he notes that one of the sentences in her *True Relation* "is twelve pages long" (something I certainly failed to note as a reader), and that the contents of her books are so jumbled they look like nothing so much as "a lady's overturned work-basket." One of Robertson's most interesting judgments about Cavendish is that she was "a kind of over-grown,

---

[234] Whitaker, *Mad Madge*, 353-54. Whitaker has also tracked down—or attempted to track down—the source of the unfortunate nickname "Mad Madge of Newcastle," first recorded by Mark Anthony Lower in his 1872 preface to a new edition of Margaret's biography of her husband. Whitaker searched in vain for any source for the nickname, concluding that "there might well be no seventeenth-century source for the Mad Madge nickname" (p. 355).

[235] Eric Robertson, *English Poetesses: A Series of Critical Biographies* (London: Cassell, 1883), 13-34.

spoilt girl"; such infantilization seems to be intended as a way of smoothing over the oddities of her behavior, for Robertson is not entirely critical of Cavendish. Robertson has consulted Jenkins's edition of Cavendish's work, and he is clearly familiar with Lamb's Elia essays, noting that "no later critic has supported in writing the emphatic praises of Elia." And so, he is forced to "confess, with the object of surprising many readers with a style not far removed from Lamb himself," that he "cannot refrain from at once quoting a specimen of the Duchess's prose." What follows is an essay from *The World's Olio*, previously published by Jenkins, Cavendish's "Of Gentlewomen That are Sent to Board Schools."[236] In addition to this essay, he includes selections from her *True Relation* and from her biography of her husband, both woven into his biographical narrative. He recognizes that, of all her verse, only "The Pastime of the Queen of the Fairies" and the "Dialogue between Melancholy and Mirth" are at all known, but he reprints portions of both, as well as Lady Happy's song from the *Convent of Pleasure*, though it is clear from his brief remarks about the play that he has not read it. Like Jenkins, Robertson also claims that, at times, Cavendish achieves "smooth passages" in her work, passages in which her "diction is almost as perfect as that which the most fastidious artifice could have devised," reproducing here a few of the "aphorisms" that Jenkins had printed in *The Cavalier and His Lady*. For Robertson, Cavendish's "aphoristic tendency" is "quite masculine," and he goes even farther in his praise of her aphorisms when he adds that on occasion they are "Baconian, almost."

While interest in Margaret Cavendish had never disappeared, her reputation was certainly tattered before the twentieth century began, and the first two books about her in the new century did not do anything to change the earlier critical views. In his 1910 *The First Duke and Duchess of Newcastle-upon-Tyne*, Thomas Longueville published a book-length study of the pair, primarily biographical and primarily focused on William Cavendish, drawing a great deal of his information about the duke from Margaret's biography of her husband.[237] In addition to his biographical narrative, Longueville devotes two chapters

---

[236] Cavendish, *The Worlds Olio*, 61-62.

[237] Thomas Longueville, *The First Duke and Duchess of Newcastle-upon-Tyne* (London: Longmans, Green, 1910).

to William's writing, followed by two chapters that focus on Margaret's. He relies a great deal on Langbaine, adding in comments by Cibber and Lamb. Longueville's judgments are not enthusiastic; he expresses appreciation for Cavendish's *Life*, noting it as a rich source of information about William Cavendish, but about the best he can muster about the rest of the duchess's work is a less-than-halfhearted and back-handed compliment: "It would be easy to sneer at her poetry," he says, "but, at its best, it is not so very bad."[238] He includes some lines from "The Pastime of the Queen of the Fairies" and some from "Melancholy and Mirth," which by 1910 had been published and republished many times, before slamming the poems praising the duchess published by William Cavendish after his wife's death. The volume is filled with "the grossest and most fulsome panegyric," he writes, adding, "I know no flattery, ancient or modern, that is, in any degree, comparable to it, except the deification of Augustus and the erection of altars to him in his lifetime."[239]

Uniquely, however, at least up to this point in discussions of Cavendish's work, Longueville devotes an entire chapter to Cavendish's plays—or, rather, what he regards as the "formidable array" of her plays. He began by citing a dozen lines from her "General Prologue" in the 1662 *Plays*, judging them to be "not the happiest of her poetical efforts," though he also acknowledges that since "even Dryden" failed in writing a prologue, perhaps "we may well make excuses" for Cavendish. The lines he reproduces are those where Cavendish contrasted herself to Jonson, Shakespeare, and Beaumont and Fletcher; because she did not know Greek and Latin and thus did not have access to their sources, she argues that she couldn't "steal" the "wit" or the plots of those sources, as her male predecessors had. To Cavendish's assertions, Longueville asks, in an aghast note, "Is this a slap on Shakespeare?" Immediately following, he prints three selected scenes from her plays: to illustrate her "heavy, wearisome style," he includes a scene from *The Presence*; to illustrate her "attempts at comedy," one from *The Bridals*, and to show her wit, one from *The Wit's Cabal*. While at least *considering* Cavendish's dramatic efforts, his conclusions about her plays are entirely negative. "They combine

---

[238] Longueville, *The First Duke and Duchess*, 254.
[239] Longueville, *The First Duke and Duchess*, 258.

indecency and obscenity with the stagnate [sic] dullness so usually the accompaniment of literary ditchwater," he writes. He follows up this very brief look at only a three of her plays (he began his bibliography by quoting Langbaine's list of all the titles of her plays, so he knew the extent of her dramatic output) with a series of anecdotes and comments drawn from her correspondents and contemporaries, giving particular emphasis to Pepys's gossipy diary entries, and finishing off with a terrible anecdote about Cavendish that, he admits, is not really about Cavendish at all but about someone else entirely. Even knowing that, this mistold story is his final word on the duchess of Newcastle—and he notes the misidentification only in a footnote.[240]

In another dual study of Margaret Cavendish and her husband, Henry Ten Eyck Perry gives Margaret preeminence: *The First Duchess of Newcastle and Her Husband as Figures in Literary History*. As Perry tells us in his introduction, the book began as a Harvard Ph.D. dissertation and was published as a monograph "in substantially its original form."[241] Interestingly, Perry conducted much of his research "on this side of the Atlantic," and found that often only one copy of some of Cavendish's works was to be found, and that with "exceeding difficulty." He was given access to several of Cavendish's books in Henry E. Huntington's personal library, then in New York—thus documenting something of the dissemination of Cavendish's published volumes.[242] Perry's introduction is generous in its assessment of Cavendish; while she can be "verbose and tiresome," she is also "at times stimulating and readable." Like so many of his predecessors, Perry regards her best work as her biography of William Cavendish, though he judges it to be less a history and more "an early species of glory-story," arguing that it was written in a period "when fictitious material was beginning to masquerade as veracious record." As the *Life* was both literature and history, Perry thus devotes the first chapter of his book to an extended

---

[240] For the chapter on Cavendish's plays, Longueville, *The First Duke and Duchess*, 262-72.

[241] Henry Ten Eyck Perry, *The First Duchess of Newcastle and Her Husband as Figures in Literary History* (Boston: Ginn, 1918).

[242] In 1919 Henry E. Huntington established the Huntington Library in San Marino, California. The Library owns a significant number of original Cavendish works in its rare books collection; the library's catalogue can be accessed online http://catalog.huntington.org/#.

analysis of the life of William Cavendish as portrayed in *The Life of William Cavendish*.

After spending the following chapter on the work of William Cavendish, Perry then moves on to Margaret Cavendish's work, an analysis of which occupies the rest of his literary study. Perry believes the real significance of her literary production lay in its quantity, not its quality—the value "does not consist in form or contents, but in the mere fact that they exist." Perry fully recognizes the almost insurmountable obstacles for early-modern women writers: "one needs to remember that masterpieces have seldom been produced by a pioneer," he cautions, emphasizing that "Margaret Cavendish was one of the first English women seriously to undertake written composition."[243] Perry devotes an entire chapter to her "minor writings," including an overview of her "poems and pseudo-science," an extended analysis of *The World's Olio* and *Nature's Pictures*, and a detailed examination of her plays. Perry sees in her drama the "limitless scope" of her "fancy," even though he regards her "dramatic technique" as "completely lacking." While noting that her plays could not be acted when they were published, he also points out that "time went on and conditions changed," but that her plays "remained unacted and unactable." Her drama is "lifeless" and "so dull that one shrinks from it even on the printed page"; her plays represent the "lowest ebb" of Cavendish's literary output. Nevertheless, Perry manfully works through all of them, producing summaries and brief analyses for every play included in Cavendish's two folio collections. This chapter on her minor writings concludes with a discussion of her orations, the *Sociable Letters*, and *The Blazing World* and is followed next by a chapter about "The Duchess Herself."[244] After all this careful reading and effort, the best Perry can muster in the end is this assessment: if Cavendish and her husband were not "of supreme moment" as "producers of literature," they were at least "individual and attractive personages."

---

[243] Perry, *The First Duchess of Newcastle*, 171.

[244] The minor writings are covered in Perry, *The First Duchess of Newcastle*, Chapter 3 (pp. 171-264); the following chapter (pp. 265- 313) is on Cavendish's life, focusing primarily on her autobiography, but Perry also includes Margaret Cavendish's love letters to her husband, as transcribed and printed by Richard William Goulding, ed., *Letters of Margaret Lucas to Her Future Husband* (London: John Murray, 1909).

Such was the state if affairs when Virginia Woolf came to write about Margaret Cavendish, condemning her as some kind of kudzu-like vine, strangling everything and anything in her pathway. The three progressively more sympathetic biographies produced in the late twentieth and early twenty-first centuries—Douglas Grant's *Margaret the First* (1957), Kathleen Jones's *A Glorious Fame* (1988), and Katie Whitaker's *Mad Madge* (2002)—provided correctives to the apocryphal stories about Cavendish without sacrificing any of the pleasures of juicy gossip or the occasional absurdities of Cavendish's life. And it has been the work of a generation of feminist scholars to vault Margaret Cavendish right into the canon of British literature, where we find her comfortably established today.

A Note on the Text

This edition of *The Convent of Pleasure* began with my transcription from a British Library copy of the 1668 *Plays, Never before Printed.*[245] In preparing this edition, I have also relied on the copy of *Plays, Never before Printed* now in the collection of the University of Illinois at Urbana-Champaign, which has digitized the book and makes the facsimile fully and freely available online.[246] In this way, a reader interested in looking at the original play, as published by Cavendish, can read *The Convent of Pleasure* in its 1668 version alongside the carefully edited version in the pages that follow in this volume.

With the aim of presenting a more readable Cavendish for those unfamiliar with the peculiarities of seventeenth-century printed books, I have modernized the spelling and capitalization throughout. Punctuation presents a more complicated set of problems. As is the norm in the period, the commas, semi-colons, colons, and periods are used more rhetorically, as a guide to reading, than grammatically, following the kind of systematic rules we find today in a handbook like Diana Hacker's *A Writer's Reference*. My aim has been to bring the punctuation more into conformity with twenty-first century norms without erasing completely the texture and flavor of the original. I have

---

[245] The British Library owns three copies of Cavendish's 1668 *Plays*, including the one I refer to here, General Reference Collection 79.I.15.

[246] University of Illinois at Urbana-Champaign, Rare Book & Manuscript Library UIQ01743, available at http://hdl.handle.net/10111/UIUCRB:5544586.

retained Cavendish's original paragraphing throughout. I have emended infrequently, and such emendations are indicated by square brackets. As an aid to readers, I have footnoted words and phrases where definitions, clarifications, and explanations might be helpful. When the meaning of a word is complicated or difficult, or where the meaning of the word has changed significantly from Cavendish's time, I have quoted relevant definitions from the *Oxford English Dictionary*.

The layout and format have also been modernized. In the 1668 volume, all stage directions are set in italic type, a font that has been retained here. All proper nouns, but not titles, are also set in italics in the original (for example "Lady *Happy*" and "Madam *Mediator*"); these italics have not been retained. Character names in the speech headings are abbreviated and italicized in the original, but they have been written in full and set in capital letters in this edition. In the 1668 edition of *The Convent of Pleasure*, all lyrics, like the song that ends 1.2, are indented and set in italics, but verse speeches, like those at the end of 3.1, are not; all of the poetry has been set in a roman font in this edition.

The Convent of Pleasure

A Comedy

ACT 1, Scene 1

Enter three gentlemen.

FIRST GENTLEMAN. Tom, where have you been, you look so sadly[1] of it?

SECOND GENTLEMAN. I have been at the funeral of the Lord Fortunate, who has left his daughter, the Lady Happy, very rich, having no other daughter but her.[2]

FIRST GENTLEMAN. If she be so rich, it will make us all young men spend all our wealth in fine clothes, coaches, and lackeys[3] to set out[4] our wooing hopes.

---

[1] "Seriously; in earnest; gravely, soberly" (*Oxford English Dictionary* [online], www.oed.com, hereafter *OED*).

[2] Since Lord Fortunate has died without a son (or any other male heir), his entire estate will pass to his only daughter—a situation that disrupts male control of wealth and destabilizes the traditional marriage market. On this situation and its effect, see Introduction, 71-72, and below, n. 5.

[3] A *lackey* could be a footman, a member of a gentleman's household who attended him at table and to his carriage, or a valet, a gentleman's servant who attended to his clothing and his personal care, like bathing and shaving.

[4] The phrase *to set out* can not only mean to "fit out (a ship, fleet) for a voyage," but it can also have martial connotations: "to fit out," or "to equip for an expedition," or "to send out (forces)" (*OED*). The suggestion that the pursuit of Lady Happy represents a kind of military assault appears again in 2.1.

THIRD GENTLEMAN. If all her wooers be younger brothers, as most of us gallants are, we shall undo ourselves upon bare hopes, without probability.[5] But is she handsome, Tom?

SECOND GENTLEMAN. Yes, she is extremely handsome, young, rich, and virtuous.

FIRST GENTLEMAN. Faith,[6] that is too much for one woman to possess.

SECOND GENTLEMAN. Not if you were to have her.

FIRST GENTLEMAN. No, not for me but, in my opinion, too much for any other man.

Exeunt.[7]

ACT 1, Scene 2

Enter the Lady Happy and one of her attendants.

SERVANT. Madam, you being young, handsome, rich, and virtuous, I hope you will not cast away those gifts of nature, fortune,[8] and heaven upon a person which cannot merit you.

---

[5] The word *gallant* referred generally to a gentleman "of fashion and pleasure," though it could also refer more specifically to a man "who pays court to ladies" (*OED*). The third young gentleman claims that "most" of the men who are interested in pursuing Lady Happy, her father's sole heir, are "younger sons." Under the principle of primogeniture, lands, titles, and estates are inherited by the eldest son, while younger sons have to acquire wealth and social position some other way— through marriage, for example. But in order to pursue a wealthy bride and be successful in their "wooing hopes," the third gentleman suggests that these disadvantaged younger sons will have to borrow money they don't have and, perhaps, ruin themselves in the process.

[6] From "in faith," a mild interjection meaning "truly" or "really."

[7] Literally "they go out" (from the Latin), a stage direction indicating that all of the actors leave the stage.

[8] With a play on Lord Fortunate's name.

LADY HAPPY. Let me tell you that riches ought to be bestowed on such as are poor and want means to maintain themselves, and youth on those that are old, beauty on those that are ill-favored, and virtue on those that are vicious. So that if I should place my gifts rightly, I must marry one that's poor, old, ill-favored, and debauched.

SERVANT. Heaven forbid.

LADY HAPPY. Nay, heaven doth not only allow of it, but commands it, for we are commanded to give to those that want.[9]

Enter Madam Mediator to the Lady Happy.[10]

MADAM MEDIATOR. Surely, madam, you do but talk and intend not to go where you say.

---

[9] Throughout *The Convent of Pleasure*, Cavendish, like other contemporary playwrights, is careful in her handing of religion, avoiding specific references to the Christian god and to the Christian faith. In addition to the Master of the Revels, empowered to control and censor plays for challenging or mocking orthodox religious views and "prophaning" the sacraments, the "Act to Restrain Abuses of Players" had been passed by parliament in 1606 with the aim of "preventing and avoiding of the great abuse of the Holy Name of God in stage plays, interludes, May games, shows and such like"; the law made it a crime for "any person or persons" in such a public performance to "jestingly or profanely speak or use the Holy Name of God, or of Christ Jesus, or of the Holy Ghost, or of the Trinity." Quoted in Glynne Wickham, Herbert Berry, and William Ingram, eds., *English Professional Theatre, 1530-1660*, Theatre in Europe: A Documentary History (New York: Cambridge University Press, 2000), 131. The legislation was later extended from performance to publication; on this see Geoffrey Hughes, *An Encyclopedia of Swearing: The Social History of Oaths, Profanity, Foul Language, and Ethnic Slurs in the English-Speaking World* (New York: Routledge, 2006), 63.

Nevertheless, Lady Happy's assertion that "heaven . . . commands" us "to give to those that want," echoes Jesus's response to the young man who has kept the commandments but asks, "what lacke I yet?" Jesus replies, "If thou wilt be perfect, goe and sell that thou hast, and give to the poore, and thou shalt have treasure in heaven" (Matthew 19:20-21; see also Mark 10:21 and Luke 14:13). All biblical references are from *The Holy Bible: A Facsimile . . . of the Authorized Version Published in the Year 1611* (New York: Oxford University Press, 1911).

[10] Madam Mediator, like several of the characters in this play, appears first in *The Bridals*, which immediately precedes *The Convent of Pleasure* in the 1668 *Plays, Never before Printed*. On the relationship between these two plays, see Introduction, 70

LADY HAPPY. Yes, truly, my words and intentions go even together.

MADAM MEDIATOR. But surely you will not encloister yourself, as you say.

LADY HAPPY. Why, what is there in the public world that should invite me to live in it?

MADAM MEDIATOR. More than if you should banish yourself from it.

LADY HAPPY. Put the case[11] I should marry the best of men, if any best there be, yet would a married life have more crosses and sorrows than pleasure, freedom, or happiness. Nay, marriage to those that are virtuous is a greater restraint than a monastery. Or should I take delight in admirers? They might gaze on my beauty and praise my wit, and I receive nothing from their eyes nor lips, for words vanish as soon as spoken, and sights are not substantial. Besides, I should lose more of my reputation by their visits than gain by their praises. Or should I quit reputation and turn courtesan? There would be more lost in my health than gained by my lovers; I should find more pain than pleasure. Besides, the troubles and frights I should be put to, with the quarrels and *brouilleries*[12] that jealous rivals make, would be a torment to me, and 'tis only for the sake of men when women retire not. And since there is so much folly, vanity, and falsehood in men, why should women trouble and vex themselves for their sake, for retiredness bars the life from nothing else but men.

MADAM MEDIATOR. Oh, yes, for those that encloister themselves bar themselves from all other worldly pleasures.

---

[11] The phrase Lady Happy uses here, *put the case*, is a technical one, meaning "to propound a hypothetical instance or illustration, to suppose; . . . to present a set of facts or arguments in support of a particular person, course of action, or version of events" (*OED*).

[12] The French word *brouilleries* means "conflicts," "disagreements," or "disturbance."

LADY HAPPY. The more fools they.

MADAM MEDIATOR. Will you call those fools that do it for the gods' sake?

LADY HAPPY. No, madam, it is not for the gods' sake, but for opinion's sake, for can any rational creature think or believe the gods take delight in the creature's uneasy life? Or did they command or give leave to nature[13] to make senses for no use, or to cross, vex and pain them? For what profit or pleasure can it be to the gods to have men or women wear coarse linen or rough woolen, or to flay their skin with haircloth,[14] or to eat or saw through their flesh with cords? Or what profit or pleasure can it be to the gods to have men eat more fish than flesh or to fast unless the gods did feed on such meat themselves, for then, for fear the gods should want it, it were fit for men to abstain from it.[15] The like for garments, for fear the gods should want fine clothes to adorn themselves, it were fit men should not wear them. Or what profit or pleasure can it be to the gods to have men to lie uneasily on the hard ground unless the gods and nature were at variance, strife, and wars, as if what is displeasing unto nature were pleasing to the gods and to be enemies to her were to be friends to them?

---

[13] Throughout the play, Lady Happy personifies nature and, as below, uses feminine pronouns when referring to nature.

[14] A rough cloth made from goat or horse hair and designed to irritate—or "flay"—the skin.

[15] Although there is no specific reference here to the Christian god or devotional practices, many of the questions Lady Happy poses in this speech challenge traditional Christian notions of "mortification of the flesh"—forms of penance that respond to the apostle Paul's injunctions to discipline the body: "For if ye live after the flesh, ye shall die: but if ye through the spirit doe mortifie the deeds of the body, ye shall liue" (Romans 8:13); "But I keepe under my body, and bring it into subjection: lest that by any meanes when I have preached to others, I my selfe should be a castaway" (1 Corinthians 9:27); and "Mortifie therefore your members which are upon the earth: fornication, uncleannesse, inordinate affection, evill concupiscence, and covetousnesse, which is idolatrie" (Colossians 3:5), for example. Lady Happy refers to the practice of wearing a hairshirt, an undergarment worn in order to chafe the skin; the practice of wearing a *cincture*, or knotted cord or rope, tied around the waist or thigh; and the practice of fasting.

MADAM MEDIATOR. But being done for the gods' sake, it makes that which in nature seems to be bad, in divinity to be good.

LADY HAPPY. It cannot be good, if it be neither pleasure nor profit to the gods; neither do men anything for the gods but [for] their own sake.

MADAM MEDIATOR. But when the mind is not employed with vanities nor the senses with luxury,[16] the mind is more free to offer its adorations, prayers, and praises to the gods.

LADY HAPPY. I believe the gods are better pleased with praises than fasting, but when the senses are dulled with abstinency,[17] the body weakened with fasting, the spirits tired with watching, the life made uneasy with pain, the soul can have but little will to worship; only the imagination doth frighten it into active zeal, which devotion is rather forced than voluntary, so that their prayers rather flow out of their mouth than spring from their heart, like rain water that runs through gutters or like water that's forced up a hill by artificial pipes and cisterns. But those that pray not unto the gods or praise them more in prosperity than adversity, more in pleasures than pains, more in liberty than restraint, deserve neither the happiness of ease, peace, freedom, plenty, and tranquility in this world nor the glory and blessedness of the next. And if the gods should take pleasure in nothing but in the torments of their creatures and would not prefer those prayers that are offered with ease and delight, I should believe the gods were cruel, and what creature that had reason or rational understanding would serve cruel masters when they might serve a kind mistress or would forsake the service of their kind mistress to serve cruel masters? Wherefore,[18] if the gods be cruel, I will serve nature, but the gods are bountiful and give all that's good and bid us freely please ourselves in that which is best for us, and that is best what is most temperately used and longest may be enjoyed, for excess doth waste itself and all it feeds upon.

---

[16] "The habitual use of, of indulgence in what is choice or costly, whether food, dress, furniture, or appliances of any kind" (*OED*).

[17] "The quality or fact of being abstinent" (*OED*); deprivation.

[18] For which reason, therefore.

MADAM MEDIATOR. In my opinion your doctrine and your intention do not agree together.

LADY HAPPY. Why?

MADAM MEDIATOR. You intend to live encloistered and retired from the world.

LADY HAPPY. 'Tis true, but not from pleasures, for I intend to encloister myself from the world to enjoy pleasure and not to bury myself from it, but to encloister myself from the encumbered cares and vexations, troubles, and perturbance[19] of the world.

MADAM MEDIATOR. But if you encloister yourself, how will you enjoy the company of men, whose conversation is thought the greatest pleasure?

LADY HAPPY. Men are the only troublers of women, for they only cross and oppose their sweet delights and peaceable life; they cause their pains but not their pleasures. Wherefore those women that are poor and have not means to buy delights and maintain pleasures are only fit for men, for having not means to please themselves, they must serve only to please others, but those women where fortune, nature, and the gods are joined to make them happy, were mad to live with men, who make the female sex their slaves; but I will not be so enslaved but will live retired from their company. Wherefore, in order thereto, I will take so many noble persons of my own sex as my estate will plentifully maintain, such whose births are greater than their fortunes and are resolved to live a single life and vow virginity. With these I mean to live encloistered with all the delights and pleasures that are allowable and lawful. My cloister shall not be a cloister of restraint, but a place for freedom, not to vex the senses but to please them.

> For every sense shall pleasure take,
> And all our lives shall merry make;
> Our minds in full delight shall joy,

---

[19] Agitation or disturbance.

Not vexed with every idle toy;
Each season shall our caterers be,
To search the land and fish the sea,
To gather fruit and reap the corn
That's brought to us in plenty's horn[20]
With which we'll feast and please our taste,
But not luxurious make a waste;
We'll clothe ourselves with softest silk
And linen fine, as white as milk;
We'll please our sight with pictures rare,
Our nostrils with perfumed air,
Our ears with sweet melodious sound
Whose substance can be nowhere found,
Our taste with sweet delicious meat,[21]
And savory sauces we will eat;
Variety each sense shall feed,
And change in them new appetites breed;
Thus will in pleasure's convent I
Live with delight and with it die.[22]

Exeunt.

---

[20] The horn of plenty, or cornucopia, was an ancient symbol of fruitfulness, frequently represented as "overflowing with flowers, fruit, and corn" (*OED*).

[21] Rather than flesh, *meat* is used to mean food, in general, or a particular meal or dish.

[22] Lady Happy's lyric echoes Christopher Marlowe's song "Come live with me and be my love" (now commonly printed under the title "The Passionate Shepherd to His Love") and reproduces the poem's tetrameter couplets. Marlowe's lyric was printed in part by William Jaggard in his *The Passionate Pilgrime* (London, 1599), the complete poem, attributed to Marlowe, published in John Flasket's anthology of pastoral poems titled *Englands Helicon* (London 1600; a second, expanded, edition was published in 1614).

ACT 2, Scene 1

Enter Monsieur Take-Pleasure[23] and his man, Dick.

MONSIEUR TAKE-PLEASURE. Dick, am I fine[24] to day?

DICK. Yes, sir, as fine as feathers, ribbons, gold, and silver can make you.

MONSIEUR TAKE-PLEASURE. Dost thou think I shall get the Lady Happy?

DICK. Not if it be her fortune to continue in that name.

MONSIEUR TAKE-PLEASURE. Why?

DICK. Because if she marry your worship,[25] she must change her name, for the wife takes the name of her husband and quits her own.

MONSIEUR TAKE-PLEASURE. Faith, Dick, if I had her wealth I should be happy.

DICK. It would be according as your worship would use it but, on my conscience, you would be more happy with the lady's wealth than the lady would be with your worship.

MONSIEUR TAKE-PLEASURE. Why should you think so?

DICK. Because women never think themselves happy in marriage.

---

[23] Like Madam Mediator (see n. 10, above), Monsieur Take-Pleasure is a character who appears first in *The Bridals*, where he is one of several "bridemen," young men charged with "performing ceremonial duties at a wedding" (*OED*).

[24] "Smartly dressed" (*OED*).

[25] As Monsieur Take-Pleasure's "man," or personal attendant, Dick addresses his master as "your worship," indicating Monsieur Take-Pleasure's superior social status.

MONSIEUR TAKE-PLEASURE. You are mistaken, for women never think themselves happy until they be married.

DICK. The truth is, sir, that women are always unhappy in their thoughts, both before and after marriage, for before marriage they think themselves unhappy for want of a husband, and after they are married, they think themselves unhappy for having a husband.

MONSIEUR TAKE-PLEASURE. Indeed, women's thoughts are restless.

Enter Monsieur Facil and Monsieur Adviser to Monsieur Take-Pleasure, all in their wooing accouterments.[26]

MONSIEUR TAKE-PLEASURE. Gentlemen, I perceive you are all prepared to woo.

MONSIEUR FACIL. Yes, faith, we are all prepared to be wooers. But whom shall we get to present us to the Lady Happy?

MONSIEUR ADVISER. We must set on bold faces and present ourselves.

MONSIEUR TAKE-PLEASURE. Faith, I would not give my hopes for an indifferent portion.[27]

MONSIEUR FACIL. Nor I.

---

[26] Monsieur Facil (his name suggests he may be easy-going or that he likes to take the easy way out), Monsieur Adviser, and Monsieur Courtly, who soon arrives on the scene to join the wooing gentlemen, were also "bridemen" (see n. 23, above) in *The Bridals*. The men are in their "wooing accouterments" (from the French *accoutrement*), the fine clothing and accessories they've decked themselves out in so that they will attract the attention of Lady Happy. The word is frequently used to refer to the equipment of a soldier or military man—appropriate here, since these men intend to lay siege to Lady Happy until someone conquers her by marriage.

[27] A marriage *portion* is money or property that is passed from a woman's father to her husband at the time of her marriage. An *indifferent portion* would be modest, or, by extension, "Not particularly good; poor, inferior; rather bad" (*OED*).

MONSIEUR ADVISER. The truth is we are all stuffed with hopes, as cushions are with feathers.

Enter Monsieur Courtly.

MONSIEUR COURTLY. Oh, gentlemen, gentlemen, we are all utterly undone.

MONSIEUR ADVISER. Why, what's the matter?

MONSIEUR COURTLY. Why, the Lady Happy hath encloistered herself with twenty ladies more.

MONSIEUR ADVISER. The devil she hath?

MONSIEUR FACIL. The gods forbid.

MONSIEUR COURTLY. Whether it was the devil or the gods that have persuaded her to it, I cannot tell, but gone in she is.

MONSIEUR TAKE-PLEASURE. I hope it is but a blast of devotion which will soon flame out.

Enter Madam Mediator.

MONSIEUR TAKE-PLEASURE. Oh, Madam Mediator, we are all undone—the Lady Happy is encloistered.

MADAM MEDIATOR. Yes, gentlemen, the more is the pity.

MONSIEUR ADVISER. Is there no hopes?

MADAM MEDIATOR. Faith, little.

MONSIEUR FACIL. Let us fee[28] the clergy to persuade her out for the good of the commonwealth.

---

[28] Offer a fee—in other words, a bribe.

MADAM MEDIATOR. Alas, gentlemen! They can do no good, for she is not a votaress[29] to the gods but to nature.

MONSIEUR COURTLY. If she be a votaress to nature, you are the only person fit to be lady prioress,[30] and so by your power and authority you may give us leave to visit your nuns sometimes.

MADAM MEDIATOR. Not but at a grate, unless in time of building or when they are sick; but howsoever,[31] the Lady Happy is lady prioress herself and will admit none of the masculine sex, not so much as to a grate, for she will suffer no grates about the cloister.[32] She has also women physicians, surgeons,[33] and apothecaries,[34] and she is the chief confessor herself and gives what indulgences or absolutions she pleaseth.[35] Also, her house, where she hath made

---

[29] From the Latin *vovere*, "to vow," a votary (or, here, in a feminine form, *votaress*) is a man or woman who has taken the religious vows of a monk or nun.

[30] A prioress is a nun who governs a religious house.

[31] In any case.

[32] In addition to admitting male builders and doctors, Madam Mediator says that if she were prioress of the convent she would grant men permission to visit the nuns inside by means of a *grate*. A grate is a barred window or opening that allows some communication between the women inside a convent and the outside world, but it prevents them from leaving—or escaping—and prevents any unauthorized person— like these young men—from entering. But, as Madam Mediator immediately makes clear, Lady Happy has other ideas about giving men access in any capacity to her convent.

In *The Female Academy*, a play from Cavendish's earlier *Playes* (London, 1662), a grate allows communication between the young women inside the Female Academy and the young men outside the school. Throughout the play, the men closed out of the all-female school can see what's going on inside. As the stage direction describes the scene, "Enter a company of young ladies and with them two grave matrons, where through the hanging a company of men look on them, as through a grate." Margaret Cavendish, *The Female Academy*, in *Playes*, 653.

[33] "One who practises the art of healing by manual operation; a practitioner who treats wounds, fractures, deformities, or disorders by surgical means" (*OED*).

[34] An earlier name for a pharmacist: "One who prepared . . . drugs for medicinal purposes" (*OED*).

[35] A *confessor* is a religious functionary (a priest in the Catholic tradition) whose role is to hear a penitent's confession of sin and then prescribe a form of penance (in theological terms, "satisfaction," a penalty to be paid by the penitent, frequently prayers or an act of mortification of the flesh; see above, n. 15), the performance of which is crucial in the sacrament of penance. As part of the sacrament, the confessor also grants *absolution* (a forgiveness of sin). As chief confessor, Lady Happy claims the

her convent, is so big and convenient and so strong as it needs no addition or repair. Besides, she has so much compass of ground within her walls as there is not only room and place enough for gardens, orchards, walks, groves, bowers, arbors, ponds, fountains, springs and the like, but also conveniency for much provision, and hath women for every office and employment, for though she hath not above twenty ladies with her, yet she hath a numerous company of female servants, so as there is no occasion for men.

MONSIEUR TAKE-PLEASURE. If there be so many women, there will be the more use for men. But pray,[36] Madam Mediator, give me leave rightly to understand you by being more clearly informed. You say the Lady Happy is become a votaress to nature, and if she be a votaress to nature, she must be a mistress to men.

MADAM MEDIATOR. By your favor,[37] sir, she declares that she hath avoided the company of men by retirement merely[38] because she would enjoy the variety of pleasures which are in nature, of which, she says, men are obstructers, for instead of increasing pleasure, they produce pain, and instead of giving content, they increase trouble, instead of making the female sex happy, they make them miserable, for which she hath banished the masculine company forever.

MONSIEUR ADVISER. Her heretical opinions ought not to be suffered, nor her doctrine[39] allowed, and she ought to be examined by a masculine synod[40] and punished with a severe husband or tortured with a deboist[41] husband.

---

privilege not only of granting absolution but also of offering an *indulgence*, a formal remission of a sin and of the necessity of completing of an act of penance.

[36] For "I pray you," an expression comparable to "please."

[37] "Pardon" or "with your permission," used to introduce a correction.

[38] Only, or for no other reason than.

[39] Set of principles or beliefs, frequently used in a religious context, as Monsieur Adviser's use here suggests.

[40] A governing body of a church, frequently functioning as an ecclesiastical court.

[41] Debauched (from the French *débauché*).

MADAM MEDIATOR. The best way, gentlemen, is to make your complaints and put up a petition to the state with your desires for a redress.[42]

MONSIEUR COURTLY. Your counsel is good.

MONSIEUR FACIL. We will follow it and go presently about it.

Exeunt.

ACT 2, Scene 2

Enter the Lady Happy with her ladies, as also Madam Mediator.

LADY HAPPY. Ladies, give me leave to desire your confession,[43] whether or no you repent your retirement.

LADIES. Most excellent lady, it were as probable a repentance could be in heaven amongst angels as amongst us.

LADY HAPPY. Now, Madam Mediator, let me ask you, do you condemn my act of retirement?

MADAM MEDIATOR. I approve of it with admiration and wonder that one that is so young should be so wise.

LADY HAPPY. Now give me leave to inform you how I have ordered this, our Convent of Pleasure. First, I have such things as are for our ease and convenience; next, for pleasure and delight, as I have change of furniture[44] for my house according to the four seasons of the year, especially our chambers. As in the spring, our chambers are

---

[42] A formal claim for compensation from a loss or for having suffered a wrong.

[43] As Madam Mediator notes in 2.1, Lady Happy has decided to act as the confessor for the women in her convent.

[44] All of the items in a house, not only the cupboards and beds, mentioned here, but all of the furnishings, including the carpets, curtains, art, linen, and tableware.

hung with silk damask[45] and all other things suitable to it, and a great looking glass in each chamber, that we may view ourselves and take pleasure in our own beauties whilst they are fresh and young; also, I have in each chamber a cupboard of such plate[46] as is useful, and whatsoever is to be used is there ready to be employed; also, I have all the floor strewn with sweet flowers.[47] In the summer, I have all our chambers hung with taffeta[48] and all other things suitable to it, and a cupboard of porcelain and of plate, and all the floor strewn every day with green rushes[49] or leaves, and cisterns[50] placed near our bed-heads, wherein water may run out of small pipes made for that purpose. To invite repose in the autumn, all our chambers are hung with gilt leather[51] or frangipane[52]; also, beds and all other things suitable, and the rooms matted with very fine mats. In the winter our chambers must be hung with tapestry and our beds of velvet lined with satin, and all things suitable to it, and all the floor spread over with Turkey carpets,[53] and a cupboard of gilt plate, and

---

[45] Sumptuous textile wall hangings could serve for decoration and as well as for insulation. In the spring, the individual *chambers*, or bedrooms, in Lady Happy's convent will have their walls covered with *damask*, a "rick silk fabric woven with elaborate designs and figures, often of a variety of colours" (*OED*).

[46] Expensive tableware, frequently made from gold or silver or gold- or silver-plate.

[47] Various plant materials were laid down on floors from the Middle Ages through the eighteenth century, some sweet-smelling, as the flowers prescribed here, some to insure warmth, and some to serve as insecticides.

[48] A glossy silk fabric.

[49] *Green rushes* were freshly strewn rushes spread onto a floor in honor of a guest or a stranger—but in the Convent of Pleasure, they are to be spread every day in summer, not for guests but for the enjoyment of the women themselves.

[50] Large basins, often decorated, that hold water for bathing.

[51] Gilded leather wall hangings (*cuir de Cordoue*), embossed with patterns and painted, were produced in several Dutch cities in the seventeenth century.

[52] *Frangipane* is a scent made from the flower of the red jasmine. Here, however, it is associated with a chamber's wall hangings, and in particular with a gilded leather wall hanging. Lady Happy may have in mind either leather wall hangings perfumed with frangipane or perhaps scented wallpaper. On perfumed leather, see Katia Johansen, "Perfumed Textiles," *Textile Society of America Symposium Proceedings* (2008), http://digitalcommons.unl.edu/tsaconf/104.

[53] "A carpet manufactured in or imported from Turkey, or of a style in imitation of this; made in one piece of richly-coloured wools, without any imitative pattern, . . . and having a deep pile, cut so as to resemble velvet" (*OED*).

all the wood for firing to be cypress and juniper,[54] and all the lights[55] to be perfumed wax. Also, the bedding and pillows are ordered according to each season, *viz.*,[56] to be stuffed with feathers in the spring and autumn and with down in the winter, but in the summer to be only quilts, either of silk or fine Holland.[57] And our sheets, pillows, tablecloths, and towels to be of pure, fine Holland, and every day clean. Also, the rooms we eat in and the vessels we feed withal,[58] I have according to each season, and the linen[59] we use to our meat to be pure fine diaper[60] and damask, and to change it fresh every course of meat. As for our galleries, staircases, and passages, they shall be hung with various pictures and, all along the wall of our gallery, as long as the summer lasts, do stand upon pedestals flowerpots with various flowers and, in the winter, orange trees. And my gardens to be kept curiously[61] and flourish in every season of all sorts of flowers, sweet herbs, and fruits, and kept so as not to have a weed in it, and all the groves, wildernesses,[62] bowers, and arbors pruned and kept free from dead boughs, branches, or leaves, and all the ponds, rivulets, fountains, and spring kept clear, pure, and fresh. Also, we will have the choicest meats every season doth afford, and that every day our meat be dressed[63] several ways, and our drink cooler or hotter according to the several seasons, and all our drinks fresh and pleasing. Change of garments are also provided, of the newest fashions for every season, and rich trimming, so as we may be accoutered properly and according to our several pastimes. And our shifts[64] shall be of the finest and purest linen that can be bought or spun.

---

[54] Aromatic woods that would produce a pleasant fragrance when burned.

[55] Candles.

[56] The abbreviation for *videlicet*, "that is to say" or "namely," and "used to introduce an amplification, or more precise or explicit explanation, of a previous statement or word" (*OED*).

[57] A finely woven cloth, linen or cotton, imported from Holland.

[58] Likewise.

[59] Table linen.

[60] A cotton or linen fabric "woven with a small and simple pattern" (*OED*).

[61] Carefully.

[62] "A piece of ground in a large garden or park, planted with trees, and laid out in an ornamental or fantastic style, often in the form of a maze or labyrinth" (*OED*).

[63] Prepared.

[64] A woman's smock or chemise, an undergarment of linen or cotton.

LADIES. None in this world can be happier.

LADY HAPPY. Now, ladies, let us go to our several pastimes, if you please.

Exeunt.

ACT 2, Scene 3

Enter two ladies.[65]

LADY AMOROUS. Madam, how do you since you were married?

LADY VIRTUE. Very well, I thank you.

LADY AMOROUS. I am not so well as I wish I were.

Enter Madam Mediator to them.

MADAM MEDIATOR. Ladies, do you hear the news?

LADY VIRTUE. What news?

MADAM MEDIATOR. Why, there is a great foreign princess arrived, hearing of the famous Convent of Pleasure, to be one of nature's devotees.

LADY AMOROUS. What manner of lady is she?

---

[65] The two women who enter in 2.3, Lady Amorous and Lady Virtue, made their first appearance in *The Bridals*, the play that precedes *The Convent of Pleasure* in Cavendish's 1668 *Plays, Never before Printed*. *The Bridals* opens with a scene in which Monsieur Take-Pleasure, Monsieur Adviser, and Monsieur Facil discuss two marriages that have just taken place, that of Sir John Amorous and the Lady Coy (whom Monsieur Facil tries to seduce) and of Sir William Sage and the Lady Virtue. Here, the two recently married women appear again, with Lady Amorous, the former Lady Coy, suggesting that marriage is not all that she might have hoped it would be.

MADAM MEDIATOR. She is a princely brave[66] woman truly, of a masculine presence.[67]

LADY VIRTUE. But, Madam Mediator, do they live in such pleasure as you say? For they'll admit you, a widow, although not us, by reason we are wives.

MADAM MEDIATOR. In so much pleasure as nature never knew before this convent was and, for my part, I had rather be one in the Convent of Pleasure than empress of the whole world, for every lady there enjoyeth as much pleasure as any absolute monarch can do without the troubles and cares that wait on royalty. Besides, none can enjoy those pleasures they have unless they live such a retired or retreated life free from the world's vexations.

LADY VIRTUE. Well, I wish I might see and know what pleasures they enjoy.

MADAM MEDIATOR. If you were there, you could not know all their pleasure in a short time, for their varieties will require a long time to know their several changes. Besides, their pleasures and delights vary with the seasons, so that what with the several seasons and the varieties of every season, it will take up a whole life's time.

LADY VIRTUE. But I could judge of their changes by their single principles.[68]

MADAM MEDIATOR. But they have variety of one and the same kind.

LADY VIRTUE. But I should see the way or manner of them.

---

[66] A word that may mean "courageous," but here perhaps means "worthy" or "finely dressed"—that is, the princess is dressed in a manner befitting her royal status.

[67] "Demeanour, carriage, esp. when stately or impressive; nobleness or handsomeness of bearing or appearance, esp. the capacity to project or suggest inner strength, force of personality, etc., merely by being present" (*OED*).

[68] General rules.

MADAM MEDIATOR. That you might.

Exeunt.

ACT 2, Scene 4

Enter Monsieur Adviser, Monsieur Courtly, Monsieur Take-pleasure, and Monsieur Facil.

MONSIEUR COURTLY. Is there no hope to get those ladies out of their convent?

MONSIEUR ADVISER. No, faith, unless we could set the convent on fire.

MONSIEUR TAKE-PLEASURE. For Jupiter's sake,[69] let us do it, let's everyone carry a firebrand[70] to fire it.

MONSIEUR COURTLY. Yes, and smoke them out, as they do a swarm of bees.

MONSIEUR FACIL. Let's go presently[71] about it.

MONSIEUR ADVISER. Stay, there is a great princess there.

MONSIEUR TAKE-PLEASURE. 'Tis true, but when that princess is gone, we will surely do it.

---

[69] Monsieur Take-Pleasure's oath, like "by Jove" or "by the gods," appears frequently in contemporary plays, a result of the "Act to Restrain Abuses of Players," which made it a crime for actors to "jestingly or profanely speak or use the Holy Name of God, or of Christ Jesus, or of the Holy Ghost, or of the Trinity" (see above, n. 9). As Geoffrey Hughes notes, this "restrictive legislation" produced "minced oaths," like the one Cavendish uses here, frequently employing pagan deities rather than the name of the Christian god. Even after the Restoration, while there were "oaths in profusion" on stage, they were still usually "either minced or secular" (*Encyclopedia of Swearing*, 64). Not coincidentally, Monsieur Take-Pleasure swears by the Roman god who is a notorious seducer and rapist of women.

[70] A spark or a piece of burning wood used to ignite a fire.

[71] At once, right now.

MONSIEUR ADVISER. Yes, and be punished for our villainy.

MONSIEUR TAKE-PLEASURE. It will not prove villainy, for we shall do nature good service.

MONSIEUR ADVISER. Why, so we do nature good service when we get a wench with child, but yet the civil laws[72] do punish us for it.

MONSIEUR COURTLY. They are not civil laws that punish lovers.

MONSIEUR ADVISER. But those are civil laws that punish adulterers.

MONSIEUR COURTLY. Those are barbarous that make love adultery.

MONSIEUR ADVISER. No, those are barbarous laws that make adultery love.

MONSIEUR FACIL. Well, leaving love and adultery, they are foolish women that vex us with their retirement.

MONSIEUR ADVISER. Well, gentlemen, although we rail at the Lady Happy for retiring, yet if I had such an estate as she and would follow her example, I make no doubt but you would all be content to encloister yourselves with me upon the same conditions as those ladies encloister themselves with her.

MONSIEUR TAKE-PLEASURE. Not unless you had women in your convent.

MONSIEUR ADVISER. Nay, faith, since women can quit the pleasure of men, we men may well quit the trouble of women.

---

[72] In their exchange, the men engage in punning wordplay with the meaning of *civil laws*: when Monsieur Adviser refers to "civil" laws, he means the laws of a city or state that regulate the lives of its citizens, while Monsieur Courtly's reference to "civil" laws means laws that are humane or benevolent.

MONSIEUR COURTLY. But is there no place where we may peek into the convent?

MONSIEUR ADVISER. No, there are no grates but brick and stone walls.

MONSIEUR FACIL. Let us get out some of the bricks or stones.

MONSIEUR ADVISER. Alas! The walls are a yard thick.

MONSIEUR FACIL. But nothing is difficult to willing minds.[73]

MONSIEUR ADVISER. My mind is willing, but my reason tells me it is impossible; wherefore I'll never go about it.

MONSIEUR TAKE-PLEASURE. Faith, let us resolve to put ourselves in women's apparel and so by that means get into the convent.

MONSIEUR ADVISER. We shall be discovered.[74]

MONSIEUR TAKE-PLEASURE. Who will discover us?

MONSIEUR ADVISER. We shall discover ourselves.

MONSIEUR TAKE-PLEASURE. We are not such fools as to betray ourselves.

MONSIEUR ADVISER. We cannot avoid it, for our very garb and behavior, besides our voices, will discover us, for we are as untoward[75] to make curtseys in petticoats as women are to make

---

[73] A proverbial expression. See John Ray, *A Collection of English Proverbs, Digested into a convenient Method for the speedy finding any one upon occasion* . . . , 2nd ed. (Cambridge, 1678), 29.

[74] Another punning exchange follows, with Monsieur Adviser claiming the disguised men would *discover*—reveal or betray—themselves, and Monsieur Take-Pleasure, misunderstanding, asking who would *discover*—find—them.

[75] Inept or awkward.

legs[76] in breeches, and it will be as great a difficulty to raise our voices to a treble sound as for women to press down their voices to a base. Besides, we shall never frame our eyes and mouths to such coy, dissembling looks and pretty, simpering mops[77] and smiles as they do.

MONSIEUR COURTLY. But we will go as strong, lusty country wenches that desire to serve them in inferior places and offices, as cook maids, laundry maids, dairy maids, and the like.

MONSIEUR FACIL. I do verily believe I could make an indifferent[78] cook maid, but not a laundry nor a dairy maid, for I cannot milk cows nor starch gorgets,[79] but I think I could make a pretty shift[80] to wash some of the ladies' night linen.

MONSIEUR TAKE-PLEASURE. But they employ women in all places in their gardens and for brewing, baking, and making all sorts of things. Besides, some keep their swine, and twenty such-like offices and employments there are which we should be very proper for.[81]

MONSIEUR FACIL. Oh, yes, for keeping of swine belongs to men. Remember the prodigal son.[82]

MONSIEUR ADVISER. Faith, for our prodigality we might be all swineherds.

---

[76] *To make legs* is to bow.

[77] "A grotesque grimace or grin, as made by a monkey" (*OED*), from the verb *mop*, "To make a grimace, to make faces."

[78] Fair or tolerable.

[79] "An article of female dress, covering the neck and breast" (*OED*).

[80] While Monsieur Facil thinks he could manage (*make a . . . shift*) to wash some of the women's bedclothes, he also puns on the word *shift* (see above, n. 64), a woman's undergarment.

[81] Suited for or fit for.

[82] The parable of the prodigal son, in which the younger son is reduced to living as a swineherd, appears in Luke 15:11-32.

MONSIEUR COURTLY. Also we shall be proper for gardens, for we can dig and set and sow.

MONSIEUR TAKE-PLEASURE. And we are proper for brewing.

MONSIEUR ADVISER. We are more proper for drinking, for I can drink good beer or ale when 'tis brewed, but I could not brew such beer or ale as any man could drink.

MONSIEUR FACIL. Come, come, we shall make a shift one way or other. Besides, we shall be very willing to learn and be very diligent in our services, which will give good and great content; wherefore let us go and put these designs into execution.[83]

MONSIEUR COURTLY. Content, content.

MONSIEUR ADVISER. Nay, faith, let us not trouble ourselves, for it 'tis in vain.

Exeunt.

---

[83] Monsieur Facil's assurance that the men will *make a shift* and *be very diligent* in their *services*—which will *give great and good content*—continues his sexually suggestive double-entendres.

ACT 3, Scene 1

Enter the princess and the Lady Happy, with the rest of the ladies belonging to the convent.

LADY HAPPY. Madam, Your Highness has done me much honor to come from a splendid court to a retired convent.

PRINCESS. Sweet Lady Happy, there are many that have quit their crowns and power for a cloister of restraint;[84] then well may I quit a court of troubles for a Convent of Pleasure, but the greatest pleasure I could receive were to have your friendship.

LADY HAPPY. I should be ungrateful should I not be not only your friend but humble servant.

PRINCESS. I desire you would be my mistress and I your servant, and upon this agreement of friendship I desire you will grant me one request.

LADY HAPPY. Anything that is in my power to grant.

PRINCESS. Why then, I observing in your several recreations some of your ladies do accouter themselves in masculine habits[85] and act lovers' parts, I desire you will give me leave to be sometimes so accoutered and act the part of your loving servant.[86]

---

[84] The princess is correct in saying that kings and queens have been known to leave behind "their crowns and power" and enter monasteries or convents. Most immediately, and as only one example, Cavendish had served in the court of Queen Henrietta Maria; the widowed English queen founded the convent of the Sisters of the Visitation of Holy Mary at Chaillot (Paris) in 1651, after the execution of her husband Charles I, and spent much of the rest of her life there; see Introduction, 37. (Although it was still in the future, Mary of Modena, James II's wife and, briefly, queen of England [1685-1688], would also retreat to the convent at Chaillot after the death of her husband, the exiled English king.)

[85] Clothing.

[86] In this exchange, Lady Happy uses the word *servant* in a customary sense when she addresses the princess, as a way of welcoming the new arrival and expressing her generosity and her willingness to be of use to the princess, but the princess employs the word in a more specific sense, coming from the literature of courtly love, as a way

LADY HAPPY. I shall never desire to have any other loving servant than yourself.

PRINCESS. Nor I any other loving mistress than yourself.

LADY HAPPY. More innocent lovers never can there be,
Than my most princely lover that's a she.

PRINCESS. Nor never convent did such pleasures give,
Where lovers with their mistresses may live.

Enter a lady asking whether they will see the play.

LADY. May it please Your Highness, the play is ready to be acted.

The scene is opened, the princess and Lady Happy sit down, and the play is acted within the scene, the princess and the Lady Happy being spectators. [87]

Enter one dressed like a man that speaks the prologue.

Noble spectators, you shall see tonight
A play which, though't be dull, yet's short to sight;
For, since we cannot please your ears with wit,
We will not tire your limbs long here to sit. [88]

---

of declaring herself as a "professed lover; one who is devoted to the service of a lady" (*OED*). The princess also says that she would like Lady Happy to be her *mistress*, another word with multiple meanings: "A woman having control or authority," "A woman who employs others in her service," and "A woman loved and courted by a man" (*OED*). Lady Happy seems quick to adapt herself to the princess's desire for her as a love object, though she also expresses some doubt (see below, 4.1).

[87] This stage direction seems to signal not only the beginning of the play-within-a-play (*the scene is opened*) but also the staging as Cavendish imagines it (*the play is acted within the scene*), suggesting that she might envision an outer stage, where the princess and Lady Happy sit, and an inner stage, a recessed space at the back of the outer stage. This second playing space can be enclosed by curtains that open to reveal it when it is needed.

[88] The scenes that follow in *The Convent of Pleasure*'s extended play-within-a-play all present the woes of marriage from women's perspectives. Western literature depicting the pains of marriage—for men—has a long tradition, stretching back to the classical period, but the early-modern *querelle des femmes* ("debate about women") brought

ACT 3, Scene 2

Enter two mean[89] women.

FIRST WOMAN. Oh, neighbor, well met. Where have you been?

SECOND WOMAN. I have been with my neighbor, the cobbler's wife, to comfort her for the loss of her husband who is run away with Goody Mettle,[90] the tinker's wife.

FIRST WOMAN. I would to heaven my husband would run away with Goody Shred, the botcher's[91] wife, for he lies all day drinking in an alehouse, like a drunken rogue as he is, and when he comes home, he beats me all black and blue when I and my children are almost starved for want.

SECOND WOMAN. Truly, neighbor, so doth my husband, and spends not only what he gets,[92] but what I earn with the sweat of my

---

women's voices into the discussion, beginning with Christine de Pizan (1364-c. 1430), and with those new voices a counternarrative to the discussion of the pains of marriage. Like Cavendish's play-within-a-play, Pizan's *Book of the City of Ladies* illustrates the sorrows and difficulties of marriage from the female point-of-view. On the male anti-marriage tradition, see Katharine M. Wilson and Elizabeth M. Makowski, *Wykked Wyves and the Woes of Marriage: Misogamous Literature from Juvenal to Chaucer* (Albany: State University of New York, 1990) and, for the primary texts, Alcuin Blamires, ed., *Woman Defamed and Woman Defended: An Anthology of Medieval Texts* (New York: Oxford University Press, 1992; despite its title, Blamires's anthology contains Greek and Latin texts as well as texts of the Church Fathers). On women and the *querelle des femmes*, see Margaret L. King and Albert Rabil, "The Other Voice in Early Modern Europe," an introductory essay published in the sixty volumes of the University of Chicago's Other Voice in Early Modern Europe series, and now available online at www.othervoiceineme.com/othervoice.html.

[89] A person of low social status—as the two women's conversation makes clear, their neighbors are the wives of cobblers, tinkers, and botchers (see n. 91, below).

[90] *Goody*, from "goodwife," is a "title of courtesy prefixed to the surname of a woman, usually a married woman of humble social status" (*OED*). Since her husband is a tinker, a man who repairs pots, pans, kettles, and other household utensils, Goody Mettle's name suggests her character (her lively and vigorous *mettle*) while it also alludes to her husband's craft—she is Mrs. Metal.

[91] Since a *botcher* is a tailor who mends and patches clothes, his wife, Goody Shred, is also appropriately named.

[92] Earns.

brows, the whilst my children cry for bread, and he drinks that away that should feed my small children, which are too young to work for themselves.

FIRST WOMAN. But I will go and pull my husband out of the alehouse, or I'll break their lattice-windows[93] down.

SECOND WOMAN. Come, I'll go and help, for my husband is there too, but we shall be both beaten by them.

FIRST WOMAN. I care not, for I will not suffer him to be drunk, and I and my children starve—I had better be dead.

Exeunt.

ACT 3, Scene 3

Enter a lady and her maid.

LADY. Oh, I am sick!

MAID. You are breeding a child,[94] madam.

LADY. I have not one minute's time of health.

Exeunt.

ACT 3, Scene 4

Enter two ladies.

FIRST LADY. Why weep you, madam?

---

[93] "A window of lattice-work (usually painted red), . . . formerly a common mark of an alehouse or inn" (*OED*).

[94] Pregnant.

SECOND LADY. Have I not cause to weep when my husband hath played all his estate away at dice and cards, even to the clothes on his back?

FIRST LADY. I have as much cause to weep, then, as you, for though my husband hath not lost his estate at play, yet he hath spent it amongst his whores and is not content to keep whores abroad,[95] but in my house, under my roof, and they must rule as chief mistresses.[96]

SECOND LADY. But my husband hath not only lost his own estate but also my portion[97] and hath forced me with threats to yield up my jointure,[98] so that I must beg for my living, for anything I know as yet.

FIRST LADY. If all married women were as unhappy as I, marriage were a curse.

SECOND LADY. No doubt of it.

Exeunt.

ACT 3, Scene 5

Enter a lady, as almost distracted,[99] running about the stage, and her maid follows her.

LADY. Oh, my child is dead, my child is dead, what shall I do, what shall I do?

---

[95] Away from home.

[96] Again Cavendish plays with the many possible meanings of *mistress*, used here to refer to the female head of a household and to a man's extra-marital sexual partner.

[97] From "marriage portion." See n. 27, above.

[98] In addition to specifying a woman's marriage portion, or dowry, a marriage settlement contract determined her *jointure*, the portion of a man's estate set aside for her support if her husband should die and leave her a widow. In financial straits because of his gambling, the second lady's husband has forced his wife to relinquish her legally contracted protection.

[99] As if she were mad or insane.

MAID. You must have patience, madam.

LADY. Who can have patience to[100] lose their only child? Who can? Oh, I shall run mad, for I have no patience.

Runs off the stage. Exit maid after her.

ACT 3, Scene 6

Enter a citizen's[101] wife, as into a tavern where a bush is hung out,[102] and meets some gentlemen there.

CITIZEN'S WIFE. Pray, gentlemen, is my husband, Mr. Negligent, here?

FIRST GENTLEMAN. He was, but he is gone some quarter of an hour since.

CITIZEN'S WIFE. Could he go, gentlemen?[103]

SECOND GENTLEMAN. Yes, with a supporter.

CITIZEN'S WIFE. Out upon[104] him! Must he be supported? Upon my credit,[105] gentlemen, he will undo himself and me too with his drinking and carelessness, leaving his shop and all his commodities at sixes and sevens,[106] and his prentices[107] and journeymen[108] are as

---

[100] At the very moment of, as a result of.

[101] "An ordinary (city- or town-dwelling) person as opposed to a member of the landed nobility or gentry on one hand or an artisan, labourer, etc. on the other" (*OED*).

[102] "A branch or bunch of ivy (perhaps as the plant sacred to Bacchus) hung up as a vintner's sign; hence, the sign-board of a tavern" (*OED*).

[103] The citizen's wife is asking whether her husband had drunk too much to make his way home.

[104] An expression that corresponds to "curses upon, damnation to" (*OED*).

[105] Believe me.

[106] A phrase "originally denoting the hazard of one's whole fortune, or carelessness as to the consequences of one's actions, and in later use the creation or existence of, or neglect to remove, confusion, disorder, or disagreement" (*OED*).

[107] Apprentices.

careless and idle as he. Besides, they cozen[109] him of his wares. But was it a he- or she-supporter my husband was supported by?

FIRST GENTLEMAN. A she-supporter, for it was one of the maidservants which belong to this tavern.

CITIZEN'S WIFE. Out upon him, knave, must he have a she-supporter, in the devil's name? But I'll go and seek them both out with a vengeance.

SECOND GENTLEMAN. Pray, let us entreat your stay to drink a cup of wine with us.

CITIZEN'S WIFE. I will take your kind offer, for wine may chance to abate choleric vapors and pacify the spleen.[110]

FIRST GENTLEMAN. That it will, for wine and good company are the only abaters of vapors.

SECOND GENTLEMAN. It doth not abate vapors so much as cure melancholy.

CITIZEN'S WIFE. In truth, I find a cup of wine doth comfort me sometimes.

FIRST GENTLEMAN. It will cheer the heart.

SECOND GENTLEMAN. Yes, and enlighten the understanding.

---

[108] After serving his apprenticeship, a journeyman becomes an employee of a master (in this case, Mr. Negligent), qualified to earn wages for a trade or in a business.

[109] Cheat.

[110] An excess of *choler*, one of the four bodily humors believed to control physical and mental health, resulted in anger; here the citizen's wife agrees that a little wine might help to cure her of her choleric *vapors*, "exhalations supposed to be developed within the organs of the body . . . and to have an injurious effect upon the health" (*OED*). While yellow bile (choler) was believed to derive from the liver, black bile—which produces melancholy—was believed to come from the spleen, so the citizen's wife is both angry and depressed.

CITIZEN'S WIFE. Indeed, and my understanding requires en-lightening.[111]

Exeunt.

ACT 3, Scene 7

Enter a lady big with child, groaning as in labor, and a company of women with her.

LADY. Oh, my back, my back will break. Oh! Oh! Oh!

FIRST WOMAN. Is the midwife sent for?

SECOND WOMAN. Yes, but she is with another lady.

LADY. Oh, my back! Oh! Oh! Oh! Juno,[112] give me some ease.

Exeunt.

ACT 3, Scene 8

Enter two ancient ladies.

FIRST LADY. I have brought my son into the world with great pains, bred him with tender care, much pains, and great cost, and must he now be hanged for killing a man in a quarrel? When he should be a comfort and staff of my age, is he to be my age's affliction?

---

[111] While it is possible that the two gentlemen are sincerely concerned about the citizen's wife and interested only in comforting her and relieving her of her sorrow, there are no other scenes in this play-within-a-play where men are generous and supportive of women. It may well be that the gentlemen have ulterior motives in offering to ply the distraught woman with wine—particularly since a "light" woman—or an *en*lightened one?—was a wanton or unchaste woman.

[112] Juno is not only Jupiter's long-suffering wife (see above, n. 69), she is a goddess of childbirth (and marriage).

SECOND LADY. I confess it is a great affliction, but I have had as great, having had but two daughters, and them fair ones, though I say it, and might have matched them well. But one of them was got with child to my great disgrace, the other run away with my butler, not worth the droppings of his taps.[113]

FIRST LADY. Who would desire children, since they come to such misfortunes?

Exeunt.

ACT 3, Scene 9

Enter one woman meeting another.

FIRST WOMAN. Is the midwife come, for my lady is in a strong labor?[114]

SECOND WOMAN. No, she cannot come, for she hath been with a lady that hath been in strong labor these three days of a dead child, and 'tis thought she cannot be delivered.

Enter another woman.

THIRD WOMAN. Come away, the midwife is come.

FIRST WOMAN. Is the lady delivered she was withal[115]?

---

[113] In Cavendish's day, rather than being the head servant in a household, the *butler* was the "servant who has charge of the wine-cellar and dispenses the liquor" (*OED*)—and thus the second lady's assessment that the man with whom her daughter has run away is not worth the drops that fall from a *tap*, "a hollow or tubular plug through which liquid may be drawn, . . . used especially in drawing liquor from a cask" (*OED*).

[114] Although there is no specific link here to 3.7, this scene may continue the action of the earlier one.

[115] *She* meaning the midwife, who was attending the lady who has died in childbirth; *withal* "substituted for WITH, *prep.* in postposition," used with a question (*OED*). More simply, "Has the lady whom the midwife was attending given birth?"

Various studies of childbirth during the early modern period have demonstrated that the rates of maternal mortality in the seventeenth century, especially in London,

THIRD WOMAN. Yes, of life, for she could not be delivered, and so she died.

SECOND WOMAN. Pray tell not our lady so, for the very fright of not being able to bring forth a child will kill her.

Exeunt.

ACT 3, Scene 10

Enter a gentleman who meets a fair young lady.

GENTLEMAN. Madam, my lord desires you to command whatsoever you please, and it shall be obeyed.

LADY. I dare not command, but I humbly entreat I may live quiet and free from his *amours*.[116]

GENTLEMAN. He says he cannot live and not love you.

LADY. But he may live and not lie with me.

GENTLEMAN. He cannot be happy unless he enjoy you.[117]

LADY. And I must be unhappy if he should.

GENTLEMAN. He commanded me to tell you that he will part from his lady for your sake.

"were comparable with some of the highest rates recorded for any human community"; in the later seventeenth century, the rate has been calculated as sixteen maternal deaths per 1,000 births, counting only women who died in labor, the number rising if women who died within a month of childbirth were included. See Louis Schwarz, *Milton and Maternal Mortality* (New York: Cambridge University Press, 2009), 29-31. (By way of contrast, today in developed countries the rate of maternal mortality is six to eight maternal deaths per 100,000 live births [31].)

[116] His "courtship" of her—here, his efforts to seduce her.

[117] Possesses her, whether she is willing or not; "to have one's will of (a woman)" (*OED*).

LADY. Heaven forbid I should part man and wife.

GENTLEMAN. Lady, he will be divorced for your sake.[118]

LADY. Heaven forbid I should be the cause of a divorce between a noble pair.

GENTLEMAN. You had best consent, for otherwise he will have you against your will.

LADY. I will send His Lordship an answer to morrow; pray him to give me so much time.

GENTLEMAN. I shall, lady.

Exit gentleman. Lady sola.[119]

LADY. I must prevent my own ruin, and the sweet, virtuous lady's, by going into a nunnery; wherefore I'll put myself into one tonight.

---

[118] Despite the gentleman's casual promise that his friend will divorce his wife for the lady, a divorce in the modern sense was not a likely option. Following Matthew 19:3-9, the English church generally regarded marriage as indissoluble. Attempts to legalize divorce in England were opposed by the Church of England throughout the reigns of Edward VI, Mary, and Elizabeth. On this, see Roderick Phillips, *Untying the Knot: A Short History of Divorce* (New York: Cambridge University Press, 1991), 36. In 1604, after the accession of James I, the "first systematic revision of canon law of the Anglican church was promulgated"; while "it permitted separations," it "explicitly ruled out the possibility of divorce" (24). Reform continued to be debated through the Commonwealth period, but as late as 1660, when Charles II was restored to the English throne, "no progress had been made toward the legalization of divorce in England" (36). The first divorce to be granted in England was that of John Manners, lord Roos, who in 1670 cleverly "circumvented" the "barriers to divorce" by having a bill, introduced in the House of Lords, "to have his marriage dissolved and to permit him to marry again" (37). See also Lawrence Stone, *Broken Lives: Separation and Divorce in England, 1660-1857* (New York: Oxford University Press, 1993). The gentleman may be equivocating when he speaks to the lady here, suggesting his friend will somehow dissolve his marriage, when all he really means is that his friend will *divorce* in a more general way, by simply leaving his wife (an idea which the lady has already rejected).

[119] Alone on stage.

There will I live and serve the gods on high,
And leave this wicked world and vanity.

Exeunt.

One enters and speaks the epilogue.

Marriage is a curse we find,
Especially to womankind;
From the cobbler's wife, we see,
To ladies, they unhappy be.

LADY HAPPY (to the princess). Pray, servant, how do you like this play?

PRINCESS. My sweet mistress, I cannot in conscience approve of it, for though some few be unhappy in marriage, yet there are many more that are so happy as they would not change their condition.

LADY HAPPY. Oh, servant, I fear you will become an apostate.[120]

PRINCESS. Not to you, sweet mistress.

Exeunt.

[Act 3, Scene 11][121]

Enter the gentlemen.

FIRST GENTLEMAN. There is no hopes of dissolving this Convent of Pleasure.

SECOND GENTLEMAN. Faith, not as I can perceive.

---

[120] Someone who denies his or her religious faith, deserts his or her political party, or who abandons his or her moral principles.

[121] There is no scene break here in Cavendish's original, but since Lady Happy and the princess leave the stage empty before the three gentlemen appear, moving the action outside the convent, a new scene seems to be needed.

THIRD GENTLEMAN. We may be sure this convent will never be dissolved, by reason it is ennobled with the company of great princesses and glorified with a great fame, but the fear is that all the rich heirs will make convents and all the young beauties associate themselves in such convents.

FIRST GENTLEMAN. You speak reason; wherefore, let us endeavor to get wives before they are encloistered.

Exeunt.

ACT 4, Scene 1

Enter Lady Happy, dressed as a shepherdess. She walks, very melancholy, then speaks as to herself.

LADY HAPPY. My Name is Happy, and so was my condition before I saw this princess, but now I am like to be the most unhappy maid alive. But why may not I love a woman with the same affection I could a man?
No, no, nature is nature and still will be
The same she was from all eternity.

Enter the princess in masculine shepherd's clothes.[122]

PRINCESS. My dearest mistress, do you shun my company? Is your servant become an offence to your sight?

LADY HAPPY. No, servant! Your presence is more acceptable to me than the presence of our goddess, nature, for which she, I fear, will punish me for loving you more than I ought to love you.

PRINCESS. Can lovers love too much?

LADY HAPPY. Yes, if they love not well.

---

[122] In wearing the costumes of shepherd and shepherdess, the princess and Lady Happy enter into the fantasy world of the pastoral, a literary tradition long associated with homoeroticism, from Theocritus and Virgil in the ancient world through early-modern writers like John Lyly, Christopher Marlowe, William Shakespeare, Edmund Spenser, and Richard Barnfield. As Valerie Traub notes, "As if in homage to the pastoral of Shakespeare and Lyly, much of the homoeroticism of [*The Convent of Pleasure*] arises out of the amorous pastime of pastoral 'Recreations.'" Noting the exchange in this scene, she adds, "The amorous freedom associated with pastoral, combined with the gender fluidity of transvestism, lead [sic] to an expression of love." Valerie Traub, *The Renaissance of Lesbianism in Early Modern England* (New York: Cambridge University Press, 2002), 178-79. See also Harriette Andreadis, *Sappho in Early Modern England: Female Same-Sex Literary Erotics, 1550-1714* (Chicago: University of Chicago Press, 2001), 84-88.

PRINCESS. Can any love be more virtuous, innocent, and harmless than ours?

LADY HAPPY. I hope not.

PRINCESS. Then let us please ourselves as harmless lovers use to do.

LADY HAPPY. How can harmless lovers please themselves?

PRINCESS. Why, very well—as to discourse, embrace, and kiss, so mingle souls together.

LADY HAPPY. But innocent lovers do not use to kiss.

PRINCESS. Not any act more frequent amongst us womankind; nay, it were a sin in friendship should not we kiss. Then let us not prove ourselves reprobates.[123]

They embrace and kiss and hold each other in their arms.

PRINCESS. These my embraces, though of female kind,
May be as fervent as a masculine mind.

The scene is opened;[124] the princess and Lady Happy go in.

A pastoral[125] within the scene.

The scene is changed into a green, or plain, where sheep are feeding and a maypole[126] in the middle.

---

[123] Sinners (having sinned against friendship by not kissing).

[124] See above, n. 87.

[125] Rural scene.

[126] A long pole, decorated with flowers and painted with stripes, raised on a *green* (a piece of public land in a town or village) for May Day celebrations. Long before Freud, the maypole was given phallic significance. The *OED* offers several examples of *maypole* used as a slang reference for an erect penis.

Lady Happy, as a shepherdess, and the princess, as a shepherd, are sitting there.

Enter another shepherd and woos the Lady Happy.

SHEPHERD. Fair shepherdess, do not my suit[127] deny,
    Oh, grant my suit, let me not for love die;
    Pity my flocks, oh, save their shepherd's life,
    Grant you my suit, be you their shepherd's wife.

LADY HAPPY. How can I grant to everyone's request?
    Each shepherd's suit lets me not be at rest,
    For which I wish the winds might blow them far,
    That no love-suit might enter to my ear.

Enter Madam Mediator in a shepherdess dress and another shepherd.

SHEPHERD. Good dame, unto your daughter speak for me,
    Persuade her I your son-in-law may be;
    I'll serve your swine, your cows bring home to milk,
    Attend your sheep, whose wool's as soft as silk;
    I'll plow your grounds, corn I'll in winter sow,
    Then reap your harvest, and your grass I'll mow,
    Gather your fruits in autumn from the tree—
    All this and more I'll do, if you speak for me.

SHEPHERDESS.[128] My daughter vows a single life
    And swears she ne'er will be a wife,
    But live a maid and flocks will keep,
    And her chief company shall be sheep.

The princess as a shepherd speaks to the Lady Happy.

PRINCESS. My shepherdess, your wit flies high,
    Up to the sky,

---

[127] "Wooing or courting of a woman; solicitation for a woman's hand" (*OED*).
[128] Here the costumed Madam Mediator.

And views the gates of heaven,
Which are the planets seven,[129]
Sees how fixed stars[130] are placed,
And how the meteors waste,
What makes the snow so white,
And how the sun makes light,
What makes the biting cold
On everything take hold,
And hail, a mixed degree
'Twixt snow and ice; you see
From whence the winds do blow,
What thunder is you know,
And what makes lightning flow
Like liquid streams you show;
From sky you come to th'earth
And view each creature's birth,
Sink to the center deep,
Where all dead bodies sleep,
And there observe to know
What makes the minerals grow,
How vegetables sprout,
And how the plants come out,
Take notice of all seed
And what the earth doth breed,
Then view the springs below
And mark how waters flow,
What makes the tides to rise
Up proudly to the skies
And shrinking back descend,
As fearing to offend;
Also your wit doth view
The vapor and the dew
In summer's heat, that wet

---

[129] In classical antiquity, there were seven visible planets ("wanderers"): the sun, the moon, Mercury, Venus, Mars, Jupiter, and Saturn.

[130] The *fixed stars*, unlike the planets, remain in the same relative position in the night sky. (In the second century CE, the astronomer Ptolemy identified some 1,022 fixed stars.)

Doth seem like the earth's sweat;
In wintertime that dew
Like paint's white to the view,
Cold makes that thick, white, dry,
As cerusse[131] it doth lie
On th'earth's black face, so fair
As painted ladies are,
But when a heat is felt,
That frosty paint doth melt;
Thus heaven and earth you view,
And see what's old, what's new,
How bodies transmigrate,[132]
Lives are predestinate;[133]
Thus doth your wit reveal
What nature would conceal.[134]

LADY HAPPY. My shepherd,
All those that live do know it,
That you are born a poet;

---

[131] White lead, used as a cosmetic foundation to cover the skin.

[132] Transform. Hero Chalmers notes Cavendish's essay "On Transmigrations" (*The Philosophical and Physical Opinions*, 1655), where the process of transmigration within the body is illustrated by the example of "the transformation of food into blood"; Hero Chalmers, Julie Sanders, and Sophie Tomlinson, eds., *Three Seventeenth-Century Plays on Women and Performance*, The Revels Plays Companion Library (Manchester: Manchester University Press, 2006), 294.

[133] "Destined or fated, esp. to a particular office, condition, type of existence, etc." (*OED*). Again, Chalmers is extremely helpful, quoting Cavendish's essay "The Predestination of Nature" (*The Worlds Olio*, 1655): "there is a predestination in Nature, that whatever she gives Life to, she gives Death to; she hath also predestinated such Effects from such Causes"; *Three Seventeenth-Century Plays*, 294.

[134] By the time she publishes *Plays, Never before Printed* in 1668, Cavendish has written a great deal on the subject of natural philosophy. From *Poems, and Fancies* (1653), where she includes essays about "Ebbing and Flowing of the Sea" and "Of Dewes, and Mists from the Earth," for example, to *Grounds of Naturall Philosophy* (1668), her "much altered" new edition of *Philosophical and Physical Opinions*, where she includes several essays on the "human humours," "human appetites and passions," and "passionate love," Cavendish has published about most of the scientific topics mentioned here and in the following speech. For a detailed listing of Cavendish's essays and reflections on these topics, see Chalmers, *Three Seventeenth-Century Plays*, 292-94.

Your wit doth search[135] mankind,
In body and in mind,
The appetites you measure
And weigh each several pleasure,
Do figure every passion
And every humor's fashion,
See how the fancy's wrought
And what makes every thought,
Fathom conceptions low[136]
From whence opinions flow,
Observe the memory's length
And understanding's strength;
Your wit doth reason find
The center of the mind,
Wherein the rational soul
Doth govern and control;
There doth she[137] sit in state,
Predestinate by fate
And by the gods' decree,
That sovereign she should be;
And thus your wit can tell
How souls in bodies dwell,
As that the mind dwells in the brain,
And in the mind the soul doth reign,
And in the soul the life doth last,
For with the body it doth not waste,
Nor shall wit like the body die,
But live in the world's memory.

PRINCESS. May I live in your favor and be possessed with your love
and person is the height of my ambitions.[138]

---

[135] Examine or investigate rigorously.

[136] Deep.

[137] The *rational soul*.

[138] A grammatically mixed construction that might be clarified as "That I may live in your favor and be possessed with your love and person is the height of my ambitions." It is important to note here the princess's emphasis on possessing not only the *love* but the *person* (body) of Lady Happy.

LADY HAPPY. I can neither deny you my love nor person.

PRINCESS. In amorous pastoral verse we did not woo
  As other pastoral lovers use to do.

LADY HAPPY. Which doth express we shall more constant be,
  And in a married life better agree.

PRINCESS. We shall agree, for we true love inherit,
  Join as one body and soul or heavenly spirit.

Here come rural sports, as country dances about the maypole; that pair
which dances best is crowned king and queen of the shepherds that year,
which happens to the princess and the Lady Happy.

LADY HAPPY *to the Princess.* Let me tell you, servant, that our custom
  is to dance about this maypole, and that pair which dances best is
  crowned king and queen of all the shepherds and shepherdesses this
  year, which sport, if it please you, we will begin.

PRINCESS. Nothing, sweetest mistress, that pleases you can displease
  me.

They dance; after the dancing, the princess and Lady Happy are crowned
with a garland of flowers. A shepherd speaks.

Written by my Lord Duke.[139]

You've won the prize and justly, so we all
Acknowledge it with joy and offer here

---

[139] A pasted-on strip, inserted into the printed text of *The Convent of Pleasure* in
some copies of *Plays, Never before Printed,* attributes authorship of the following lyric to
Cavendish's husband, William Cavendish, duke of Newcastle. For a discussion of the
variety of ways this strip and the one immediately below might be interpreted, see
Introduction, 78-80.

Our hatchments[140] up, our sheep-hooks, as your due,
And scrips of cordwain and oaten pipe;
So all our pastoral ornaments we lay
Here at your feet, with homage to obey
All your commands, and all these things we bring
In honor of our dancing queen and king,
For dancing heretofore has got more riches
Than we can find in all our shepherds' breeches—
Witness rich Holmby.[141] Long then may you live,
And for your dancing what we have we give.

A wassail[142] is carried about and syllabubs.[143]

Another shepherd speaks or sings this that follows.

Written by my Lord Duke.

The jolly wassail now do bring,
With apples drowned in stronger ale,

---

[140] "An escutcheon or ensign armorial" (*OED*). The shepherds' "armorial bearings" are their shepherd's crooks, small leather satchels (*scrips of cordwain*), and pipes (an *oaten pipe* was made of straw or an oatgrass stem).

[141] Holdenby House (pronounced and sometimes spelled *Holmby*) was built by Sir Christopher Hatton. Hatton reportedly came to the attention of Elizabeth Tudor because of his skill as a dancer. He ultimately became Lord Chancellor of England and, not entirely coincidentally, one of the wealthiest men in the country. When Holdenby was constructed in 1583, it was the "largest private house in Elizabethan England—with 123 huge glass windows around two courtyards" ("The House," *Holdenby House*, 2016, http://www.holdenby.com). For Holdenby's significance to Cavendish, Charles I and Henrietta Maria were entertained by a masque staged there, in their honor, in 1634. When King Charles I was captured by parliamentary forces in 1647, he was a kept as a prisoner at Holdenby for several months. After the civil wars, the Elizabethan house was sold by parliament to Adam Baynes, who destroyed all but one wing of house Hatton had built. After 1660, the house—or what was left of it—reverted to royal ownership and was then sold. (In the eighteenth century it was rebuilt).

[142] For "wassail bowl," a "large bowl or cup in which wassail was made and from which healths were drunk," the liquor *wassail* being a "spiced ale used in Twelfth-night and Christmas-eve celebrations" (OED).

[143] "A drink or dish made of milk . . . or cream, curdled by the admixture of wine, cider, or other acid, often sweetened and flavoured" (OED).

And fresher syllabubs, and sing;
Then each to tell their lovesick tale;
So home by couples and thus draw
Ourselves by holy Hymen's law.[144]

The scene vanishes.

Enter the princess, sola, and walks a turn or two in a musing posture, then views herself and speaks.

PRINCESS. What, have I on a petticoat?[145] Oh, Mars, thou god of war, pardon my sloth, but yet remember thou art a lover, and so am I. But you will say my kingdom wants me, not only to rule and govern it, but to defend it. But what is a kingdom in comparison of a beautiful mistress? Base thoughts, fly off, for I will not go did not only a kingdom, but the world, want me.

Exeunt.[146]

---

[144] The pairs of lovers (*couples*)—each pair consisting of two women, one of whom is cross-dressed—are drawn together by *Hymen*, the god of wedding ceremonies. The myths of Hymen incorporate various stories of cross-gendered sexual desire, including one in which Apollo is so in love with Hymen that he (Apollo) won't leave him (Hymen) alone and another in which Hymen disguises himself as a woman to pursue a young woman with whom he is in love.

[145] Some readers see in this speech the princess's revelation that "she" is, in fact, *not* someone used to wearing a female garment, a *petticoat*. Notice, however, the feminine pronoun (*herself*) is retained in Cavendish's stage direction, as is the feminine ending in the Latin adjective *sola*. (Contrast to 5.3, where the stage directions specify that Mimic is alone, *solus*, on stage.) But it is also important to know that, even in the princess's speech, Cavendish continues the gender ambiguity—the word "petticoat" originally referred not to an item of women's clothing but to a "man's tight-fitting undercoat, usually padded and worn under a doublet and over a shirt" (*OED*), a meaning it retained into Cavendish's own day. So is the "princess" a man who isn't used to wearing a female garment? Or is the "princess" a woman who isn't used to wearing a man's garment—the princess assumed male clothing just after her arrival at the convent (3.1), and from that point on, she has only appeared in male costume.

[146] After the second shepherd's song, the stage directions indicate that the pastoral scene *vanishes*, and the princess is described as alone on stage. But the plural *exeunt* here complicates the staging—who, besides the princess, is left on stage to exit? It is hard to decide just what Cavendish may have imagined. In any case, the rapid shifts—the pastoral celebration, the princess's soliloquy and exit, and Lady Happy's

Enter the Lady Happy, sola and melancholy, and after a short musing speaks.

LADY HAPPY. Oh, nature, oh, you gods above,
Suffer me not to fall in love;
Oh, strike me dead here in this place
Rather than fall into disgrace.

Enter Madam Mediator.

MADAM MEDIATOR. What, Lady Happy, solitary, alone and musing like a disconsolate lover!

LADY HAPPY. No, I was meditating of holy things.

MADAM MEDIATOR. Holy things! What holy things?

LADY HAPPY. Why, such holy things as the gods are.

MADAM MEDIATOR. By my truth, whether your contemplation be of gods or of men, you are become lean and pale since I was in the convent last.

Enter the princess.

PRINCESS. Come, my sweet mistress, shall we go to our sports and recreations?

MADAM MEDIATOR. Beshrew me,[147] Your Highness hath sported too much I fear.[148]

---

entrance—are not marked as separate scenes by Cavendish but seem to reflect one continuous action on stage.

[147] Curse you. A mild oath, "often humorous or playful" (*OED*).

[148] Madam Mediator's comment—that the princess has *sported* too much—is a double entendre. The verb "to sport" can mean "to amuse or entertain oneself," and thus Madam Mediator might simply be saying that the princess has already played around enough. But "to sport" can also mean "to engage in amorous behaviour or sexual activity" (*OED*), and thus Madam Mediator may be suggesting that the

PRINCESS. Why, Madam Mediator, say you so?

MADAM MEDIATOR. Because the Lady Happy looks not well; she is become pale and lean.[149]

PRINCESS. Madam Mediator, your eyes are become dim with time, for my sweet mistress appears with greater splendor than the god of light.[150]

MADAM MEDIATOR. For all you are a great princess, give me leave to tell you:
I am not so old nor yet so blind,
But that I see you are too kind.[151]

PRINCESS. Well, Madam Mediator, when we return from our recreations, I will ask your pardon for saying your eyes are dim, conditionally[152] you will ask pardon for saying my mistress looks not well.

Exeunt.

---

princess has been the cause of a more serious problem, raised in the next part of their exchange.

[149] Lady Happy's symptoms—she is described by Madam Mediator here as being *pale and lean* and, above, as *lean and pale*—seem to suggest she is suffering from greensickness or "virgin's disease," a common medical "disease" of young, unmarried women. Its symptoms included weakness, dietary disturbance, loss of weight, a lack of menstruation, and, as its name suggests, a change in skin color (a form of anemia that contributes to paleness). This diagnosis turned puberty and virginity into medical problems, the cure for which was marriage, sex, and, ultimately, pregnancy. See Helen King, *The Disease of Virgins: Green Sickness, Chlorosis, and the Problems of Puberty* (New York: Routledge, 2004).

[150] In addition to being the god of music, truth, and poetry, Apollo is also the god of sun and light; while he is usually depicted with a lyre, in Cavendish's frontispiece he is depicted with a scepter topped with a sun. See Introduction, 59, and Figure 1.

[151] Madam Mediator's description of the princess as *too kind* offers a number of interpretive possibilities. Most simply, she may mean that the princess is too nice, but—more pointedly—she may mean that the princess is too "affectionate" or that her relationship with Lady Happy is too "intimate" (*OED*). Madam Mediator's insistence that she is capable of seeing just what's what when it comes to the princess may also suggest that she has begun to suspect the princess is not all she seems to be, with *kind* referring to the princess's inner nature (*OED*).

[152] On the condition that.

The scene is opened, and there is presented a rock as in the sea, whereupon sits the princess and the Lady Happy, the princess as the sea god Neptune, the Lady Happy as a sea goddess.[153] The rest of the ladies sit somewhat lower, dressed like water nymphs. The princess begins to speak a speech in verse, and after her the Lady Happy makes her speech.

PRINCESS. I am the king of all the seas,
    All watery creatures do me please,
    Obey my power and command
    And bring me presents from the land;
    The waters open their floodgates[154]
    Where ships do pass, sent by the Fates,[155]
    Which Fates do yearly, as May dew,
    Send me a tribute from Peru,[156]

---

[153] Like the pastoral frolics that have just occurred, the following scene, which borrows from Stuart and Caroline court masques, draws on a dramatic tradition familiar to Cavendish.

[154] "A gate or gates that may be opened or closed, to admit or exclude water, *esp.* the water of a flood; *spec.* the lower gates of a lock" (*OED*).

[155] The three goddesses who control human destiny: Clotho, who spins the thread of every individual's life; Lacnesis, who measures out the thread of each person's life; and Atropos, who cuts the thread of life.

[156] It is impossible to know whether Cavendish had in mind any particular current event when she included these rather gruesome lines about Neptune's yearly "tribute" of ships and men *from Peru*, but several possibilities suggest themselves. During the sixteenth and seventeenth centuries, many ships returning to Spain and Portugal laden with treasure from their South American colonies were lost at sea, sunk by bad weather, pirates, or rival European powers. A series of disasters for ships carrying Peruvian treasure occurred in the 1650s, including the wreck of the *Capitana* in 1654 and the *Nuestra Señora de las Maravillas* in 1656. Other kinds of vessels were also lost, including courier ships like the *San Miguel Arcangel*, a dispatch ship sent by the count of Alba de Liste, viceroy of Peru, to Spain in 1659. This shipwreck is particularly interesting, because the *Arcangel* was not only carrying documents and sealed letters for Philip IV of Spain but also a significant amount of silver and gold—not usually transported on a small ship like the *Arcangel*—and because the courier ship had a brief encounter with several Royal Navy vessels while on its voyage to Spain. After stopping in Havana, the *Arcangel* had to avoid a British blockade in order to leave port; the small ship, carrying 120 passengers and eight crewmembers, made it as far as the Florida Keys, where it was hit by a tremendous storm with hurricane-force winds. News of the disaster reached Spain in July 1660. Of the 128 people onboard, only thirty-four survived, found stranded at Jupiter Inlet, in southwest Florida. J. A. Ruth, "1659: The Last Voyage of the Aviso *San Miguel Archangel*," *South American Explorer*, Summer 1997, 4-11.

From other nations besides,
Brought by their servants, winds and tides;
Ships fraught[157] and men to me they bring,
My watery kingdom lays them in;
Thus from the earth a tribute I
Receive, which shows my power thereby;
Besides, my kingdom's richer far
Than all the earth and every star.

LADY HAPPY. I feed the sun, which gives them light
And makes them shine in darkest night;
Moist vapor from my breast I give,
Which he sucks forth and makes him live,
Or else his fire would soon go out,
Grow dark, or burn the world throughout.

PRINCESS. What earthly creatures like to me
That hath such power and majesty?
My palaces are rocks of stone
And built by nature's hand alone;
No base, dissembling, cozening[158] art

Another event that Cavendish may have in mind here took place during the British blockade of Cadiz in September 1656. A Spanish treasure fleet, carrying the governor of Peru and his family, arrived without an escort of warships; the British blockaders attacked and captured one of the richly laden galleons, but three others sank, with most of their crew and all of their cargo lost. In the disaster, the governor of Peru, his wife, and his daughter were killed, his son taken prisoner by the English. The boy was "entertained" by Edward Montagu, General-at-Sea for the operation against Cadiz. An account of the disaster was published as *A True Narrative of the late Success . . . against the King of Spain's West-India Fleet in its return to Cadiz* (London, 1656).

Finally, Cavendish's reference to Peru is also topical in terms of contemporary drama. William Davenant's masque, *The Cruelty of the Spaniards in Peru*, had first been performed in 1657 (as a masque, it circumvented proscriptions against theatrical productions still in place during the Commonwealth period), and it was incorporated into his 1663 anthology stage play, *The Playhouse to Be Let*. This was followed by his *History of Sir Francis Drake*, set in colonial Peru, staged during the winter of 1658-59. The *Indian Queen*, a collaborative work by Sir Robert Howard and John Dryden, was performed in 1664; the play's principal characters include the Peruvian king Ynca and his daughter, Orazia, and the action includes the conquest of Peru by Moctezuma.

[157] "Of a vessel: Laden" (*OED*).

[158] Deceptive or cheating.

Do I employ in any part
In all my kingdom large and wide;[159]
Nature directs and doth provide
Me all provisions which I need
And cooks my meat on which I feed.

LADY HAPPY. My cabinets are oyster shells,
    In which I keep my orient pearls;[160]
    To open them I use the tide
    As keys to locks, which opens wide
    The oyster shells; then out I take
    Those orient pearls and crowns do make;
    And modest coral I do wear,
    Which blushes when it touches air;
    On silver waves I sit and sing,
    And then the fish lie listening;
    Then, sitting on a rocky stone,
    I comb my hair with fish's bone,
    The whilst Apollo, with his beams,
    Doth dry my hair from watery streams;
    His light doth glaze the water's face,
    Make the large sea my looking glass;
    So when I swim on water's high,
    I see myself as I glide by;
    But when the sun begins to burn,
    I back into my waters turn
    And dive unto the bottom low;
    Then on my head the waters flow
    In curled waves and circles round,
    And thus with waters am I crowned.

---

[159] Cavendish addresses herself to the ongoing philosophical debate between nature and art on many occasions, in particular taking the part of "Wise Nature," for "art is not onely gross in comparison to Nature, but, for the most part, deformed and defective" (*Observations upon Experimental Philosophy* [1666], 12-13).

[160] A pearl "from the seas around India, as distinguished fro those of less beauty found in European mussels; (hence, more generally) a brilliant or precious pearl" (*OED*).

PRINCESS. Besides, within the waters deep,
 In hollow rocks my court I keep;
 Of ambergris[161] my bed is made,
 Whereon my softer limbs are laid;
 There take I rest, and whilst I sleep,
 The sea doth guard and safe me keep
 From danger, and when I awake,
 A present of a ship doth make;
 No prince on earth hath more resort,
 Nor keeps more servants in his court;
 Of mermaids you're waited on,
 And mermen do attend upon
 My person—some are councilors,
 Which order all my great affairs
 Within my watery kingdom wide;
 They help to rule and so to guide
 The commonwealth and are by me
 Preferred[162] unto an high degree;
 Some judges are and magistrates,
 Decide each cause[163] and end debates,
 Others, commanders in the war,
 And some to governments prefer;
 Others are Neptune's priests, which pray
 And preach when is a holy day;
 And thus with method order I
 And govern all with majesty;
 I am sole monarch of the sea,
 And all therein belongs to me.

A sea nymph sings this following song.[164]

We watery nymphs rejoice and sing
About God Neptune, our sea's king,

---

[161] A waxy substance, from sperm whales, used in the making of perfume.
[162] Promoted.
[163] Legal question; "a matter before a court for decision" (*OED*).
[164] In the 1668 *Plays, Never before Printed*, each of the three stanzas of the sea nymph's song is numbered.

In sea-green habits[165] for to move
His godhead for to fall in love,

That with his trident[166] he doth stay
Rough foaming billows which obey,
And when in triumph he doth stride
His managed dolphin for to ride;

All his sea people to his wish,
From whale to herring, subject fish,
With acclamations do attend him
And pray more riches still to send him.

Exeunt.

The scene vanishes.

---

[165] Clothing; in a specialized sense, *habit* can also refer to "dress or attire characteristic of a particular rank, degree, profession, or function" (OED), which seems to be the sense of the *sea-green habits* here.

[166] A three-pronged spear associated with depictions of the god Neptune.

ACT 5, Scene 1

Enter the princess and the Lady Happy. The princess is in a man's apparel as [if] going to dance; they whisper some time, then the Lady Happy takes a ribbon from her arm and gives it to the princess, who gives her another instead of that[167] and kisses her hand. They go in and come presently out again with all the company to dance. The music plays, and after they have danced a little while, in comes Madam Mediator wringing her hands and spreading her arms and full of passion cries out.

MADAM MEDIATOR. Oh, ladies, ladies! You're all betrayed, undone, undone, for there is a man disguised in the convent— search and you'll find it.

They all skip from each other, as afraid of each other. Only the princess and the Lady Happy stand still together.

PRINCESS. You may make the search, Madam Mediator, but you will quit[168] me, I am sure.

MADAM MEDIATOR. By my faith, but I will not, for you are most to be suspected.

PRINCESS. But you say the man is disguised like a woman, and I am accoutered like a man.

MADAM MEDIATOR. Fiddle-faddle,[169] that is nothing to the purpose.

Enter an ambassador to the prince(ss).[170] The ambassador kneels, the prince bids him rise.

---

[167] The two exchange ribbons, as love-tokens. Such favors usually consisted of ribbons or a glove and were worn conspicuously as a sign of love.

[168] Acquit.

[169] Nonsense.

[170] In her stage directions, Cavendish for the first time identifies the princess as "prince." I've used the parentheses here to indicate the collapse of one identity into

PRINCE. What came you here for?

AMBASSADOR. May it please Your Highness, the lords of your council sent me to inform Your Highness that your subjects are so discontented at your absence that if Your Highness do not return into your kingdom soon, they'll enter this kingdom, by reason[171] they hear you are here, and some report as if Your Highness were restrained as prisoner.

PRINCE. So I am, but not by the state, but by this fair lady, who must be your sovereigness.

The ambassador kneels and kisses her hand.

PRINCE. But since I am discovered, go from me to the councilors of this state and inform them of my being here, as also the reason, and that I ask their leave I may marry this lady; otherwise, tell them I will have her by force of arms.

Exit ambassador.

MADAM MEDIATOR. Oh, the lord! I hope you will not bring an army to take away all the women, will you?

PRINCE. No, Madam Mediator, we will leave you behind us.

Exeunt.

ACT 5, Scene 2

Enter Madam Mediator, lamenting and crying with a handkerchief in her hand.

---

the other. Throughout the play, Cavendish has used the abbreviation *Princ.* in the speech headings, expanded in this edition to *Princess* and, from this point on, *Prince*.
[171] Because.

Written by my Lord Duke.[172]

MADAM MEDIATOR. Oh, gentlemen, that I never had been born! We're all undone and lost!

MONSIEUR ADVISER. Why, what's the matter?

MADAM MEDIATOR. Matter? Nay, I doubt there's too much matter.[173]

MONSIEUR ADVISER. How?

MADAM MEDIATOR. How? Never such a mistake. Why, we have taken[174] a man for a woman.

MONSIEUR ADVISER. Why, a man is for a woman.

MADAM MEDIATOR. Fiddle-faddle! I know that as well as you can tell me, but there was a young man dressed in woman's apparel and entered our convent, and the gods know what he hath done. He is mighty handsome, and that's a great temptation to virtue, but I hope all is well. But this wicked world will lay aspersion upon anything or nothing,[175] and therefore I doubt all my sweet young birds are undone, the gods comfort them.

---

[172] Once more the play includes material written by Cavendish's husband. For the pasted-on strip here, and for just how much the duke contributes to the play at this point, see Introduction, 78-80.

[173] When Monsieur Adviser asks, simply, what's wrong (*what's the matter*), Madam Mediator responds that she's afraid (*doubt*, to be in dread of or fearful of) there's been too much going on (*too much matter*)—perhaps with a double entendre, since the "princess" seems to have some extra "matter" (a penis) that a woman wouldn't have.

[174] Mistaken.

[175] Since the word "thing" could be used to refer to male genitals, Madam Mediator's worry here may be a sexual double entendre. Whether the convent has been invaded by a man (with a "thing") masquerading as a woman or a woman (with "no thing") masquerading as a man, it really won't make a difference to the damaging gossip about the young women in the convent.

MONSIEUR COURTLY. But could you never discover it? Nor have no hint he was a man?

MADAM MEDIATOR. No, truly, only once I saw him kiss the Lady Happy, and you know women's kisses are unnatural, and methought[176] they kissed with more alacrity[177] than women use, a kind of titillation,[178] and more vigorous.

MONSIEUR ADVISER. Why did you not then examine it?

MADAM MEDIATOR. Why, they would have said I was but an old jealous fool and laughed at me. But experience is a great matter; if the gods had not been merciful to me, he[179] might have fallen upon[180] me.

MONSIEUR COURTLY. Why, what if he had?

MADAM MEDIATOR. Nay, if he had, I care not, for I defy[181] the flesh as much as I renounce the devil and the pomp of this wicked world,[182] but if I could but have saved my young, sweet virgins, I would willingly have sacrificed my body for them, for we are not born for ourselves but for others.[183]

---

[176] It seemed to me.

[177] Willingness or readiness.

[178] Excitement or stimulation.

[179] The prince.

[180] "To come with violence; to make an attack" or to "assault" (OED), with a sexual suggestion here, given Madam Mediator's response, below, that she would have sacrificed her own body if it meant saving the "sweet virgins" in the convent.

[181] Reject or renounce.

[182] In the service of the "Publick Baptism of Infants to be used in the Church," the priest asks godfathers and godmothers, "Dost thou, in the name of this child, renounce the devil and all his works, the vain pomp and glory of the world. . . ." *The Book of Common Prayer, and Administration of the Sacraments, and Other Rites and Ceremonies of the Church. . . .* (Cambridge: John Baskerville, 1662).

[183] Cavendish might have in mind the apostle Paul's "For we preach not our selves, but Christ Jesus the Lord, and our selves your servants for Jesus sake" (2 Corinthians 4:5) or, more closely, the Latin motto *non nobis, sed omnibus* ("not for us, but for everyone"), from Cicero's *De officiis*, "humans have been created for the sake of others of their kind, indeed, to benefit each other as much as possible." In either

MONSIEUR ADVISER. 'Tis piously said, truly, lovingly and kindly.

MADAM MEDIATOR. Nay, I have read the *Practice of Piety*;[184] but further, they say he is a foreign prince and, they say, they're very hot.[185]

MONSIEUR COURTLY. Why, you are Madam Mediator, you must mediate and make a friendship.

MADAM MEDIATOR. 'Od's body,[186] what do you talk of mediation? I doubt[187] they are too good friends. Well, this will be news for

---

case a wonderful sentiment for Madam Mediator, who says she would have sacrificed herself to a man for the sake of the young women in the Convent of Pleasure.

[184] Lewis Bayly, bishop of Bangor's *The Practice of Piety: Directing a Christian how to walk, that he may please God* was an extremely popular devotional work. Since Bayly was an ardent Puritan and Cavendish herself went into exile with Queen Henrietta Maria's court during the English Civil Wars, her husband a general leading royalist forces against the Puritan army, Madam Mediator's reference to this Puritan-authored book undoubtedly contributes a bit more humor to her already humorous character. Although the date of the first publication of *The Practice of Piety* is unknown, it had run through many editions by the time Cavendish published *The Convent of Pleasure*. A 1612 edition has been identified as the second edition, and the 1636 edition (n.p.) is noted as the third. Subsequent editions are dated 1637 (London), 1640 (London), 1642 (Amsterdam), 1643 (London), 1647 (London), 1648 (n.p.), 1648 (Rotterdam), 1649 (Edinburgh), 1654 (London), 1656 (London), 1660 (Delft), 1661 (London), 1663 (London), 1665 (London), and 1668 (London), the same year that *Plays, Never before Printed* was published. (By 1821 *The Practice of Piety* had gone through 74 editions, and several modern editions are currently in print.)

Interestingly, Ben Jonson's last comedy, *The Magnetick Lady, or Humours Reconcil'd*, first published in the 1640 edition of his *Works*, contains a similar reference to Bayly's book (4.4.39)—in Jonson's play, *The Practice of Piety* has been used as book upon which Mistress Keep, a nurse to Mistress Placentia, has sworn an oath. Like *The Convent of Pleasure*, Jonson's *Magnetic Lady* dramatizes a world turned upside-down— Lady Loadstone is in command of her own all-female household, but as Jonson depicts it, the household is out of control. In the end, all is restored to its "natural" order: men are back in control, Lady Magnetic and her niece "suitably" married to Captain Ironside, a soldier, and Mr. Compass, "a scholar matahematick."

[185] "Full of or characterized by sexual desire, lustful; sexually aroused" (*OED*); in the medical and psychological system of the four humors, the choleric humor is hot and dry, associated with fire, and its heat excites the passions.

[186] An oath: "by God's body."

[187] I have no doubt.

court, town, and country, in private letters, in the *Gazette*,[188] and in abominable ballads,[189] before it be long, and jeered to death by the pretending wits.[190] But, good gentlemen, keep this as a secret and let not me be the author, for you will hear abundantly of it before it be long.

MONSIEUR ADVISER. But, Madam Mediator, this is no secret. It is known all the town over, and the state is preparing to entertain the prince.

MADAM MEDIATOR. Lord! To see how ill news will fly so soon abroad!

MONSIEUR COURTLY. Ill news indeed for us wooers.

MONSIEUR ADVISER. We only wooed in imagination but not in reality.

MADAM MEDIATOR. But you all had hopes.

MONSIEUR ADVISER. We had so, but she only has the fruition,[191] for it is said the prince and she are agreed to marry, and the state is so willing as they account it an honor and hope shall reap much advantage by the match.

---

[188] The *Gazette* was first published on 7 November 1665 as *The Oxford Gazette*, since Charles II had moved his court to Oxford in order to avoid the plague. When the court returned to London in 1666, the paper became *The London Gazette*. While the setting for *The Covent of Pleasure* has not been clearly delineated by Cavendish, with this reference we get a sense of a contemporary London connection. The paper is still publishing today; see *The Gazette*, https://www.thegazette.co.uk/.

[189] "A popular, usually narrative, song, *spec.* one celebrating or scurrilously attacking persons or institutions. In the 17th and 18th centuries such songs were often printed as broadsheets, without accompanying music" (*OED*).

[190] Young men of fashion who pride themselves on being clever. Madam Mediator is concerned here about would-be or pretentious (*pretending*) young men, joining in the general ridiculing of the Convent of Pleasure and its inhabitants.

[191] Fulfillment.

MADAM MEDIATOR. Yes, yes, but there is an old and true saying, "There's much between the cup and the lip."[192]

Exeunt.

ACT 5, Scene 3

Enter the prince as bridegroom and the Lady Happy as bride, hand in hand under a canopy born over their heads by men. The magistrates march before, then the oboes, and then the bridal guests, as coming from the church where they were married.

All the company bids them joy; they[193] thank them.

MADAM MEDIATOR. Although Your Highness will not stay to feast with your guests, pray dance before you go.

PRINCE. We will both dance and feast before we go; come, madam, let us dance to please Madam Mediator.

The prince and princess[194] dance.

PRINCE. Now, noble friends, dance you, and the princess and I will rest ourselves.

After they have danced, the Lady Happy, as now princess, speaks to the Lady Virtue.

LADY HAPPY. Lady Virtue, I perceive you keep Mimic[195] still.

LADY HAPPY *to the Prince.* Sir, this is the Mimic I told you of.

---

[192] A proverbial expression. See Ray, *A Collection of English Proverbs*, 121. The proverb may be more familiar as "There's many a slip between cup and lip."

[193] The newly married couple.

[194] In the stage direction, Cavendish gives Lady Happy her new title, *princess*.

[195] Mimic, Lady Virtue's household "fool," was a character in *The Bridals*. Lady Virtue and Mimic must be among the "bridal guests" noted in the stage directions.

LADY HAPPY *to Mimic.* Mimic, will you leave your lady and go with me?

MIMIC. I am a married man and have married my lady's maid, Nan, and she will keep me at home do what I can. But you've now a mimic of your own, for the prince has imitated a woman.

LADY HAPPY. What, you rogue, do you call me a fool?

MIMIC. Not I, please, Your Highness, unless all women be fools.

PRINCE. Is your wife a fool?

MIMIC. Man and wife, 'tis said, makes but one fool.[196]

He kneels to the prince.

MIMIC. I have a humble petition to Your Highness.

PRINCE. Rise. What petition is that?

MIMIC. That Your Highness would be pleased to divide the convent in two equal parts, one for fools, and th'other for married men, as madmen.[197]

PRINCE. I'll divide it for virgins and widows.

MIMIC. That will prove a Convent of Pleasure indeed, but they will never agree, especially if there be some disguised prince amongst them. But you had better bestow it on old, decrepit, and bed-rid matrons, and then it may be called the Convent of Charity, if it cannot possibly be named the Convent of Chastity.

---

[196] Though Mimic implies ("'tis said") this is a recognized proverb, it is not italicized as the earlier proverbial expressions were (see n. 73 and n. 192), nor is this expression found in Ray's *Collection of English Proverbs*.

[197] Mimic seems to suggest that the Convent of Pleasure should be transformed into an asylum for the mentally ill—for *fools* in the now obsolete sense of those who are born with mental handicaps, and *married men*, who must be also be insane.

PRINCE. Well, to show my charity and to keep your wife's chastity, I'll bestow my bounty in a present, on the condition you speak the epilogue. Come, noble friends, let us feast before we part.

Exeunt.

Mimic solus.

MIMIC. An epilogue says he, the devil[198] an epilogue have I. Let me study.

He questions and answers himself.

I have it, I have it. No, faith, I have it not. I lie, I have it! I say, I have it not. Fie,[199] Mimic, will you lie? Yes, Mimic, I will lie, if it be my pleasure. But I say, it is gone. What is gone? The epilogue. When had you it? I never had it. Then you did not lose it. That is all one,[200] but I must speak it, although I never had it. How can you speak it and never had it? I, marry,[201] that's the question; but words are nothing, and then an epilogue is nothing, and so I may speak nothing: then nothing be my speech.

He speaks the epilogue.

MIMIC. Noble spectators by this candlelight,
I know not what to say, but bid, "Good night";
I dare not beg applause—our poetess then
Will be enraged and kill me with her pen,
For she is careless and is void of fear;
If you dislike her play, she doth not care,
But I shall weep, my inward grief shall show

---

[198] Used as "an expression of impatience, irritation, . . . or vexation" (*OED*).

[199] "An exclamation expressing . . . disgust or indignant reproach" (*OED*).

[200] That is one and the same thing—that is, it doesn't matter whether he had it and lost it or never had it, it's all the same.

[201] A variation of "Mary," invoking the Virgin Mary, used as an interjection to express surprise or outrage or simply to give emphasis; "Often in response to a question, expressing surprise or indignation that it should be asked" (*OED*).

Through floods of tears that through my eyes will flow,
And so, poor Mimic, he for sorrow die
And then through pity you may chance to cry;
But, if you please, you may a cordial[202] give,
Made up with praise, and so he long may live.

Finis

---

[202] A stimulating or restorative beverage, usually alcoholic.

The Actors' Names[203]

Three gentlemen
Lady Happy
Madam Mediator
Monsieur Take-pleasure and Dick, his man
Monsieur Facil
Monsieur Adviser
Monsieur Courtly
Lady Amorous
Lady Virtue
The princess
Two mean women
A lady and her maid
Two ladies
A distracted lady and her maid
A citizen's wife
Two ancient ladies
A gentleman and a young lady
A shepherd
Sea nymphs
An ambassador

---

[203] The list of *dramatis personae* at the end of the play is oddly selective—it does not include Lady Happy's attendant, who speaks in 1.1, nor the twenty young ladies who join Lady Happy in her Convent of Pleasure, though they have lines in 2.2., and they are mentioned in the stage directions for 3.1. Several of the characters in the scenes of the third-act play-within-a-play are listed here as characters, but presumably these "characters" are played by the young women inside the convent. Notably, Mimic is also absent from this list.

Select Bibliography

Primary Sources

Original Collections of Plays Published by Margaret Cavendish

Cavendish, Margaret. *Playes*. London, 1662.

———. *Plays, Never before Printed*. London, 1668.

Modern Editions of Margaret Cavendish's *The Convent of Pleasure*

Cavendish, Margaret. *The Convent of Pleasure*. A Celebration of Women Writers. Edited by Mary Mark Ockerbloom. http://digital.library.upenn.edu/women/.

———. *The Convent of Pleasure*. In *The Broadview Anthology of British Literature*, 2nd ed. Vol. 3, *The Restoration and Eighteenth Century*. Edited by Joseph Black et al., 13-31. Peterborough, ON [Canada]: Broadview Press, 2012.

———. *The Convent of Pleasure: A Comedy*. In *The Convent of Pleasure and Other Plays*. Edited by Anne Shaver, 218-47. Baltimore: Johns Hopkins University Press, 1999.

———. *The Convent of Pleasure: A Comedy*. In *Paper Bodies: A Margaret Cavendish Reader*. Edited by Sylvia Bowerbank and Sara Mendelson, 97-135. Broadview Literary Texts. Peterborough, ON [Canada]: Broadview Press, 1999.

———. *The Convent of Pleasure*. In *Three Seventeenth-Century Plays on Women and Performance: John Fletcher's "The Wild-Goose Chase," James*

Shirley's "The Bird in a Cage," and Margaret Cavendish's "The Convent of Pleasure." Edited by Hero Chalmers, Julie Sanders, and Sophie Tomlinson, 267-308. The Revels Plays Companion Library. Manchester: Manchester University Press, 2006.

————. *The Convent of Pleasure.* In *Women's Writing of the Early Modern Period, 1588–1688.* Edited by Stephanie Hodgson-Wright, 257-87. New York: Columbia University Press, 2002.

————. *The Convent of Pleasure: A Comedy, Written by the Thrice Noble, Illustrious, and Excellent Princesse, the Duchess of Newcastle.* Edited by Jennifer Rowsell. Oxford: Seventeenth Century Press, 1995.

Additional Primary Sources

Cavendish, Margraet. *The Blazing World and Other Writings.* Edited by Kate Lilley. New York: Penguin Books, 1994.

————. *The Life of the thrice Noble, High and Puissant Prince William Cavendishe, Duke, Marquess, and Earl of Newcastle. . . .* London, 1667. In *The Life of William Cavendish, Duke of Newcastle, . . . by Margaret, Duchess of Newcastle.* Edited by C. H. Firth, 1-147. 2nd rev. ed. New York: E. P. Dutton, 1907.

————. *A True Relation of my Birth, Breeding and Life.* London, 1656. In Firth, ed., *The Life of William Cavendish*, 155-78.

Cavendish, William, ed. *Letters and Poems in Honour of the Incomparable Princess, Margaret, Dutchess of Newcastle.* London, 1676.

Cerasano, S. P., and Marion Wynne-Davies, eds. *Renaissance Drama by Women: Texts and Documents.* New York: Routledge, 1996.

Evelyn, John. *The Diary of John Evelyn.* Vol. 2. Edited by William Bray. London: George Bell, 1889.

Evelyn, Mary. "Letters of Mrs. Evelyn." In *The Diary and Correspondence of John Evelyn.* Vol. 4. Edited by William Bray, 3-43. London: Henry Colburn, 1857.

Huygens, Constijn. *Die Briefwisseling van Constantijn Huygens, 1608-1687.* 6 vols. Edited by J. A. Worp. The Hague: Martinus Nijhoff, 1911-16. Reprinted Huygens ING, 2010, http://resources.huygens.knaw.nl/briefwisseling-constantijnhuygens.

Osborne, Dorothy. *The Letters of Dorothy Osborne to Sir William Temple.* Edited by Edward A. Parry. New York: E. P. Dutton, 1914,

Pepys, Samuel. *The Diary of Samuel Pepys . . . .* 8 vols. Edited by Henry B. Wheatley. New York: Macmillan, 1892-96.

Prynne, William. *Histrio-mastix: The Players Scourge, or, Actors Tragedie, Divided into Two Parts. . . .* London, 1633.

Thompson, Edward M. *Correspondence of the Family of Hatton . . . 1607-1704.* Camden Society n. s., vol. 22. London: Camden Society, 1878.

Select Secondary Sources

Complete bibliographical information for all sources consulted in this edition is provided in the notes. Included here are biographies of Margaret Cavendish, works that focus on women and drama in early-modern England, and critical studies of Margaret Cavendish's plays, in particular of *The Convent of Pleasure.*

Andrea, Bernadette. "Coming Out in Margaret Cavendish's Closet Dramas." *In-between* 9 (2000): 219-41.

Baker-Putt, Alyce R. "Redefining the Female Self through Female Communities: Margaret Cavendish's *The Female Academy*, *The Convent of Pleasure*, and *Bell in Campo.*" *Shakespeare and Renaissance Association of West Virginia* 29 (2006): 37-46.

Bennett, Alexandra G. "Fantastic Realism: Margaret Cavendish and the Possibilities of Drama." In Cottegnies and Weitz, *Authorial Conquests*, 179-94.

————. "Happy Families and Learned Ladies: Margaret Cavendish, William Cavendish, and Their Onstage Academy Debate." *Early Modern Literary Studies: A Journal of Sixteenth- and Seventeenth-Century English Literature* Special Issue 14 (2004): 3.1-14. http://extra.shu.ac.uk/cmls/si-14/bennhapp.html.

Billing, Valerie. "'Treble marriage': Margaret Cavendish, William Newcastle, and Collaborative Authorship Author(s)." *Journal for Early Modern Cultural Studies* 11, no. 2 (2011): 94-122.

Bonin, Erin Lang. "Margaret Cavendish's Dramatic Utopias and the Politics of Gender." *Studies in English Literature, 1500-1900* 40, no. 2 (2000): 339-54.

Britland, Karen. *Drama at the Courts of Henrietta Maria.* New York: Cambridge University Press, 2006.

Brown, Pamela, and Peter Parolin, eds. *Women Players in England, 1500–1650: Beyond the All-Male Stage.* Studies in Performance and Early Modern Drama. Burlington, VT: Ashgate Publishing, 2005.

Bullard, Rebecca. "Gatherings in Exile: Interpreting the Bibliographical Structure of *Natures Pictures Drawn by Fancies Pencil to the Life* (1656)." *English Studies* 92, no. 7 (2011): 786-805.

Cerasano, S. P., and Marion Wynne-Davies, eds. *Readings in Renaissance Women's Drama: Criticism, History, and Performance, 1594-1998.* New York: Routledge, 1998.

Chalmers, Hero. "'The Gallery of Heroick Women': Margaret Cavendish and the Images of the Author." In *Royalist Women Writers, 1650-1680,* 16–55. Oxford English Monographs. New York: Oxford University Press, 2004.

————. "The Politics of Feminine Retreat in Margaret Cavendish's *The Female Academy* and *The Convent of Pleasure.*" *Women's Writing* 6, no. 1 (1999): 81-94.

Clucas, Stephen, ed. *A Princely Brave Woman: Essays on Margaret Cavendish, Duchess of Newcastle.* Burlington, VT: Ashgate Publishing, 2003.

Cottegnies, Line. "Gender and Cross-dressing in the Seventeenth Century: Margaret Cavendish Reads Shakespeare." *Testi e Linguaggi* 7 (2013): 257-266.

Cottegnies, Line, and Nancy Weitz, eds. *Authorial Conquests: Essays on Genre in the Writing of Margaret Cavendish.* Madison, NJ: Fairleigh Dickinson University Press, 2003.

Cotton, Nancy. *Women Playwrights in England, c. 1363-1750.* Lewisburg, PA: Bucknell University Press, 1980.

Crawford, Julie. "Convents and Pleasures: Margaret Cavendish and the Drama of Property." *Renaissance Drama* 32 (2003): 177-223.

Cuder-Dominguez, Pilar. "Re-Crafting the Heroic, Constructing a Female Hero: Margaret Cavendish and Aphra Behn." *SEDERI: Yearbook of the Spanish and Portuguese Society for English Renaissance* 17 (2007): 27-45.

———. *Stuart Women Playwrights, 1613-1713.* Studies in Performance and Early Modern Drama. Burlington, VT: Ashgate Publishing, 2010.

Dash, Irene G. "Single-Sex Retreats in Two Early Modern Drams: *Love's Labor's Lost* and *The Convent of Pleasure." Shakespeare Quarterly* 47, no. 4 (1996): 387-95.

Findlay, Alison. *Playing Spaces in Early Women's Drama.* New York: Cambridge University Press, 2006.

Findlay, Alison, Gweno Williams, and Stephanie J. Hodgson-Wright. "'The play is ready to be acted': Women and Dramatic Production, 1570-1670." *Women's Writing* 6, no. 1 (1999): 129-48.

Findlay, Alison, Stephanie Hodgson-Wright, and Gweno Williams, eds. *Women and Dramatic Production, 1550-1700.* Longman Medieval and Renaissance Library. New York: Routledge, 2000.

Finke, Laurie A. *Women's Writing in English: Medieval England*. Women's Writing in English. New York: Longman, 1999.

Fitzmaurice, James. "Cavendish, Margaret, duchess of Newcastle upon Tyne (1623?-1673)." *Oxford Dictionary of National Biography* [online]. Oxford: Oxford University Press, 2004-. Article published 2004. http://oxforddnb.com.

———. "Fancy and the Family: Self-Characterizations of Margaret Cavendish." *Huntington Library Quarterly* 53 (1990): 198-209.

———. "Margaret Cavendish on Her Own Writing: Evidence from Revision and Handmade Correction." *Papers of the Bibliographical Society of America* 85, no. 3 (1991): 297-307.

Grant, Douglas. *Margaret the First: A Biography of Margaret Cavendish, Duchess of Newcastle, 1623-1673*. London: Rupert Hart-Davis, 1957.

Greenstadt, Amy. "Margaret's Beard." *Early Modern Women: An Interdisciplinary Journal* 5 (2010): 171-82.

Hiscock, Andrew. "'Here's No Design, No Plot, nor Any Ground': The Drama of Margaret Cavendish and the Disorderly Woman." *Women's Writing* 4, no. 3 (1997): 401-20.

Holmesland, Odvaar. "*The Convent of Pleasure* (1668), Cross-gendering Negotiation." In *Utopian Negotiation: Aphra Behn and Margaret Cavendish*, 111-43. Syracuse, NY: Syracuse University Press, 2013.

Howe, Elizabeth. *The First English Actresses: Women and Drama, 1660-1700*. New York: Cambridge University Press, 1992.

Jagodzinski. Cecile M. *Privacy and Print: Reading and Writing in Seventeenth-Century England*. Charlottesville: University Press of Virginia, 1999.

Jankowski, Theodora A. "Critiquing the Sexual Economies of Marriage." In *The History of British Women's Writing*, vol. 3. *1610-1690*. Edited by Mihoko Suzuki, 221-37. New York: Palgrave Macmillan, 2011.

————. *Pure Resistance: Queer Virginity in Early Modern English Drama.* Philadelphia: University of Pennsylvania Press, 2000.

————. "Pure Resistance: Queer(y)ing Virginity in William Shakespeare's *Measure for Measure* and Margaret Cavendish's *The Convent of Pleasure.*" *Shakespeare Studies* 26 (1998): 218-55.

Jansen, Sharon L. *Reading Women's Worlds from Christine de Pizan to Doris Lessing: A Guide to Six Centuries of Women Writers Imagining Rooms of Their Own.* New York: Palgrave Macmillan, 2011.

Jones, Kathleen. *A Glorious Fame: The Life of Margaret Cavendish, Duchess of Newcastle, 1623-1673.* London: Bloomsbury Publishing, 1988.

Kellett, Katherine R. "Performance, Performativity, and Identity in Margaret Cavendish's *The Convent of Pleasure.*" *Studies in English Literature, 1500-1900* 48, no. 2 (2008): 419-42.

Kelly, Erna. "Playing with Religion: Convents, Cloisters, Martyrdom, and Vows." *Early Modern Literary Studies: A Journal of Sixteenth- and Seventeenth-Century English Literature* Special Issue 14 (2004): 4.1-24. http://extra.shu.ac.uk/emls/si-14/kellplay.html.

Liebert, Elisabeth. "'In Spight of the Criticks': Generic Complexity in Cavendish's *Convent.*" *Restoration and 18th Century Theatre Research* 25, no. 2 (2010): 35-47, 77.

Masten, Jeffrey. "Material Cavendish: Paper, Performance, 'Sociable Virginity.'" *Modern Language Quarterly* 65, no. 1 (2004): 49–68.

————. *Textual Intercourse: Collaboration, Authorship, and Sexualities in Renaissance Drama.* Cambridge Studies in Renaissance Literature and Culture. New York: Cambridge University Press, 1997.

McManus, Clare. *Women on the Renaissance Stage: Anna of Denmark and Female Masquing in the Stuart Court, 1590-1619.* Manchester, UK: Manchester University Press, 2002.

Mendelson, Sara. "Playing Games with Gender and Genre: The Dramatic Self-Fashioning of Margaret Cavendish." In Cottegnies and Weitz, *Authorial Conquests*, 195-212.

Mosher, Joyce Devlin. "Female Spectacle as Liberation in Margaret Cavendish's Plays." *Early Modern Literary Studies: A Journal of Sixteenth- and Seventeenth-Century English Literature* 11, no. 1 (2005): 7.1-28. http://extra.shu.ac.uk/emls/11-1/moshcave.htm.

Normington, Katie. *Gender and Medieval Drama*. Gender in the Middle Ages. Cambridge, UK: D. S. Brewer, 2004.

Orgel, Stephen. *Impersonations: The Performance of Gender in Shakespeare's England*. New York: Cambridge University Press, 1996.

Payne, Linda R. "Dramatic Dreamscape: Women's Dreams and Utopian Vision in the Works of Margaret Cavendish, Duchess of Newcastle." In *Curtain Calls: British and American Women and the Theater, 1660-1820*. Edited by Mary Anne Schofield and Cecilia Macheski, 18-33. Athens: Ohio University Press, 1991.

Pearson, Jacqueline. "'Women May Discourse . . . as Well as Men': Speaking and Silent Women in the Plays of Margaret Cavendish, Duchess of Newcastle." *Tulsa Studies in Women's Literature* 4, no. 1 (1985): 33-45.

Pedersen, Tara. "'We shall discover our Selves': Practicing the Mermaid's Law in Margaret Cavendish's *The Convent of Pleasure*." *Early Modern Women* 5 (2010): 111-135.

Poole, William. "Margaret Cavendish's Books in New College, and around Oxford." *New College Notes* 6 (2015): 1-8. http://www.new.ox.ac.uk/-ncnotes.

Raber, Karen. *Dramatic Difference: Gender, Class, and Genre in the Early Modern Closet Drama*. Newark: University of Delaware Press, 2001.

———. "'Our Wits Joined as in Matrimony': Margaret Cavendish's *Playes* and the Drama of Authority." *English Literary Renaissance* 28, no. 3 (1998): 464-93.

Romack, Katherine, and James Fitzmaurice, eds. *Cavendish and Shakespeare, Interconnections*. Burlington, VT: Ashgate Publishing, 2006.

Schabert, Ina. "The Theatre in the Head: Performances of the Self, by the Self, for the Self." In *Solo Performances: Staging the Early Modern Self in England*. Edited by Ute Berns, 33-48. Internationale Forschungen Zur Allgemeinen Und Vergleichende. New York: Editions Rodopi, 2010.

Shaver, Anne. "Agency and Marriage in the Fictions of Lady Mary Wroth and Margaret Cavendish, Duchess of Newcastle." In *Pilgrimage for Love: Essays in Early Modern Literature in Honor of Josephine A. Roberts*, 177-90. Edited by Sigrid King and Josephine A. Roberts. Medieval & Renaissance Texts & Studies. Tempe: Arizona Center for Medieval and Renaissance Studies, 1999.

Sierra, Horacio. "Convents as Feminist Utopias: Margaret Cavendish's *The Convent of Pleasure* and the Potential of Closeted Dramas and Communities. *Women's Studies: An Interdisciplinary Journal* 38, no. 6 (2009): 647-669.

Straznicky, Marta. *Privacy, Playreading, and Women's Closet Drama, 1550–1700*. New York: Cambridge University Press, 2004.

———. "Reading the Stage: Margaret Cavendish and Commonwealth Closet Drama." *Criticism* 37, no. 3 (1995): 355-90.

Tomlinson, Sophie. *Women on Stage in Stuart Drama*. New York: Cambridge University Press, 2005.

Venet, Gisele. "Margaret Cavendish's Dramas: An Aesthetic of Fragmentation." In Cottegnies and Weitz, *Authorial Conquests*, 213-28.

Whitaker, Katie. *Mad Madge: The Extraordinary life of Margaret Cavendish, Duchess of Newcastle, the First Woman to Live by her Pen*. New York: Basic Books, 2002.

Wiseman, Susan. *Drama and Politics in the English Civil War*. New York, Cambridge University Press, 1998.

Wood, Tanya. "Margaret Cavendish, Duchess of Newcastle, *The Convent of Pleasure* (1668), Ending Revised by Her Husband, the Duke of Newcastle." In *Reading Early Modern Women: An Anthology of Texts in Manuscript and Print, 1550-1700*. Edited by Helen Ostovich and Elizabeth Sauer, 435-37. New York: Routledge, 2004.

Woolf, Virginia. *The Common Reader, First Series*. 1925. Reprint, New York: Houghton Mifflin / Mariner Books, 2002.

———. *A Room of One's Own*. 1929. Reprint, New York: Harcourt / Harvest Edition, 1989.

Wynne-Davies, "The Theater." In *The History of British Women's Writing*, vol. 2, *1500-1610*. Edited by Caroline Bicks and Jennifer Summit, 175-95. New York: Palgrave Macmillan, 2010.

Suggestions for Further Reading

Listed here are a few key resources for readers who may be interested in further discussion of Cavendish's philosophical, theological, scientific, and political work, as well as her writing in other genres, including prose, poetry, biography, autobiographical narrative, and letters.

Battigelli, Anna. *Margaret Cavendish and the Exiles of the Mind*. Studies in the English Renaissance. Lexington: University of Kentucky Press, 1998.

Broad, Jacqueline. "Margaret Cavendish." In *Women Philosophers of the Seventeenth Century*, 35–64. New York: Cambridge University Press, 2003.

Broad, Jacqueline, and Karen Green. "Margaret Cavendish, Duchess of Newcastle." In *A History of Women's Political Thought in Europe, 1400–1700*, 199–224. New York: Cambridge University Press, 2009.

Clucas, Stephen, ed. *A Princely Brave Woman: Essays on Margaret Cavendish, Duchess of Newcastle*. Burlington, VT: Ashgate Publishing, 2003.

Cunning, David. "Margaret Lucas Cavendish." In *The Stanford Encyclopedia of Philosophy* [online]. Stanford University, 1997-. Article published 24 May 2012. http://plato.stanford.edu/archives/sum2012/entries/margaret-cavendish/.

Dodds, Lara. *The Literary Invention of Margaret Cavendish*. Pittsburgh, PA: Duquesne University Press, 2013.

James, Susan, ed. *Margaret Cavendish: Political Writings*. Cambridge Texts in the History of Political Thought. New York: Cambridge University Press, 2003.

Larson, Katherine R. *Early Modern Women in Conversation*. New York: Palgrave Macmillan, 2011.

Malcolmson, Cristina. *Studies of Skin Color in the Early Royal Society: Boyle, Cavendish, and Swift*. Literary and Scientific Cultures of Early Modernity. Burlington, VT: Ashgate Publishing, 2013.

O'Neill, Eileen. "Early Modern Women Philosophers and the History of Philosophy." *Hypatia* 20 (2005): 185-97.

Rees, Emma L. E. *Margaret Cavendish: Gender, Genre, Exile*. New York: Manchester University Press, 2003

Sarasohn, Lisa T. *The Natural Philosophy of Margaret Cavendish: Reason and Fancy during the Scientific Revolution*. 2010.

Siegfried, Brandie R. and Lisa T. Sarsohn, eds. *God and Nature in the Thought of Margaret Cavendish*. Burlington, VT: Ashgate Publishing, 2014.

Weise, Wendy S. "Recent Studies in Margaret Cavendish, Duchess of Newcastle (2001-2010)." *English Literary Renaissance* 42, no. 1 (2012): 146-76.

Appendix

A Brief Chronology of Margaret Cavendish's Published Work

This list includes the various names under which Margaret Cavendish published her work as well as each book's printer and bookseller as specified on title pages. It also includes all editions and reissues.

Poems, and Fancies, "written by the Right Honourable, the Lady Margaret Countess of Newcastle." London, 1653. Printed by T[homas] R[ycroft] for J[ohn] Martin and J[ames] Allestrye "at the Bell in Saint Pauls Church Yard."[1]

Philosophicall Fancies, "written by the Right Honourable, the Lady New-castle." London, 1653. Printed by Tho[mas] R[y]croft for J[ohn] Martin and J[ames] Allestrye "at the Bell in St. Pauls Church-yard."

The Worlds Olio, "written by the Right Honorable, the Lady Margaret Newcastle." London, 1655. Printed for J[ohn] Martin and J[ames] Allestrye "at the Bell in St. Pauls Church-Yard."

The Philosophical and Physical Opinions, "written by her Excellency, the Lady Marchionesse of Newcastle." London, 1655. Printed for J[ohn] Martin and J[ames] Allestrye "at the Bell in St. Pauls Church-Yard."

---

[1] Cameron Kroetsch notes the existence of at least one different title page, this one omitting the reference to "countess" and simply attributing the book's authorship to "the Right Honourable, the Lady Newcastle." Kroetsch, "List of Margaret Cavendish's Texts, Printers, and Booksellers (1653-1675)," *Digital Cavendish Project* (2013), http://www.digitalcavendish.org/texts-printers-booksellers/.

Natures Pictures Drawn by Fancies Pencil to the Life. In This Volume There are Several Feigned Stories of Natural Descriptions, as Comical, Tragical, and Tragi-Comical, Poetical, Romancical, Philosophical, and Historical, Both in Prose and Verse, Some All Verse, Some All Prose, Some Mixt, Partly Prose, and Partly Verse. Also, There Are Some Morals, and Some Dialogues, But They Are as the Advantage Loaves of Bread to a Bakers Dozen, and a True Story at the Latter End, Wherein There is no Feignings, "written by the Thrice Noble, Illustrious, and Excellent Princess, the Lady Marchioness of Newcastle." London, 1656. Printed for J[ohn] Martin, and J[ames] Allestrye "at the Bell in Saint Paul's Church-yard." [2]

Playes, "written by the Thrice Noble, Illustrious and Excellent Princess, the Lady Marchioness of Newcastle." London, 1662. Printed by A[lice] Warren for John Mart[i]n, James Allestry[e], and Tho[mas] Dicas "at the Bell in Saint Pauls Church Yard."

Orations of Divers Sorts, Accommodated to Divers Places, "written by the Thrice Noble, Illustrious, and Excellent Princess, the Lady Marchioness of Newcastle." London, 1662. [3]

The Philosophical and Physical Opinions, written by "the Thrice Noble, Illustrious, and Excellent Princess, the Lady Marchioness of Newcastle." 2nd ed. London, 1663. Printed by William Wilson. [4]

CCXI Sociable Letters, written by "the Thrice Noble, Illustrious, and Excellent Princess, the Lady Marchioness of Newcastle." London, 1664. Printed by William Wilson.

---

[2] The title pages of *The Worlds Olio*, *Philosophical and Physical Opinions*, and *Natures Pictures* list no printer, but Kroetsch suggests that the books were probably printed by Thomas Rycoft.

[3] Although the title page does not list a printer, Kroetsch indicates that the printer was William Wilson.

[4] According to Kroetsch (n15), "After 1662 the name of the bookseller does not appear on Cavendish's title pages. Since the remaining printers were not listed as being booksellers, it is possible that Allestrye, Martin, and Dicas continued to sell all of her books, or that at least Allestrye and/or Martin did. . . . Whitaker [*Mad Madge*] suggests that Margaret, at least by the time she is printing with Anne Maxwell, does not have the need for a large firm of booksellers, and arranges for printing and selling on her own (310)."

Poems and Phancies, "written by the Thrice Noble, Illustrious, and Excellent Princess the Lady Marchioness of Newcastle." 2nd ed., "much altered and corrected." London, 1664. Printed by William Wilson.

Philosophical Letters, or, Modest Reflections upon Some Opinions in Natural Philosophy, Maintained by Several Famous and Learned Authors of this Age, Expressed by Way of Letters, written by "the Thrice Noble, Illustrious, and Excellent Princess, the Lady Marchioness of Newcastle." London, 1664.[5]

Observations upon Experimental Philosophy, to Which is Added "The Description of a New Blazing World," written by "the Thrice Noble, Illustrious, and Excellent Princesse, the Duchess of Newcastle." London, 1666. Printed by A[nne] Maxwell.

The Life of the Thrice Noble, High, Puissant Prince William Cavendishe, Duke, Marquess, and Earl of Newcastle . . . , written by "the Thrice Noble, Illustrious, and Excellent Princess, Margaret, Duchess of Newcastle." London, 1667. Printed by A[nne] Maxwell.

De Vita et Rebus Gestis Nobilissima Principis, Guilielmi Ducis Novo-castrensis, commentarii. Ab Excellentissima Principe, Margareta ipsius uxore sanctissima conscripti. . . . London, 1668. Printed by T[homas] M[ilbourne].[6]

Grounds of Naturall Philosophy, Divided into thirteen Parts, with an Appendix Containing Five Parts, a reissue, "much altered," of *Philosophical and Physical Opinions,* written by "the Thrice Noble, Illustrious, and Excellent Princess, the Duchess of Newcastle." London, 1668. Printed by A[nne] Maxwell.

Observations upon Experimental Philosophy, to Which is Added "The Description of a New Blazing World," written by "the Thrice Noble, Illustrious, and Excellent Princesse, the Duchess of Newcastle." 2nd ed. London, 1668. Printed by A[nne] Maxwell.

---

[5] Although no printer is listed, Kroetsch posits that the book was printed by David Maxwell, whose widow, Anne Maxwell, becomes Cavendish's printer.

[6] Walter Charleton's Latin translation of Cavendish's biography of her husband.

The Description of a New World, Called the Blazing-World, written by "the Thrice Noble, Illustrious, and Excellent Princesse, the Duchess of Newcastle." London, 1668. Printed by A[nne] Maxwell.

Plays, Never before Printed, written by "the Thrice Noble, Illustrious, and Excellent Princesse, the Duchess of Newcastle." London, 1668. Printed by A[nne] Maxwell.

Poems, or, Several Fancies in Verse, with the Animal Parliament, in Prose, written by "the Thrice Noble, Illustrious, and Excellent Princesse, the Duchess of Newcastle." 3rd ed. of *Poems and Fancies.* London, 1668. Printed by A[nne] Maxwell.

Orations of Divers Sorts, Accommodated to Divers Places, "written by the Thrice Noble, Illustrious, and Excellent Princess, the Lady Marchioness of Newcastle." 2nd ed. London, 1668.

Natures Pictures Drawn by Fancies Pencil to the Life. Being Several Feigned Stories, Comical, Tragical, Tragi-comical, Poetical, Romancical, Philosophi⸮cal, Historical, and Moral: Some in Verse, some in Prose; some Mixt, and some by Dialogues, written by "the Thrice Noble, Illustrious, and Most Excellent Princess, the Duchess of Newcastle." 2nd ed. London, 1671. Printed by A[nne] Maxwell.

The Worlds Olio, "written by the Thrice Noble, Illustrious, and Most Excellent Princess, the Duchess of Newcastle." 2nd ed. London, 1671. Printed by A[nne] Maxwell.

The Life of the Thrice Noble, High, Puissant Prince William Cavendishe, Duke, Marquess, and Earl of Newcastle. 2nd ed. London, 1675. Printed by A[nne] Maxwell.

CPSIA information can be obtained
at www.ICGtesting.com
Printed in the USA
LVOW08s1817021017
550904LV00001B/160/P